Badmen of the West

Picture Research by Marion Geisinger

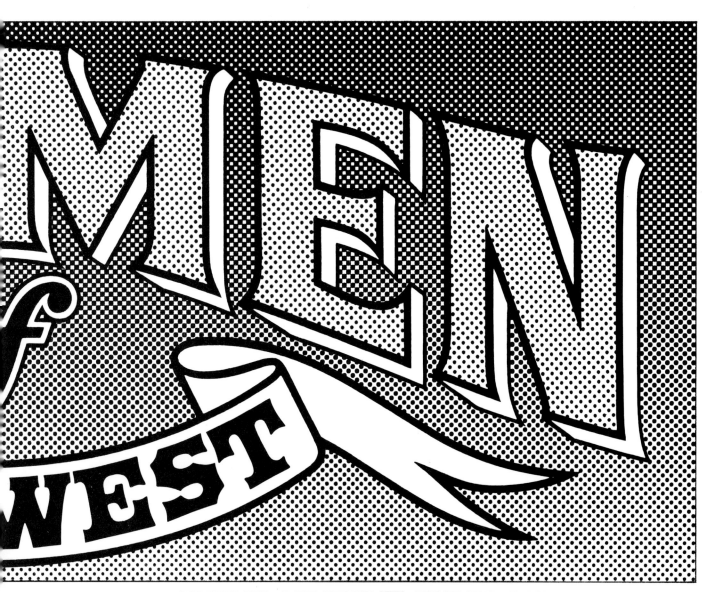

MEN of WEST

BY ROBERT ELMAN

A RIDGE PRESS/POUND BOOK

DEDICATION

To the memory of my father,

who watched the last covered wagons

roll through Fargo

Editor-in-Chief: Jerry Mason
Editor: Adolph Suehsdorf
Executive Art Director: Albert Squillace
Managing Editor: Moira Duggan
Art Associate: David Namias
Art Production: Doris Mullane

Prepared and produced by The Ridge Press, Inc.
Published in 1974 by Pound Books.
Distributed by Derbibooks, Inc.
110 Enterprise Avenue
Secaucus, New Jersey 07094
Library of Congress Catalog Card Number: 74-83646
ISBN: 0-89009-011-4
Printed in the United States of America.

Designed by Norman Snyder

FOREWORD

When my father was born this century was a mere few months old and his state, North Dakota, had not yet celebrated her eleventh anniversary. Cole Younger, awaiting parole, was planning to join Frank James on the lecture circuit, and Butch Cassidy was planning to join Kid Curry for at least one more great train robbery. My paternal grandfather was a drummer who probably could have served as model for one of the passengers in Charles M. Russell's painting of a Deadwood stage robbery, reproduced in the opening section of this book. When I was a boy I was told my grandfather sold fine cigars, and so he did. Later I discovered (with pardonable pride in his pioneering resourcefulness) that he also sold feminine novelties in the boom-town bordellos where cow hands, miners, and farmers mingled with bawds and outlaws. He fared reasonably well, and sometimes I envy his adventurous life.

One of my father's memories of his hometown of Fargo concerned a grain and feed dealer who had severe hay fever; this, the man was fond of saying, made his work more hazardous than it was in the days when he rode with the James Boys. No one ever found out whether the old feed man was truly reminiscing or just spinning dreams.

My own interest in western outlaws began with my father's recollections of those days in the Dakotas. The interest became more serious about ten years ago, when I was asked to write a series of magazine articles about gunfighters. Subsequently, the subject kept surfacing in my research books about various aspects of American history. In the course of writing one such book, for instance, I came to know Carl Seltzer, son of the noted Montana painter O. C. Seltzer. It was Carl who first showed me several of the Seltzer paintings in this book, including the dramatic portrayal of the Kid Curry holdup of the Great Northern near Malta.

My research has required extensive delving into both popular and scholarly histories. In the popular field I have been especially intrigued by Glenn Shirley and James D. Horan, whose fast-paced chronicles have not tended to sacrifice accuracy to spurious sensationalism. I have also relied on academic texts and on primary sources in the archives of state and county historical associations, research libraries, and private collections. Among scholarly works that have influenced this book are *The American West: an Interpretive History*, by Robert V. Hine, and several texts by Ray Allen Billington.

I have not always agreed with these or other historians. On occasion I have suspected scholars of seeking facts to fit academic theories rather than seeking theories to fit the discovered facts. Nonetheless, academicians have rendered an enormous service to Americana by digging beneath popular myth to the reality of frontier conditions.

I have tried to follow their example in this regard. We no longer need writers to exclaim in shocked prose that a Billy the Kid, a Grat Dalton, or a John Wesley Hardin existed. What we want to know is why and how they existed and what they actually did. I have tried here to provide some answers.

Robert Elman

Contents

Painters have often sought the essence of the American West in the nineteenth century, and this book is garlanded with pictures by many who succeeded. The best such artists have been creative historians. They built even their imagined situations on a foundation of reality. And when portraying historic incidents or personages, they made fact vivid with spontaneous drama. This pictorial history therefore begins with a selection of paintings that convey the atmosphere of the time and place where western outlawry flourished—where, in fact, desperadoes were as much a part of the environment as locoweed or rattlers.

The essential badman himself is the subject of the first painting, "The Fleeing Bandit," by William Robinson Leigh. Out of a forbidding canyon a pony lunges, given free rein by a bandit who holds his gun ready as he glances back, tense with the desperation of flight.

The next painting is Emanuel Leutze's "Westward the Course of Empire," a lofty allegory of the pioneers, determined, idealistic, full of optimism. To a modern viewer there is irony here, because many of these seemingly indomitable pioneers, brutalized by the frontier, accepted lawlessness on the empty plains and in the teeming boom towns.

Disputes in that hard country were too often settled as in the

(continued on page 17)

The Painted West

next painting, Charles M. Russell's "Smoke of a .45." Scattered playing cards and a whiskey bottle lie in the dust before The Palace, a pathetic log-cabin gambling den. A gambler dies even as he returns a cowboy's fire, and a fallen rider, one boot caught in a stirrup, is dragged under the hitching rail. It is no Hollywood melodrama but the kind of tragedy that struck when a Clay Allison or a Wes Hardin sought amusement in cow towns where reward posters decorated the saloons.

That picture is followed by another Russell work, "Hold-Up," depicting a Deadwood stage robbery. The painter has type-cast his passengers, humorously caricaturing their ethnic backgrounds and professions as well as their annoyance and dismay. But at the same time he has distilled the essence of the habitat that spawned the Sam Bass gang.

And then there is the Henry H. Cross portrait, "Wild Bill Hickok," in which the gunfighting lawman gazes pensively and caresses his .45. It is a good likeness of a corrupt man who dressed for his public, wore his hair and moustache long, and might have been handsome but for his prominent nose and lips. His image blends the proud defense of law with a paradoxical scorn for that law. The Hickoks and the Earps of the West, after all, were badmen as surely as the Jameses and Youngers.

*Preceding pages: Holding hat in one hand, quirt and
mask in the other, highwayman bows to reward poster in English
engraving captioned, "Your humble servant." Horse's
trappings include pistol in saddle holster. America's first
badmen—many of them fugitives from the Old World—
emulated such gallantly depicted English outlaws. Above:
Scene from* The Great Train Robbery, *filmed in New Jersey
in 1903. Early western movies and novels strongly
influenced popular notions about frontier desperadoes.*

It is a popular and persistent notion that the badman is a thrillingly colorful if monstrous aberration, spontaneously combusted by the wildness of the Wild West in the nineteenth century. This image was immortalized first by sensationalist newspapers, pamphlets, and almanacs, then by millions of copies of dime novels, by Wild West shows and touring "mellerdrammers," by the western novels that have proliferated since Owen Wister's *The Virginian* was published in 1902, by the Hollywood "oaters" and foreign-made "spaghetti westerns" that really began in New Jersey in 1903 with *The Great Train Robbery* (filmed on location—on the tracks of the Delaware, Lackawanna & Western), and finally by television.

This popular image is not entirely false, just somewhat askew. Though the badman often was glorified in the American West of the nineteenth century, the phenomenon of the violent, maurauding outlaw, feared yet idolized, was neither new nor uniquely American. The very words "outlaw" and "outlawry"—outside and defying the laws of society—go back to Anglo-Saxon times. "Desperado" is an old Spanish word and brigands were once Italian *brigantes*, bandits of the Mediterranean mountains. The term "road agent" seems to have originated in the American West, but those who infested travel lanes, from the Boston Post Road and the Natchez Trace to the Oregon Trail, were also known by the earlier English label "highwaymen." Significantly, they were sometimes called land pirates, just as those who preyed on the waterways were called river pirates.

Outlaw practices were simply transplanted from Europe to fertile new soil. Among the one hundred and two pilgrims who debarked from the *Mayflower* at Plymouth Rock in 1620 was a London ruffian named John Billington. On one occasion during the voyage Captain Miles Standish had squelched Billington's blasphemous rages by having his feet bound to his neck. In 1630, after a decade of feuding with other colonists, Billington found his neck encircled by a rope for the last time when he was hanged for the ambush shooting of John Newcomen. Thus he became the first convicted murderer in the American Colonies, only a small model for later badmen, but notorious among the settlers of little Plymouth Plantation.

From the Old World came the traditions of the underdog turning on its cruel master, of rebellions against authority, of flight from injustice (and often from justice), individual might seen as right, violent physical combat seen as glory. Ballads told of dashing pirates, reckless highwaymen, and Robin Hood. In print and in oral folklore, American bandits who were likened to Robin Hood included Jesse James of Missouri and Kansas, the Chicano, Juan Cortinas of Texas, Tiburcio Vasquez and Three-Fingered Jack of California, and California's legendary Gold Rush avenger, Joaquin Murieta, who —like Robin Hood when the last troubadours had done with him—probably existed only as a composite of several real men. The ghost of Sherwood Forest rode across the American plains and deserts, still pillaging the rich to give to the poor, still carrying the rebel's banner of the underdog rampant and triumphant.

The first emigrants inevitably included misfits, compulsive nomads, roguish adventurers, convicts, fugitives, indentured servants who might as well have been slaves, refugees from political chaos and economic depression—men accustomed to the savagery and gallows humor of countries where executions were public entertainments. (They continued to be so in parts of the United States as late as 1901, when citizens of Clayton, New Mexico, were disappointed by the lack of tickets to Black Jack Ketchum's hanging.) Many were driven to crime by bondage or poverty or the deprivations, dangers, and brutality of frontier life. Still, only a few had sufficient daring, color, and opportunity to become noted badmen. Circumstance was crucial. In the cities from which many emigrants came a thief might get away with a few robberies, a swindle, perhaps even homicide, but habitually violent outlaws had a short life expectancy, for there was hardly anywhere to run or hide for more than a brief period.

America, by contrast, offered a tremendous wilderness for escape and hiding. A man might flee retribution by disappearing into the backwoods or the desert. He could reappear in a distant settlement or even a city where he was unknown. Badmen often used the newly rising cities—Boston, Philadelphia, New Orleans, St. Louis, Dodge, Abilene—as both way stations and hunting grounds rich in victims. A few renegades, like the infamous Harp brothers, lived for a while with Indians, but most had visions of an easier life. Some tried to live off the land while hiding, even though the hardships of subsistence farming had originally goaded them to crime. After an interval of precarious survival in the wilds, they usually drifted back to towns or to hideaways near trails and settlements where travelers made easy prey.

At the time of Pontiac's war, a decade before the Revolution, the rattle of muskets did not always signify a defense against Algonquin or Ottawa attack. It might also punctuate a running fight between a posse and a gang of horse and cattle thieves known as the Grays, who raided the stock of farmers around Poughkeepsie. Like Indians, the raiders melted into the forests when retreating. America's first rustlers were hardly westerners, but their hit-and-run tactics spread westward with the frontier. Late in the nineteenth century, the Indian Territory —Oklahoma—remained an ideal haven for outlaws. The Cherokees and other tribes had their own police and were

"Dime novels" (which included five-centers, fifteen-centers, even twenty-five-centers) were often based on real people and events. Largely naïve audience accepted some of them as true chronicles, even when outlaws were pictured as heroes rather than villains. Men like Wild Bill Hickok and the Jameses read exaggerated accounts of their own deeds.

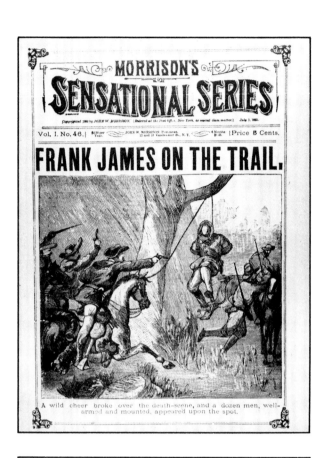

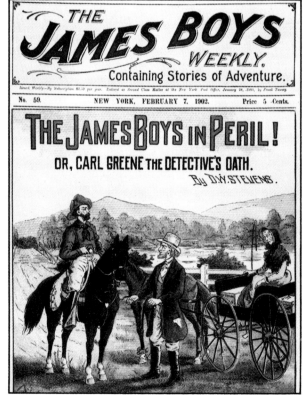

"Diamond Dick, Jr.'s Mysterious Diagram," in No. 191 of this Library.

DIAMOND-DICK LIBRARY

Entered According to Act of Congress, in the Year 1892, by Street & Smith, in the Office of the Librarian of Congress, Washington, D. C.

Entered as Second-class Matter in the New York, N. Y., Post Office.   Issued Weekly. Subscription Price, $2.50 per Year.   July 4, 1896.

No. 192.   STREET & SMITH, Publishers,   NEW YORK.   29 Rose St., N. Y.   5 Cents.

Wild Bill's Last Trail.

By NED BUNTLINE.

WILD BILL SHOUTED: "GIVE UP THAT HORSE OR DIE!"

supposed to enforce their own laws. Legally, a posse could not always pursue a badman into the Territory. Federal warrants were issued, sometimes on flimsy pretexts, so that U.S. Deputy Marshals could be dispatched into the Territory to bring back desperadoes, white or red, to stand trial before Isaac C. Parker, the "Hanging Judge" of Fort Smith, Arkansas. In twenty-one years on the bench, Judge Parker passed the death sentence on one hundred and sixty outlaws, of whom seventy-nine eventually climbed the gallows. Yet so many others evaded pursuit that the unsettled western expanses remained a haven, a temptation in the minds of the lawless, an emboldening influence on potential badmen.

Shortly after the American Revolution, a huge cavern known as Cave-in-the-Rock had drawn land and river pirates to the Illinois bank of the Ohio River. It remained a place of ambush and rendezvous, an infamous murderers' and robbers' den, for more than a generation. A century later in Wyoming, Butch Cassidy used a nearly impregnable lair that gave his famous Wild Bunch its earlier name, the Hole-in-the-Wall Gang. At one time or another whole towns became robbers' roosts.

Outlaws followed cattle trails, fur brigades, gold and oil rushes all the way to Nome, Alaska, and the era of the badman did not really end until the Klondike boom had subsided and regions of rich plunder no longer bordered regions of easy hiding.

At least two other factors molded the badman. One was the mistreatment of Indians. The other was the absence of organized government in frontier settlements. Violence begat violence. The English paid Indians a bounty for enemy scalps, and during the nineteenth century white mountain men took their turn at scalping Indians. George Frederick Ruxton, in his journal of an 1846 expedition into Arapaho country, recorded a fight in which a trapper killed and scalped an Indian. Ruxton and others also reported that parties of white traders and trappers went on horse-stealing raids, just as the Indians did. They took the mounts of white men as well as red men, killing the owners when necessary.

The Spanish, French, and English all expected easy riches on the new continent and they regarded the Indians as so far beneath humanity that Europeans had the right to take whatever they pleased. Most of them, instead of finding wealth in this promised land, found toil, disillusionment, and frustration, which led them to murder Indians and then—as human life seemed ever cheaper—to murder each other in order to take what could be taken.

In 1767, when murder and theft reached epidemic proportions in the backwoods of South Carolina, frontiersmen formed the first vigilante group. They called their mounted posses Rangers, and in some respects they might be considered forerunners of the Texas Rangers, but their usual name for themselves was Regulators. Sometimes they brought culprits to Charleston or other towns for trial. Sometimes they convened a court on the spot. Enraged by outlaws who had tortured their victims, they practiced almost equal sadism—fatal beatings, orgies of flogging to the rhythm of fiddles.

Other self-appointed avengers calling themselves Regulators arose wherever law enforcement was absent. In 1833 a band of Regulators unceremoniously gunned down Sheriff James Ford of Livingston County, Kentucky, when they discovered he was masterminding robbery-murders at Cave-in-the-Rock and nearby Ford's Ferry. The outwardly respectable sheriff has been called Satan's Ferryman.

In 1840, during an East Texas feud known as the Shelby County War, a murderer named Charles W. Jackson organized a group of Regulators whose ostensible

Paintings like "The Death Struggle," by Charles Deas, inextricably blended myth and reality. Encounters with hostile Indians were fairly common, though not atop dizzying pinnacles. In these battles the victor—whether frontiersman or Indian—was likely to scalp his adversary, and acceptance of such brutality encouraged waves of outlawry.

purpose was to suppress rustling but whose real activity was terrorizing unfriendly factions. A group called the Moderators was formed in opposition. Jackson was killed in an ambush but warfare continued, taking perhaps fifty lives before Sam Houston, president of the Republic of Texas, ended it by sending in his militia. By then the name Regulators had such horrifying overtones that later, self-appointed police groups in San Francisco and then in Montana called themselves Committees of Vigilance. The change in name did not signify any great change in attitude toward due process.

Historian Robert V. Hine has theorized that both the South Carolina outlaws and the Regulators who all but exterminated them were primed for violence by the barbarisms of the Cherokee War they had waged in 1760-1761. Indian slaughter had led to indiscriminate slaughter. Anglo-Americans felt about Mexicans pretty much as they did about Indians and blacks, and there was a marked increase in prison sentences immediately after the war with Mexico. Actually, it seems that warfare of any kind led to a thirst for more blood. In the year after the Civil War ended, crimes of violence soared by fifty percent, and throughout the Indian Wars on the plains, robbery, rustling, feuding, and gunfighting were unabated.

Not only was established law far less effective than personal force on the frontier, often the very principles of law seemed ludicrous and tyrannical to the pioneers. First the English monarchy and then the United States Government had tried to regulate expansion, letting settlement extend only as far as peacekeeping could reach, by proclaiming boundary lines beyond which frontiersmen could not legally settle. Since the boundary lines were unmarked and often unsurveyed, a man was likely to break what seemed to him an absurd law simply by moving westward. With the opening of the West came homesteading and preemption laws that frequently benefited only the land speculator and not the independent farmer or rancher. Similarly, land grants gave great slices of public domain to avaricious railroads while banks charged usurious interest rates and foreclosed relentlessly on poor dirt farmers. The man who held up a train, a gold-laden stagecoach, or a bank was seen as a Robin Hood, even though he forgot to share the loot.

The frontiersman felt he had to fight the wilderness and the Government to survive. He soon took inordinate pride in being a rugged individualist and great glee in embarrassing the establishment. Each man thus was a potential badman, an admirer and encourager of the few conscienceless wild ones who acted out their vengeful fantasies.

Left: Slavery is introduced to America's English settlements. Above: In Cherokee War, which was marked by atrocities on both sides, Southern colonists slaughter Indians. As mistreatment of blacks and Indians bred contempt for human life, some of the oppressed—as well as their oppressors—took to armed banditry to survive.

2/America's First Badmen

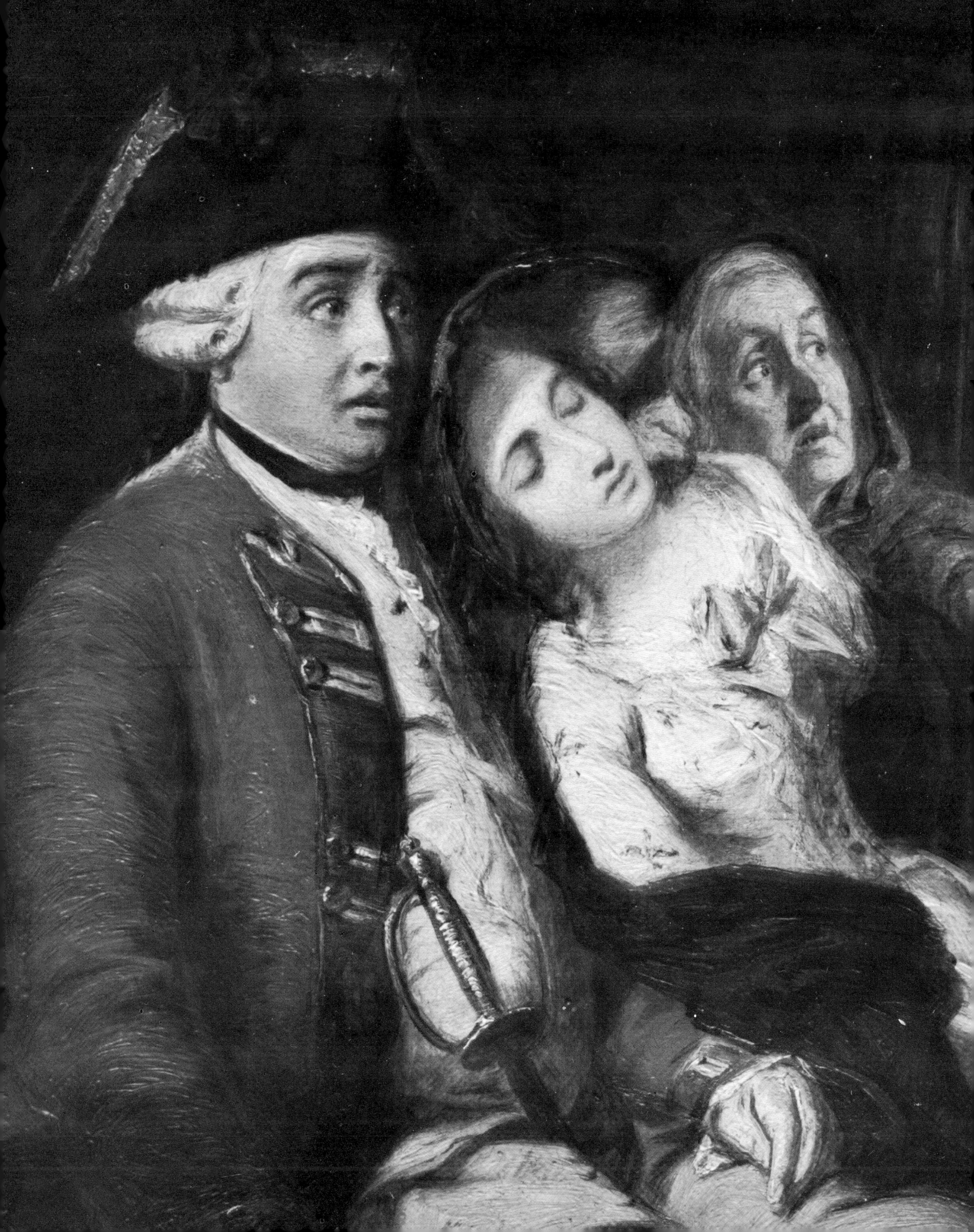

The great English lexicographer Samuel Johnson defined patriotism as the last refuge of a scoundrel. Ambrose Bierce, western satirist, journalist, prospector, and adventurer, defined it as the first. Presumably both men were thinking of hypocrites who profiteered in business, politics, and the bloody acquisition of other people's countries, all under the guise of patriotism. But their observations also applied to a more easily recognized outlawry. From the bounty-scalpers and rustlers of the French & Indian War to the train-robbing Reno brothers, the murderous William Clarke Quantrill, Bloody Bill Anderson, and the James-Younger gang, a startling number of badmen served apprenticeships as soldiers or partisan irregulars, hiring on to fight for home and country and a high moral cause. Foraging, guerrilla warfare, lightning cavalry raids employed the same tactics and garnered the same rewards as livestock theft, highway robbery, plunder, murder. Men became callous to bloodletting. Some actually seemed to enjoy it and took no great pains to break the habits of war.

Nathaniel Bacon's "rebellion" in 1676 consisted mostly of killing peaceful but "dangerous" Virginia Indians and ransacking their villages. Later, in the years before the Revolution, armed rustlers operated from the Canadian frontier around Niagara to southeastern New York. Then, in New York's Westchester County— ironically known as the Neutral Ground—the Redcoats employed marauding partisans called "cow boys," while the rebelling colonists employed a nondescript crew called the "skinners" to steal beef on the hoof, ambush patrols and supply trains, and terrorize enemy sympathizers. The same kind of activity spawned the Doane gang, scourge of Bucks County, Pennsylvania, America's first notorious outlaw brotherhood.

The six Doanes, led by Moses Doane, with brothers Abraham and Levy more or less second in command of three more brothers and perhaps a dozen henchmen, were Tory mountaineers who fought for the Crown by robbing Pennsylvania's tax collectors. Their deeds might have been reminiscent of Robin Hood except that these Merry Men kept all the booty, robbed the poor as well as the rich, and were said to commit occasional murder, mayhem, and arson.

They ranged as far as New Jersey, but their most

Preceding pages: Traditions of outlawry underwent little alteration upon crossing Atlantic. Though W. C. Firth's painting, "The Highwayman," depicts English or Scottish incident, masked outlaw could as easily have been one of America's early desperadoes—Joseph T. Hare or the Irish-American brigand Michael Martin, who became famous as Captain Lightfoot. Upper left: One of Moses Doane's cutthroats, who claimed to be Tory partisans, escaping after murder of British officer. Left: Doanes battling aroused citizens and militia.

celebrated raid took place at Newton, Pennsylvania, in 1781, when they relieved county treasurer John Hart of about $2,000 of public funds, then adjourned to the schoolhouse for a lantern-lit division of sixteen shares before riding away. They were aware that Cornwallis had surrendered three days before. It hardly mattered, since they had never entertained any notion of delivering the spoils to the British. Sometimes hiding in Pennsylvania caverns that are known to this day as Doane caves, they continued their raids for almost a decade. James Fitzpatrick, a Doane lieutenant known as "Sandy Flash," who had deserted to form his own cutthroat band, was apprehended in 1787 at Chester, Pennsylvania, where he soon encountered a hangman. Abraham and Levy Doane were finally captured a year later and hanged on the Philadelphia common. Soon Moses, too, was swaying from a rope. The reign of the Doanes was ended.

The forces fighting for independence probably spawned as many outlaws as did the Tories. The most famous was Sam Mason, one of George Rogers Clark's militiamen. Riding against the British and their Shawnee allies, Clark ranged into the wild lands that were to become Kentucky, Indiana, Illinois, and across the Mississippi into Missouri. Mason thus acquired a thorough knowledge of the early West. Unable to adjust to peaceful endeavors when the war ended, he used that knowledge to hunt victims and elude capture, sometimes along the forested banks of the Ohio and Mississippi, sometimes on the Natchez Trace, a six-hundred-mile post road following old Choctaw and Chickasaw trails from Natchez, Mississippi, northeast to Nashville, Tennessee. He was caught early in his career and ridden out of Natchez on a rail; the experience only seemed to toughen him. In the post-Revolutionary years of southwestward expansion, heavily laden flatboats were floated down the Mississippi to New Orleans. The river was virtually a one-way shipping artery before steamboats were invented with power enough to move against the current, so cargos going upstream were carried on land, along the Trace. Thus Mason prospered both as a land and river pirate.

The rise of the western badman did not wait on the coming of the six-gun. Outlaws like Mason and his gang ruled by knife and tomahawk, torch and flintlock. They raided emigrant parties, waylaid travelers, scuttled or commandeered flatboats, then boldly drifted their loot down to New Orleans, sold it, and rode north again, robbing and killing as they went. The pickings were especially rich on the waterways. In the half-century before steam replaced drifting, flatboats carried a million settlers, together with their goods, money, and livestock. During 1788 alone, more than three hundred boats came down the Ohio—close to a prize a day if they could all be taken.

Sometimes Mason or another outlaw hired on as a pilot to guide a boat through tricky channels, past shoals or hidden bars. Then he wrecked the vessel or ran it aground

Far right: Woodcut from The Piratical and Tragical Almanac of 1846 purports to show militiamen struggling with Moses Doane and about to kill him after he had killed one of them. Picture was captioned "Death of Major Kennedy and Moses Doan" but, in fact, outlaw survived to climb gallows. Near right: Coffin-decorated 18th-century broadside describing lives and hangings of two Doanes.

where an ambush party waited. Another method was to pay for passage on a boat and surreptitiously pull the caulking out of the flooring to swamp it. The favorite stratagem was for one or two outlaws and one of their women to hail a passing boat from shore or from an island. The decoys offered to buy or sell something, or claimed to be stranded. Fast canoes were hidden nearby. If a boatman was too suspicious to land he could be attacked by a boarding party. Several spots on the rivers became infamous: the Ohio's Hurricane Island, near Cave-in-the-Rock, Diamond Island, near the present site of Henderson, Kentucky, and the Mississippi's Wolf Island, near the Cairo junction of the two waterways.

Inevitably, Mason was attracted to Cave-in-the-Rock. In 1797 he turned it into an inn and stronghold for river bandits. Known today as Cave in Rock, the cavern is in a high bluff on the Illinois side of the Ohio. The site is in Hardin County, near Elizabethtown, about midway between Evansville, Indiana, and Paducah, Kentucky. The entrance is thirty-five feet wide at the base. It opens into a cavern about forty feet wide and one hundred and sixty feet long, with a huge natural chimney at the rear.

In Mason's day the entrance was screened by bushes and small trees. Eventually, when word spread about the innocent-looking bluff, flatboatmen passed it warily, ready to repel boarders. But at first there was no way to know that the bluff contained a sprawling cavern and that the cavern often contained slaves—mostly women spared for the gratification of pirates who had murdered their husbands and children. Sam Mason prospered as gang leader and tavern keeper, and long after his death outlaws flourished there with the cooperation of Sheriff James Ford, the devilish ferryman. By the 1830's the area was becoming settled and citizens were becoming suspicious of their sheriff. Ford's two sons, one of whom was a known highwayman, were murdered and Ford himself was shot by Regulators. But it was not the demise of a few outlaw chiefs that ended river piracy. It was partly the maneuverability of keelboats and steamboats, partly the notoriety of the area. Some travelers made detours. Some traveled in larger groups, well armed, ready to fight.

Mason was captured again in 1803. This time he

probably would have been executed had he not escaped. The governors of Louisiana and the Mississippi Territory put a price on his head, and forthwith his head was delivered—in a jar according to some accounts, in a ball of clay according to others—by a bounty hunter named Bill Setter. There was a certain irony in this. A citizen claimed to recognize Setter as Wiley Harp, a homicidal maniac whose life Mason once had spared. Harp was known to have a scar on his chest, and when Setter was seen to have one too the identification was upheld. In February, 1804, he and a former colleague were hanged. For some years afterward rumors were heard about Wiley Harp's continued presence in the area, but it seems likely that the right man was hanged or the rumors soon would have turned to reports of torture and slaughter.

Whereas the name Doane was sometimes spelled without the "e," the name Harp was sometimes spelled with one. The Harps, like the Doanes, were Tory sympathizers, but beyond their politics and variable spellings there were no strong similarities between the clans. Wiley, known as Little Harp, was born in about 1770 and his brother Micajah, called Big Harp, was only a couple of years older, so it is doubtful that they fought in the Revolution. But their family seems to have been vociferously loyal to George III. Historian William Daniel Snively has speculated that the brothers, always unsavory, may have been ostracized for this loyalty. In the mid-1790's they roamed (or were driven) out of the North Carolina woods into Tennessee, bringing with them their interchangeable mistresses Susan (or Susannah) and Betsy Roberts. For the next two years they lived as renegades with a group of Creek and Cherokee outcasts who preyed on other Indians. Then they rented a bit of land on Beaver Creek, near Knoxville, where Little Harp married a preacher's daughter named Sally (or Sara) Rice. She, too, was shared by the brothers and remained a loyal member of their harem even after Big Harp, who was easily annoyed by the crying of infants, killed her daughter.

Little Harp was a man of about average height with bright red hair. Big Harp stood well over six feet tall and had a very florid face. Both men were habitually ragged and dirty—frightening apparitions on the Tennessee trails. They began their major crime wave by burning the houses of Knoxville residents who objected to thefts of horses, hogs, and sheep. A posse was formed. The Harps sent their women and children to a secret meeting place in the Cumberland Mountains of western Virginia. Then they fled. They were captured, escaped, and that night began their savage robbery-murders by dragging a man out of a tavern, disemboweling him, filling the body cavity with stones, and tossing the corpse into the river.

In December of 1798 they were in Kentucky, going west with their women and children along the Wilderness Road. En route they killed at least four people. Then, on Christmas Day, they surrendered without resistance to a posse. While awaiting trial the brothers were chained by their feet to the floor of a log jail at Danville, yet somehow they broke through the wall and escaped. Each of the three women they left behind bore a child while incarcerated, and that spring the chivalrous frontier citizens released the harem and its multiplying progeny. They headed for Cave-in-the-Rock to meet the Harps, who were riding toward the Ohio but stopping frequently enough to add perhaps five names to their list of victims. One was a thirteen-year-old boy. They stole a bag of flour he was carrying and then dismembered him.

By now Kentuckians knew the Harps were sadistic maniacs. The brothers had actually faced down a posse after leaving Danville, so a stronger force was organized. The pursuers, sufficiently enraged to name themselves

Dramatic 19th-century newspaper illustration shows "A night among the robbers of the Blue Ridge." Badmen moved west with frontier, first infesting periphery of settlements from New England down through Appalachians into Blue Ridge Mountains and out over Natchez Trace and the Cumberland, Ohio, and Mississippi Rivers.

The Exterminators, combed Kentucky and succeeded only in driving the region's other outlaws toward Cave-in-the-Rock, where dozens of badmen were gathering into a formidable gang.

But the Harps did not stay long at the cavern. A flatboat was captured in May, 1799, and one survivor was kept as a prisoner. During a drunken celebration the Harps dragged him to the top of the bluff, tied him to a blindfolded horse, and whipped the horse into a panic. The bandits in the cave ran out when they heard hoofbeats, laughter, and a scream. They saw the horse and its bound rider fall from the bluff to the rocks below. This torture killing was too brutal even for them. According to tradition, Sam Mason and his henchmen would have exe-cuted the Harps, but spared them because of their women and children. They did, however, banish the clan.

The Harps wandered back through Kentucky and Tennessee, killing men, women, a small girl, and a cradled infant. At last a posse wounded Big Harp. Little Harp escaped but Big, weakened from the loss of blood, was overtaken. He was decapitated, slowly, with his own butcher knife, by a man whose wife and baby he had killed. Harpshead Road, near Henderson, is where his head was posted as a warning to other outlaws. Incredibly, the captured Harp women were set free again. This time they vanished.

Soon afterward, a far different kind of desperado named Joseph T. Hare appeared. A dapper young fellow born in Pennsylvania and raised in the burgeoning slums of New York, Philadelphia, and Baltimore, Joseph Thompson Hare was the first American highwayman to specialize in stagecoach holdups. His dash and mystery foreshadowed the exuberance of California's Black Bart, who nearly outwitted Pinkerton detectives a couple of generations later. Arriving in New Orleans as a sailor, Hare inspected the city's fleshpots and the opportunities for accosting riders where the Natchez Trace meandered through the swamps of the Choctaw and Cherokee Nations, and jumped ship. He soon discovered that lone travelers, notwithstanding their sometimes heavy purses or money belts, afforded less remunerative transactions than the stages. He tried river pirating, too, but the coach lines suited him best. Hare and his little gang of freebooters achieved a kind of anonymous fame. The failure of lawmen to obtain an accurate description enabled him to spend considerable time in New Orleans houses of entertainment. He was finally caught in 1813 and imprisoned for five years. Upon his release he headed north—not to reform but to delay the Baltimore night coach near Havre

Left: Joseph Hare, first American badman to specialize in stagecoach robbery, was memorialized in twenty-five-cent publication by 19th-century sensationalist who had also written about "The Great Western Land Pirate," John Murrell. Upper right: Woodcut of Murrell shooting unfortunate traveler on Natchez Trace. Lower right: Murrell engaged in his chief means of livelihood, kidnapping a slave for sale to unscrupulous dealers.

de Grace. This single exploit assured his lasting fame. The coach carried a bank shipment, and Hare rode off with more than $15,000, a fortune in that era, the largest prize yet taken. However, his face was now so well known that he was arrested two days later as he was buying an elegant plaid coat.

In the Baltimore jail he scrawled a few diary entries in which he cautioned others to abjure his profession: "a desperate life . . . sooner or later it ends on the gallows." So it did, in September, 1818.

A forerunner of the dime novels (selling for twenty-five cents) was entitled, *The Life and Adventures of Joseph T. Hare, the Bold Robber and Highwayman, With 16 Elegant and Spirited Engravings,* by the author of *The*

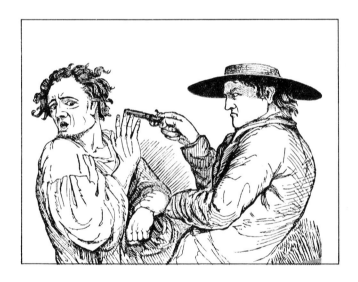

Life of John A. Murrell. The *Police Gazette* called Murrell "the Great Western Land Pirate"—"the great marauder . . . whose wonderful career has become a part of the history of the West." Actually, Murrell was a lowly horse thief turned murderer and slave stealer who had egomaniacal visions of leading a slave revolt in order to plunder New Orleans and execute the city's aristocrats—whom, for obscure reasons, he held accountable for his criminal activities. On the Natchez Trace in 1834 he met a young man named Virgil Stewart, who was trailing him in order to gather evidence of slave thefts. Evidently in need of an audience, Murrell invited Stewart to ride with him and proceeded to tell hair-raising tales of an older brother who had committed atrocities reminiscent of the Harps. Finally he revealed that he was speaking of himself. It was hardly necessary, since his thumb was branded with the letters HT, for horse thief. Stewart, in fear of his life, let himself be recruited for the planned revolt and was led into a camp of cutthroats and armed runaway slaves. He escaped during the night and directed the authorities to the camp. Murrell offered no resistance. He served ten years in the penitentiary at Nashville, after which he disappeared forever.

More colorful and clever was the Irish-American highwayman Michael Martin, alias Captain Lightfoot. Born near Kilkenny in 1775, Martin ran away from his family's reasonably thriving farm when he was seventeen to consort with what he afterward called "profligate men and women" in Dublin. In 1822, while awaiting execution at Cambridge, Massachusetts, he dictated his memoirs. At about the time he had left home, he met a distinguished gentleman riding a "splendid blooded horse," who turned out to be a celebrated Irish highwayman known as Captain Thunderbolt. Soon Martin was riding with this mentor, whose guiding principle was "to make property equal in this world . . . get as much as he could from the rich but . . . never molest the poor . . . . If there was any danger of detection, or strong opposition, he thought himself justified in taking life."

And so, with another of the latter-day Robin Hoods, Martin rode about Ireland and then Scotland taking "money from those who had more than they knew how to use." By 1818 he had his own romantic alias—Captain Lightfoot—and the rewards for Thunderbolt and Lightfoot had risen sufficiently to make Martin sail for America. He tried farming, then bought a little brewery in Salem, Massachusetts, but he was deeply in debt within a year. So he robbed a peddler of $70 with which he bought a good horse, a brace of pistols, a sword cane, and for

disguise a suit of Quaker clothing. The rejuvenated, Americanized Captain Lightfoot scandalized New England and northeastern Canada for several years, introducing to this country the traditions of highwaymen in Europe and the British Isles. Finally, near Boston, he held up a coach carrying an aide of the Massachusetts governor. Although he refused the watch of a female passenger—"Madam, I do not rob ladies!"—he had committed an unpardonable offense. In modern terms it might be compared to the hijacking of a car carrying a high-ranking state official. "Wanted" posters went up everywhere. Militiamen and civilian patrols established roadblocks and searched the countryside. Martin, in need of a fresh horse, stole one near Springfield. This was a hanging

Above: In old woodcut, Thunderbolt and Lightfoot hold up English stage, probably in 1818, just before Lightfoot fled to America and began robbing Massachusetts stages. Right: 1895 illustration entitled "The Good Old Times!" vividly recalls days of flintlock outlawry on both sides of Atlantic.

crime both in the East and West. A posse of farmers captured him and he was hanged from a tree limb at Cambridge in December, 1822.

The East was becoming too densely populated for men like Captain Lightfoot. He had found no wilderness refuge and had been captured in a suburban barn. It is true that a family called Loomis continued to steal horses in the Mohawk and Chenango valleys of New York until after the Civil War, even selling mounts to buyers for the Union Army. The Loomises maintained a network of corrals, farms, and distribution points from Canada to Pennsylvania, and when the horse market slumped a bit they did a good business in counterfeit bills drawn on the Onondaga Bank. Perhaps Wash Loomis (named for George Washington) and his five brothers were comparable to some minor western badmen. Perhaps their sister Cornelia and their mother Rhoda (a former school teacher) foreshadowed the likes of Belle Starr. All the same, the infamous and colorful badmen were moving west—farther west than the hunting grounds of the Harps—to a new frontier teeming with settlers, trappers, merchants, railroad builders, stagecoaches, unfenced livestock, gambling halls and saloons, flimsy frame-house banks, crossroads stores and way stations, a new world of prey abutting millions of square miles of wasteland where the law did not reach.

DICK TURPIN *Clearing the Old Hornsey toll bar* GATE.
TO THE SURPRISE OF HIS PURSUERS.

Far left: British retreating from Lexington under fire. Opening shots of Revolution were also, in a way, opening shots of gang warfare. Though most partisans–both Minutemen and Tories—were politically motivated, elements in colonists' guerrilla force known as "skinners" and Redcoat irregulars called "cow boys" became rustlers and marauders. Near left: Precursor of American shotgun messenger was coach guard armed with blunderbuss. Numerous historical accounts and pictures like this furnish documentation that such guards failed to deter gunmen later known as road agents. Above: Dick Turpin, England's most notorious highwayman, escapes pitchfork-wielding pursuers. An audacious stage robber, rustler, and poacher, he was captured in 1739. Though known to have murdered gamekeeper in Epping Forest, he was tried for another capital offense— horse theft. Without awaiting executioner's final adjustments of noose, he hanged himself by jumping from gallows. His fame and influence in America remained conspicuous to end of 19th century. Outlaws like Black Jack Ketchum took pride in coolness as they stood under gibbet, and newspaper illustrations of train robbers were captioned "The Modern Dick Turpin."

3 / Western Expansion

Preceding pages: N. C. Wyeth's narrative oil, entitled
"The James Gang," depicts rendezvous where bandits wait with
fresh horses for arrival of their cohorts. Jesse James
is portrayed with full beard, which he wore during his last
years. Above: Detail of Thomas Benton's mural,
"History of Missouri," in State Capital at Jefferson City,
symbolizes James gang's bank and train robberies.

At the time of the American Revolution there were fewer than three million people in the Colonies. By the mid-nineteenth century roughly that number of people lived west of the Mississippi in a vast, sparsely settled region of expansion and escape, and the country's total population had grown to thirty-one million. It was a population in flux, beset by economic growing pains and the hardships of frontier life, oozing westward from overcrowded eastern towns experiencing the stringencies of the industrial revolution. And it was a population constantly disrupted by warfare—with the Indians, with England, with Mexico, and finally with itself.

In the century after the founding of the republic the U.S. Army fought 1,240 engagements against Indians. The figure does not take into account attacks that involved only civilians, militia, or locally organized ranger forces, although some such episodes developed into massacres. Most of the Army's Indian fighting consisted of tactical sweeps, the use of starvation as a weapon, and small skirmishes resulting in surprisingly low casualties, yet bloodshed and plunder were so frequent as to become an accepted part of life.

Indians sometimes provided outlaws with predatory opportunities and a cloak for their deeds. In 1836, for instance, a punitive expedition was mounted against a "war party" rumored to be a thousand strong. The Indians turned out to be an indignant but conspicuously peaceful little band—not marauders but victims in a typical frontier horse-stealing raid. At first the affair was called the Heatherly War. Later, with some embarrassment, Missourians referred to it as the Heatherly Incident. The trouble began in 1831 when a thief named George Heatherly came west from Kentucky with four ne'er-do-well sons, an incorrigible adolescent daughter, and his wife Jenny—said to be a sister of Big and Little Harp. They

settled on the Grand River, near the present site of Chillicothe, Missouri. When a community began to develop there, they retreated to the west fork of Medicine Creek, where they built a big log cabin—later known as "Fort Heatherly"—but did almost no farming and had no visible means of livelihood.

Local settlers were warned off at gunpoint, but mysterious strangers, said to be outlaws, came and went. The family also welcomed land-hunters, prospectors, and other travelers if they looked prosperous, arrived on good horses, and were unknown in the region. These unfortunates were not seen again, and after such visits the Heatherly brothers appeared in towns on the Missouri with horses, gold watches, and other valuables for sale.

In the summer of 1836 the Heatherly gang stole eight horses from a small Indian village. There was a shooting fray but the raiders escaped. Then they began to worry that the Indians would complain to the authorities. They may have worried even more about the corpses of two former friends, a man named Dunbar and another named Thomas, left to rot in the woods. Evidently both were gang members, murdered to insure their silence when they threatened to quit. The Heatherlys rode through the settlements spreading a story of a huge war party that had stolen some of their horses and killed Dunbar and Thomas.

U.S. Army troops and the militia were called out. Fortunately, the truth was discovered without further bloodshed. Several murder trials ensued, but the testimony of Indians was not accepted, other witnesses were lacking, and the Heatherly family testified that the culprit was one of their own group, a man named Alfred Hawkins. He alone was convicted. His death sentence was commuted—perhaps because no one could believe he was the sole murderer—and he died in prison. The outlaw family rode into the wilderness and vanished. But men like George Heatherly and his boys continued to swarm through Missouri and Kansas, as far south as Texas and as far north as the Nebraska and Dakota Territories.

Some of them, assuredly, were psychopaths. Where Indians failed to provide a temptation and an excuse, there were other enemies, real or imagined. After the compromise slavery measures of 1850, battles erupted in Kansas between Free Soilers, who wanted to make the territory a slaveless state, and the proslavery faction, chiefly Missourians. Before the decade was over, the militants had formed guerrilla bands whose atrocities caused the territory to be called Bleeding Kansas. In May, 1856, proslavers sacked and burned Lawrence, the temporary capital, committing several murders during their rampage. Three days later John Brown and a small group of self-appointed avengers killed five men suspected of having participated in the raid. Depending on one's viewpoint, John Brown can be called martyr or bloodthirsty fanatic, but his motives have exempted him from the charge of outlawry in the usual sense. Still, for a while he rode with Senator Jim Lane's Red Legs, a five hundred-man partisan army that pillaged settlements on the Missouri border. It is believed that James Butler Hickok —Wild Bill—also rode with Lane for several months in 1856 or 1857. Wild Bill Hickok is remembered as a colorful lawman, yet there is strong evidence that his famous gunfighting exploits were not always to uphold the law. During the Kansas troubles, however, he had not yet emerged as badman or lawman.

By the time war came, the Unionist partisans were known as "jayhawkers" and the Rebel partisans as "bushwhackers"—both terms later used derisively for western outlaws who ambushed victims. In a few instances, according to the eminent Civil War authority

Sack of Lawrence, Kansas, in 1863 by Quantrill's bushwhackers. Frank James and Cole Younger were among raiders who shot down unarmed citizens and pillaged town. Inset shows William Clarke Quantrill, leader of guerrilla force that became outlaw brigade.

Bruce Catton, guerrilla bands "served a legitimate function, harassing enemy communications and supply lines. But in the majority of cases there was little justification for their depredations, their indiscriminate robbery and murder . . . ."

Catton describes William Clarke Quantrill as "the most murderous villain of all." Quantrill was a Kansan —originally from Ohio—whose sympathies lay with the Confederacy but whose notions of warfare had more in common with Attila than with Robert E. Lee. His chief lieutenant was Bloody Bill Anderson. By some accounts Anderson wore a hatchet, a saber, and as many as eight pistols in his belt, and he loaded his horse with rifles and two saddlebags full of pistols. One would suspect exaggeration except that weapons were valuable loot, easily removed from corpses. Moreover, Anderson was obsessed with displays of violence; Catton notes that he actually tied the scalps of victims to his bridle.

Quantrill, a former Bible-school teacher, may have earned his living as a horse thief in Utah for a brief period. By 1859 he was wanted in Kansas for horse stealing, slave stealing, and murder. Posing as an antislavery jayhawker, he raided several farms, confiscated slaves and livestock, and resold both. On one occasion he enlisted the help of five abolitionist Quakers, then betrayed them to slavers who killed three. When war came Quantrill was able to recruit a large force that included Anderson and such other rogues as John McCorkle, Little Arch Clement, Cole Younger, Jim Younger, Frank James, and—late in the war—a seventeen-year-old named Jesse James.

Lawrence was doomed to suffer a second, more vicious attack by guerrillas when Quantrill and Anderson rode in with four hundred and fifty bushwhackers in August, 1863. The town had become a target partly because it was the home of James Lane (who narrowly escaped),

partly because it had become a Union supply center, and partly because Anderson and McCorkle were thirsting for revenge wherever they could find it. Shortly before the Lawrence Massacre, dozens of women—wives, mothers, and daughters of Rebel sympathizers—had been confined in a three-story Kansas City building whose top floor had collapsed, killing a number of them. Among the dead were Bill Anderson's sister Matilda and John McCorkle's sister Christie.

Anderson led a column of men through the Lawrence streets, shooting down unarmed men and boys, forcing the women to watch. Frank James and Cole Younger were among the killers who slaughtered about one hundred and fifty citizens. A survivor afterward wrote about "the bodies of dead men . . . laying in all directions." After two hours of massacre the town was looted and burned. Two months later a similar though smaller raid was carried out at Baxter Springs.

Dissident factions now began to desert Quantrill, and he took his remaining force down to Texas, where he raided wagon trains and committed dozens of robberies and murders. With both the Confederacy and the Union

Civil War photograph at left shows three of Quantrill's bloodthirstiest rogues—Arch Clement, Dave Pool, and Bill Hendricks. At right is Quantrill's chief lieutenant, Bloody Bill Anderson, who tied scalps of victims to his bridle.

eager for his capture his band dwindled rapidly. He rode back to Missouri, fought several small skirmishes with Northern troops, then reached Kentucky with perhaps twenty men, the remnant of what he had styled his Black Flag Brigade. Shortly after the collapse of the Confederacy, Quantrill and his men decided to surrender, claiming to be regular Confederate troops and thus avoid execution. A Union contingent under Captain Edward Terrill intercepted them and cut them down. Quantrill was killed as he attempted to run away.

But Bloody Bill Anderson had decamped in the fall of 1864 with a splinter group of outlaws, among whom were the James and Younger boys. In September they burned the stores and depot at Centralia, Missouri. At noon a train arrived with more than twenty unsuspecting Union soldiers. Sergeant Thomas Goodwin was spared at the caprice of Anderson, who then ordered Arch Clement, a friend of the Jameses, to "muster out the rest of these men." As the James brothers watched, Clement shot each trooper dead.

A month later, as the band fled through Missouri, a Union force overtook some of the outlaws and shot Ander-

son out of his saddle. The Youngers and Jameses escaped.

Alexander Franklin James—known as Frank James—was born near Kearney, Missouri, in 1843. His brother, Jesse Woodson James, called "Dingus" by his friends, was born on the same farm four years later. Their widowed mother, Zerelda James, married Dr. Reuben Samuel, who became as loyal as she was to Frank and Jesse. In later years the Samuel farm served as a hideout for the James boys.

Nearby was the Younger farm. Henry Washington Younger was a gentleman farmer, one of whose brothers was a state legislator and another a peace officer. He also had a sister, Adeline, who was to marry one Lewis Dalton and become the mother of four outlaws—the famous Dalton brothers. Henry himself fathered fourteen children, of whom four also became badmen—Coleman, James, Robert, and John. John did not live long enough to become famous. In 1874, when he was in his early twenties, he and his brother Jim engaged in a shooting match with two Pinkerton detectives and a local deputy at Roscoe, Missouri. Jim killed the deputy and got away. John, who had taken part in only a few robberies with the James-Younger gang, felled one of the Pinkerton men but was fatally wounded.

Cole was the oldest, born a few months after his close friend Frank James. He was a big handsome, red-whiskered extrovert, the leader until delicately built little Dingus began planning the gang's operations. Jim Younger followed Cole into Quantrill's ranks and then into postwar banditry. Bob Younger, not yet fifteen when peace came, joined the gang as soon as they agreed to accept him.

In 1861 seventeen-year-old Frank James joined the Confederate Army. Captured, paroled, and sent home, he got into a fight with some Federal troopers, after which he

Above: Jim Younger, blood-spattered and dazed, is shown after his capture in 1876. Beardless youth is his brother John, killed by lawmen in 1874. Opposite: Famous group portrait includes (from left) Cole Younger, Jesse James, Bob Younger, and Frank James. Obsolete shoulder arms may have been studio props, but at least some of the six revolvers were part of gang's arsenal.

impulsively joined the Quantrill bushwhackers. Cole and Jim Younger joined at about the same time. A companion named Jim Cummins once described "the cool and desperate Cole who headed the advance into Lawrence." Frank James and a bushwhacker named Bill Gregg were reported to have executed fifteen Union recruits captured there. Cole Younger was said to have used fifteen others as targets to test a new gun, a report he vehemently denied in later years.

Because Frank James was known to be riding with bushwhackers, Union soldiers came to the Samuel farm to ask the family his whereabouts. They beat Dr. Samuel and his stepson Jesse, then threw Jesse into jail. A few days later they freed him and briefly jailed his mother and his sister Susan. His sister became very ill before she was released. Still, no one talked, and though Jesse was not quite sixteen, he was old enough to take pride in that and in thoughts of revenge.

He was at Centralia with his brother Frank and the Youngers. Some of the bandits with whom they later

PROCLAMATION
$5,000.00
REWARD
FOR EACH of SEVEN ROBBERS of THE TRAIN at WINSTON, MO., JULY 15, 1881, and THE MURDER of CONDUCTER WESTFALL
$ 5,000.00
ADDITIONAL for ARREST or CAPTURE
DEAD OR ALIVE
OF JESSE OR FRANK JAMES
THIS NOTICE TAKES the PLACE of ALL PREVIOUS REWARD NOTICES.
CONTACT SHERIFF, DAVIESS COUNTY, MISSOURI
IMMEDIATELY
T. T. CRITTENDEN, GOVERNOR
STATE OF MISSOURI
JULY 26, 1881

operated had also ridden with Quantrill. At the war's end amnesty seemed unlikely for known bushwhackers, especially those who had killed so wantonly, and Cole Younger excused himself with the statement that he had been forced "to take to the brush" because of persecution by state militiamen. It does not appear, however, that the Jameses and Youngers tried very hard to get jobs before starting their long series of holdups. No one knows how many stagecoach, bank, and train robberies they committed, but they were almost certainly guilty of at least two dozen between 1866 and 1882—probably many more. The loot on these occasions ranged from a few hundred dollars to nearly $60,000. And the gang killed at least ten men—again, probably many more—before the shooting ended. Here is a partial list of crimes they are known to have committed:

In 1866 they robbed the bank at Liberty, Missouri, of $15,000 in gold and about three times as much in non-negotiable securities, killing a young bystander in a gun battle; in 1867 they killed Judge William McClain during an attempted bank robbery at Savannah, Missouri, and a couple of months later they killed the mayor, sheriff, and sheriff's son during a bank holdup at Richmond, Missouri; in 1868 they took $14,000 from a bank in Russellville, Kentucky; in 1869 they killed a bank cashier in Gallatin, Missouri; in 1871 they held up the county treasurer's office at Corydon, Iowa, and on the same day robbed the local bank of $45,000; the next year they took some $10,000 in gate receipts at the Kansas City Fair; in 1873 they robbed a Chicago, Rock Island & Pacific train near Adair, Iowa, and the engineer was killed when they derailed his locomotive; in 1874, near Malvern, Arkansas, they robbed Concord stage passengers of $4,000 in cash and jewelry, then robbed a train in Missouri, and then robbed the stage running between San Antonio and Austin, Texas.

Constables, sheriffs, deputy marshals, and posses failed abysmally in attempts to catch them. Investigators and peace officers sometimes resorted to acts as ruthless as those perpetrated by the gang. On a January night in 1875, Pinkerton operatives, railroad detectives, and Clay County lawmen acted on a tip that Frank and Jesse James were hiding at the Samuel farm. Surrounding the house, they tossed in turpentine balls to light the interior, then lobbed a thirty-three-pound bomb through a window

Far left: Portrait of Jesse James, who always kept youthful, deceptively gentle appearance. Center: Reward poster distributed by Missouri's governor after 1881 train robbery in which conductor was killed. Left: Frank James in 1898, three years before Cole Younger left prison and joined him on lecture circuit, denouncing the life of crime.

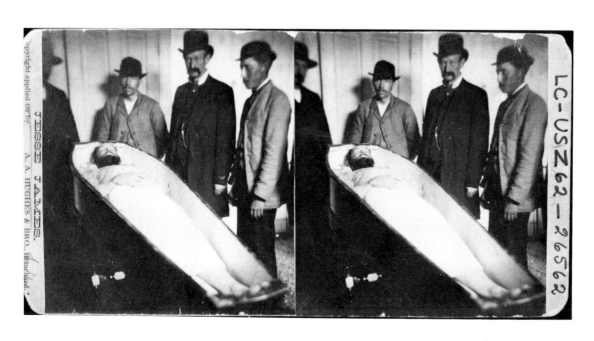

when they saw movement in the kitchen. There have been conflicting reports as to whether the James brothers were actually there. Evidence indicates that Frank and Jesse and at least one henchman came out shooting, and the detectives hastily retreated while the outlaws escaped. The bomb killed nine-year-old Archie Samuel, a half-brother of Frank and Jesse, and blew away their mother's right arm. So ended the most disgraceful attempt to stop the James-Younger robberies.

As might be expected, the Robin Hood notion flourished powerfully after such incidents. Nat Love, an old black cowpuncher who said he knew Jesse James well, wrote a memoir in which he called the James brothers "true men, brave, kind, generous and considerate, and . . . what they took from the rich they gave to the poor." There is, of course, no evidence that they ever gave to the poor, unless one counts poor relatives. Often, as a matter of fact, they took from the poor, but they also took from the rich—the banks and railroads—and that was enough to make them folk heroes. It should be noted, however, that they were idolized only at a safe distance. Some of the residents of Clay County, Missouri, accepted pay to spy on the Samuel farm, and the people in towns where they struck regarded the James-Younger gang with fear, loathing, and mounting defiance.

The defiance exploded in September, 1876, when the bank at Northfield, Minnesota, was held up by eight

Upper left: In artist's depiction of Jesse James's murder, Bob Ford raises gun as James dusts picture. Framed reward poster is fanciful touch. Lower left: Old stereoscopic print shows corpse of America's most famous outlaw displayed to public. Top: Bob Ford poses with Peacemaker—not the gun that killed James. Bottom: Revolver he actually used, with record of his deed engraved on it.

outlaws: Frank and Jesse James, Cole, Jim, and Bob Younger, Cleil Miller, Bill Chadwell, and Charlie Pitts. The supposedly cool badmen failed to notice that the safe was unlocked. When the cashier said he couldn't operate its lock, they shot him. Another clerk dashed out a back door to sound the alarm. It was unnecessary, as the shots had alerted the citizens and they attacked with shotguns, rifles, rocks, and any available weapon. Miller and Chadwell were shot down in the street. Pitts and all three Youngers were seriously wounded as they rode out of town, firing back to delay pursuit. Only the James brothers escaped uninjured.

Two weeks later, near Medalia, Minnesota, a six-man posse killed Pitts and captured the Youngers. The three brothers survived their multiple wounds and were sent to prison. Bob Younger died there, of tuberculosis, in 1889. Cole and Jim were paroled in 1901, after serving twenty-five years. Jim tried to make a living as a traveling salesman. Within a year he committed suicide. Cole Younger joined Frank James, the only other remaining gang member, on the lecture circuit, making a living by speaking on the evils of crime. Frank James died at the Samuel farm in 1915. Younger died in bed a year later.

After the Northfield debacle Frank somehow made his way to a hideout called Rest Ranch, in lower Texas. Jesse eventually joined him and the brothers rustled cattle from across the Mexican border before coming north again. By 1881 Jesse had been implicated in additional crimes with assorted gunmen in Kentucky, Alabama, and Iowa. He kept coming home, though, and in 1882 Missouri's new governor, T. T. Crittenden, determined to end the James saga. He assigned the task to Clay County Sheriff James R. Timberlake and Kansas City Police Commissioner Henry Craig. At the same time he offered a $10,000 reward. The lawmen contacted gang members Dick Liddil and Bob and Charley Ford, offering them a pardon and part of the reward. The Fords wanted James dead because they were afraid he might discover that they had killed his cousin, Wood Hite, during a row over women and loot, and because they believed he had tortured one of their relatives to make him reveal the whereabouts of an informer.

Jesse James had married his first cousin, Zerelda Mimms, and was now living with her and their two children in St. Joseph, Missouri. He had hired the Fords to help in a planned bank robbery at Platte City and, although he had little confidence in them, had given Bob Ford a nickel-plated .44 revolver. On an April morning in 1882, Jesse James stood on a chair in his frame house to dust a portrait of Stonewall Jackson. Bob Ford walked in with the nickel-plated pistol and fired three bullets into his back. Jesse James, most famous badman in American history, fell dead.

Dick Liddil, who testified at the trials of Frank James, worked as a stable hand in Ohio (far enough away from Frank to feel safe) until he died in 1893. Bob and Charley Ford toured to booing audiences in a play called *How I Killed Jesse James*. Rumors circulated that Frank James planned revenge, and in 1884 Charley Ford killed himself. Bob Ford worked in carnivals and Wild West shows until 1892, when he opened a saloon and was almost immediately slain by a drunken gunman in the employ of a competitive saloon.

Five months after the murder of Jesse James, his brother Frank appeared at Governor Crittenden's office, removed his gun belt, and quietly surrendered. The belt buckle was of Union Army issue, obtained at Centralia during the war. When asked why he had surrendered, he said that he was weary of the outlaw life after being hunted for more than twenty years. There was such strong

Typically melodramatic cover of dime novel devoted
to fictionalized exploits of Jesse James.
This one portrayed him as villainous, but some romances
made him over into America's latter-day Robin Hood.

THE JESSE JAMES STORIES

ORIGINAL NARRATIVES OF THE JAMES BOYS

Issued Weekly. By Subscription $2.50 per year. Entered as Second Class Matter at New York Post Office by STREET & SMITH, 238 William St., N. Y.

No. 1.   Price, Ten Cents.

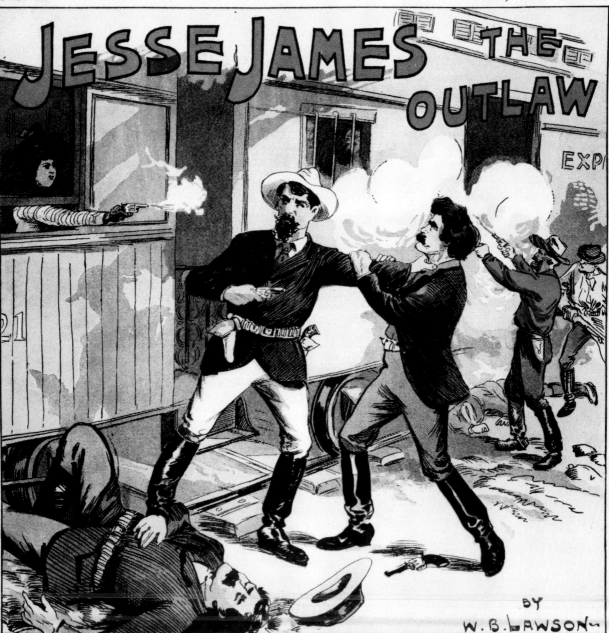

JESSE JAMES THE OUTLAW

BY
W. B. LAWSON

"HA! HA!" LAUGHED A SILVERY VOICE AS THE TIMELY LITTLE WEAPON FLASHED AND BARKED IN THE OUTLAW'S FACE.
"I OWE YOU AN OLD SCORE, JESSE JAMES!"

Reprinted December, 1938

public indignation over the connivance of lawmen in the murder of Jesse James that Frank was acquitted at two trials—in Alabama as well as Missouri. Jesse James had been using the name Thomas Howard at the time of his death. His older brother lived to hear ballad lyrics about the "the dirty little coward/who shot Mr. Howard/and laid poor Jesse in his grave."

Other dangerous men of the time attained less permanent notoriety. Among the most prominent was Henry Plummer, who was hanged by one of the first informally organized vigilante groups in Montana. His career began in the 1850's in Nevada City, California, where he killed the husband of a woman he was courting. Plummer was a seemingly respectable man, politically active, and he obtained a pardon. Almost immediately he joined a bandit gang and, in the process of robbing a stage, killed another man. Arrested, he broke out of the Nevada City jail and headed for the gold fields in Washington Territory. In what is now Lewiston, Idaho, he masqueraded as an upstanding citizen while organizing and directing a large outlaw band. In 1861 he rescued gang member Charlie Forbes from a lynch mob on Lewiston's main street by facing down the crowd and demanding due process.

Perhaps fearing exposure, he soon moved to Bannock, in what is now Montana. It was a gold-mad boom town almost unaffected by the Civil War raging in the East. In 1863 he was elected sheriff. It is said that by then his outlaw army numbered almost two hundred men, known ironically as The Innocents. One of their specialties was to waylay stages that had been marked with chalk by Plummer's informants to indicate that they carried gold shipments. He was a rich man when, at last, some captured outlaws betrayed him. Together with Charlie Forbes and two others he was arrested in January, 1864, and taken by a quickly formed vigilante group before a gallows he had built. "You wouldn't hang your own sheriff, would you?" he protested. They would and did. In an aftermath of searching, pursuit, and execution, some two dozen of his men went to the same gallows and the grip of The Innocents was broken.

A few years later Kansans were reminded of the Heatherly family that had preyed on Missourians a generation before. This time it was the Benders. Pa, or Old Man, Bender, Ma Bender, a feeble-minded son, and a buxom daughter named Kate settled at Cherryvale, in southeastern Kansas, in 1872. They built a cabin in which they established an inn and general store. Kate Bender made a modest living by holding seances and touring nearby towns with her own spiritualist show. Sometimes she returned to the Bender Inn with men who had enjoyed her performance, and travelers stopped there, too, for a meal or a night's lodging. The dining table was so situated that a customer sat flush against a canvas curtain separating the public room from the living quarters. Old Man Bender or his son stood behind the canvas, holding a sledge hammer. Corpses were dumped through a trap door into an earthen cellar, where they awaited burial on the prairie.

The murders went undetected until the spring of 1873, when a Dr. York stopped there after mentioning his intention to his brother, Colonel York. When he failed to arrive at his destination, Colonel York went to the inn and questioned the proprietors. Old Man Bender said he hadn't seen Dr. York—that perhaps the poor man had been waylaid by Jesse James or scalped by the Indians. The Colonel left but grew increasingly suspicious when his brother remained missing. After five days he returned with a posse. The Benders had fled. The posse found eleven graves, including that of Dr. York.

Pursuers could find no trace of the Benders. The case

remained officially open for many years. In 1889 two women were extradited to Kansas from Detroit but were released when they could not be positively identified as Kate and Ma Bender. There is a legend that a vengeful posse did overtake the family somewhere on the prairie, far from witnesses, and killed them—burning Kate alive for her crimes. The legend explains that the executioners vowed never to reveal their grim revenge. If the story is true, the vow was kept.

In those years James Butler Hickok was inspiring very different legends in that region. Born in 1837 in Illinois, he was the son of a New England preacher who had settled in the West as a farmer and storekeeper. His boyhood hero was Kit Carson, and early in life he began to follow the bragging, tall-tale tradition of Carson, Boone, Crockett, and Mike Fink. As he gained shooting skill, he also began to copy some of their fabled deeds, not always with fortunate results. But it is doubtful that the nickname Wild Bill was earned in recognition of reckless exploits. There is evidence that he was called Dutch Bill for a while when nonsense aliases were a fashionable form of western humor, and that he attempted to thrash anyone who called him Duck Bill—a reference to the pendulous nose and protruding lip from which he diverted attention by growing a large moustache. It was probably much later, when he toured the East with Buffalo Bill Cody in a Ned Buntline melodrama, *Scouts of the Prairie*, that he assumed the colorful stage name Wild Bill.

In the mid-1850's Hickok walked to St. Louis in quest of adventure and a livelihood. It was about then that he may have ridden for a few months with Lane's Red Legs. It was also about then that he tried farming and served as a constable at Johnson City, Kansas—until a couple of his cabins were burned by neighbors who resented his advances to their wives. He married and quickly abandoned a Shawnee girl, going off to work for the Overland Company as a stagecoach guard and driver on the Santa Fe Trail. In 1858 he and some fifty other righteous possemen raided an Indian village near St. Joseph, Missouri, killed some braves, and "captured" a herd of horses, several of which supposedly had been stolen from Overland.

Next he worked for the famous freighting firm of Russel, Majors and Waddell as manager of the Rock Creek Station, on a stretch of the Oregon Trail through Nebraska Territory. The company had bought land from David McCanles, a southern sympathizer suspected of supplying horses to the Confederates at the outbreak of the war. There had been trouble between Hickok and McCanles, possibly over horses, possibly over a woman. When McCanles and two neighbors, all unarmed, came to the Rock Creek Station to seek payment for the land, they were shot down. Afterward Hickok claimed that McCanles had ridden up with nine horse thieves. Hickok said he killed McCanles with a single-shot rifle, shot three rustlers with a revolver, stabbed several, but had to admit that a couple got away.

Court records at Beatrice, Nebraska, tell a somewhat simpler story of triple murder, and no one—least of all witnesses—had any doubt about it. However, the judge and most of the neighbors felt strong obligations to Overland and the Union. Hickok was acquitted.

He served the North as a scout, spy, and sniper, always as a civilian, and in 1865 became a more or less professional gambler in Springfield, Missouri. In July of that year he fought a duel with Dave Tutt over a gambling debt. Tutt fired first and missed. Hickok then put a bullet through his heart. Somehow he usually convinced authorities of his innocence in such affairs, and in the following years he worked as a Deputy U.S. Marshal at Fort Riley, Kansas, and as an Army scout, "pacifying" Indians with Sheridan and Custer. In 1869 he served as sheriff and city marshal in Fort Hays, where he enforced a new ordinance against carrying weapons by patrolling with a sawed-off shotgun, two revolvers, a derringer, and a Bowie knife. With his armament, his long, flowing hair, and his attire—fancy buckskins or velvet, red sash, big sombrero—he was already glamorizing his image. But in 1870 he was involved in half a dozen unglamorous gambling-hall or saloon killings. Because four of the dead were soldiers, General Sheridan ordered his arrest and Hickok left Hays as a fugitive from justice.

Next he showed up at Niagara Falls as entrepreneur of a financially disastrous Wild West show. Heading west again, he became marshal of Abilene, Kansas (where there was no Army post). He shot down two men the day he took office. Later he had an indecisive argument with John Wesley Hardin, but neither man was inclined to settle the matter with guns. Hickok did, however, shoot down a lesser gunfighter named Phil Coe in a row over a woman, and on one occasion he killed a deputy by mistake. After a year of what struck Abilene authorities as excessive violence, he was dismissed amid ugly rumors about the state of his eyesight and his mental health.

Having arranged some sort of amnesty with the Fort Hays Army post, he returned briefly as marshal, then embarked on his vaudeville tour with Colonel Cody, married a lady circus owner named Agnes Lake, and left her in Cincinnati while he went off to Deadwood to explore ways of finding cash in the new Dakota gold rush.

There, in August, 1876, he was playing poker in the Mann & Lewis No. 10 Saloon when a saddle tramp named Jack McCall walked in and shot him through the back of the head. It had been Hickok's rule to sit with his back to the wall, because of the many enemies he had made, but on this occasion he switched places with another gambler as a joke. His killer was tried, released, caught and tried again in Laramie, and finally hanged in 1877.

That did not end the Hickok saga. He had been lionized in *Harper's Monthly* shortly after the Civil War, and again in Wild West shows and Buntline dramas. After his death, dime novels made him a hero. In 1895 Sir Henry Morton Stanley, the man who had found Dr. Livingstone in Africa for the readers of the New York *Herald*, published a book about his American travels in which he recalled an interview with Hickok. "I say," Sir Henry had asked, "how many white men have you killed to your certain knowledge?"

"I suppose I have killed considerably over a hundred," Hickok had replied, adding, however, that "by heaven, I have never killed one man without good cause."

Left: James Butler Hickok—"Wild Bill"—who is still popularly depicted as one of America's great lawmen, but was tried for murder after one shocking gunfight and sought by Army troops after additional shootings. Upper right: Stage operated by Overland Mail, for which Hickok worked when he stole horses from Indians and engaged in early shoot-outs. Lower right: Sheriff Henry Plummer's band of road agents waylaying Montana stagecoach.

A claim might be made for St. Louis as the first of the western boom towns. It was, after all, the gateway to the West from the time of the Lewis and Clark expedition, if not earlier. In the 1820's and 1830's traders bound for the great fur rendezvous set out from there, and it was to St. Louis that they returned with mountains of pelts. Many of the famous plains rifles were made there, and the town supplied westering wagon trains with oxen, horses, mules, prairie schooners, gunpowder, whiskey, food, and guides.

With hooves gouging deep ruts and men brawling in the muddy streets, St. Louis remained wild by eastern standards for several generations. In 1882 *St. Louis Post-Dispatch* editorial writer John A. Cockerill wrote somewhat disparagingly of a political office seeker, and Colonel Alonzo Slayback called at the composing room to express his opposing view with a pepperbox pistol. Cockerill drew a gun from the editorial desk and slew the Colonel. The situation was rather like that in Nevada at the height of the Comstock silver rush, during the Civil War. When the *Territorial Enterprise* moved from Carson City to the raw new community of Virginia City, its editors and some of the other staff members carried six-guns to defend their views regarding the war, silver mining, imminent statehood, and local politics. On one occasion, Joe Goodman of the *Enterprise* wounded Tom Fitch of the rival *Daily Union* in a duel over editorial statements.

St. Louis, however, was essentially a southern rather than a western settlement, with a stable municipal government and constabulary to discourage violence. Swindles were more typical than gunplay. The "Pike's-Peak-or-Bust" gold rush, though it uncovered great ore deposits, began as a fraud perpetrated by St. Louis wagon dealers in the days when Denver was still called Cherry Creek. With the California gold rush slowing down, the dealers whipped up new business by dis-

playing heavy nuggets supposedly plucked from Cherry Creek. Thus they encouraged an exodus of adventurers from their own city and helped to populate wilder towns in the gold fields.

Wagon travel was too slow for many of the forty-niners and subsequent prospectors, however. After the news trickled east regarding the Mother Lode diggings at Sutter's Mill in California, newly designed clipper ships broke speed records rounding Cape Horn en route to San Francisco. There was also a shorter way—a packet voyage to Panama, a trip by mule-back or Indian-back relays across the Isthmus, and a second voyage up to San Francisco. Carrying their savings across the Panamanian gold trail, prospectors became the prey of bandits who converged on Panama City until local businessmen imported a gunfighter named Randy Runnels from Texas. Runnels and his employers organized a group of gunmen known as the Vigilantes of New Grenada (perhaps the first group to be called Vigilantes rather than Regulators). They reportedly captured seventy-eight road agents and hanged them from the sea wall. After additional lynchings, corpses were

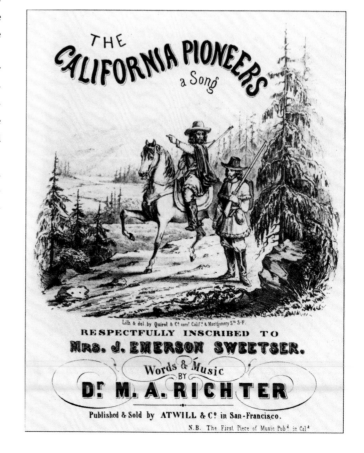

Preceding pages: "Sunday Morning in the Mines," painting by Charles C. Nahl, captures wild spirit of gold camps where miners made their own laws and settled disputes by holding informal "court sessions." Prospectors departing (left) and on trail to California (right) travel with weapons ready in case of attack by Indians or road agents.

Old photograph shows Goldfield, Nevada, one of many boom towns that retained rough frontier atmosphere after rich gold and silver strikes began to dwindle and modern telegraph poles lined Main Street. In establishments like Miner's Exchange, Esmeralda, and Grotto, liquor flowed freely enough to help professional gamblers ease gold dust away from prospectors. In drawing, top-hatted "sharpers" deal faro at California gold camp. Vigilantes failed to thwart dishonest gamblers, "the curse of California."

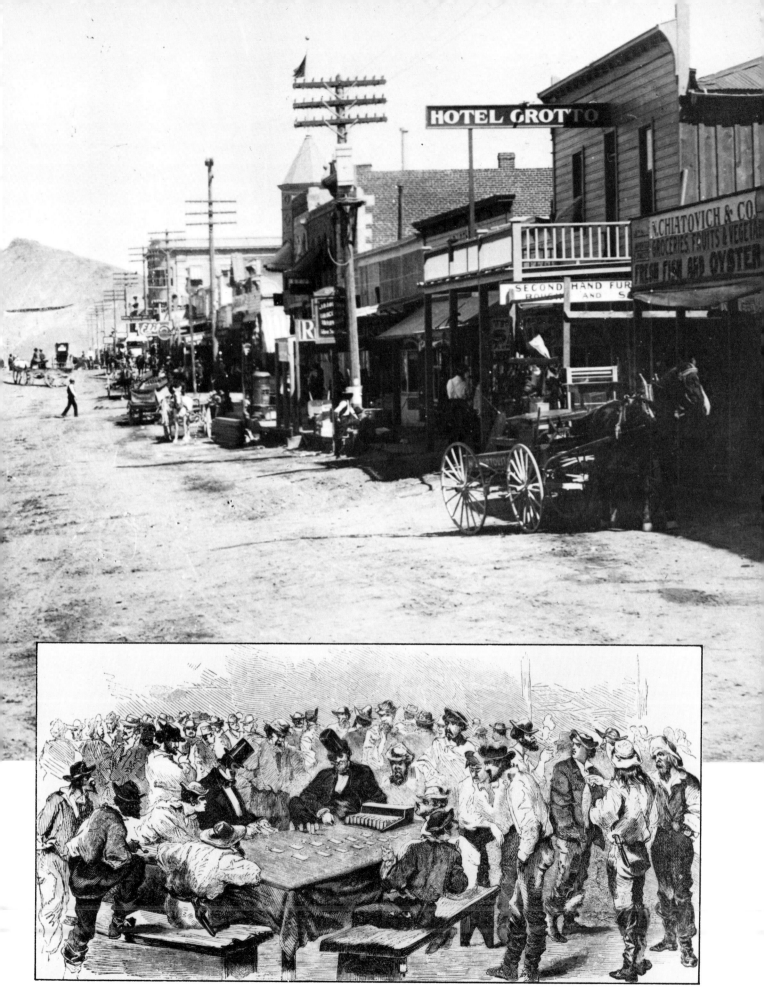

left as warnings on the jungle trails. One of the first wild towns had been tamed.

From Kansas to California boom towns arose. Most of the early ones began as mining camps. A little later came the cow towns and supply depots at railheads, the winter settlements of track-laying crews, and the sprawling tent towns on the Kansas-Oklahoma border of the Indian lands. In some instances, as at Fort Riley and Fort Hays, the proximity of an Army post made a town all the wilder as bored soldiers—like the Texas trail hands when they reached the loading-pen towns—squandered their pay in saloons, gambling halls, and bawdy houses. Frontier boredom and tension were important factors. From the writings of the noted American historian Frederick Jackson Turner, some theorists have concluded that western towns provided psychological safety valves, an emotional release from the tensions of the frontier.

A few such places have been linked by history to notorious badmen. A famous picture of Cole and Bob Younger, Frank and Jesse James, posing in a photographer's studio with a total of two rifles and six revolvers, is believed to have been taken in Kansas City during a customary spree between holdups.

Further west, Lewiston and Bannock were the lairs of the Plummer gang, and a couple of Plummer's cronies may have been the horsemen who once rode right into the Old Montana Club in Virginia City to scoop the money from the poker, keno, and roulette tables. In the same city (the Virginia City in Montana, not Nevada), on the corner of Wallace and Van Buren streets, vigilantes lynched one of Plummer's chief lieutenants, Jack Gallagher, and four of his lesser road agents in January, 1864. They were buried together at Alder Gulch cemetery, which, like the one at Dodge, acquired the name Boot Hill.

Wild Bill Hickok left bloodstains in Hays and Abilene

Illustrations published in 1850's by Gleason's Pictorial Drawing-Room Companion *and* Harper's *show typical characters and activities at California diggings. Pictures at upper left were captioned "Cradle rocking, on the Stanislaus" and "Quicksilver machine, in Mormon Gulch." Scene at lower left was labeled "Housekeeping." "A native Californian" (above) was made to look both colorful and villainous; note that Mexican has dagger in boot and one miner has gun on hip.*

69

and was himself shot down in Deadwood. Wyatt Earp, another lawman finally exposed as lawless by relentless investigation, contributed generously to the bad reputation of Tombstone—as did Doc Holliday, Sheriff John Behan, and the Clantons. Earp, Holliday, Clay Allison, and Belle Starr all loitered in the saloons of Dodge, too, though Belle Starr was better known at Fort Smith and in the Indian Territory.

Still, the really wild, lawless boom towns were more

Above: Captain Harry Love, self-styled "Ranger" who killed two Mexicans, then decapitated one and amputated hand of the other as evidence he had slain legendary bandits Joaquin Murieta and Three-Fingered Jack Garcia. Love was eventually killed in shoot-out with his estranged wife's bodyguard. Scene at right represents unruliness and squalor on one of San Francisco's main thoroughfares in 1849.

often associated with outlaws in general—little-known outlaws for the most part—than with the famous myth-makers. California's gold-rush towns were at first sprawl-ing tent-and-shanty camps that attracted gamblers, foot-pads, whiskey peddlers, usurers, swindlers, armed ban-dits, and prostitutes. Such professions were usually more profitable than placer mining. Placerville, in California's Eldorado County, was originally called Hangtown as a tribute to the zeal of an informal vigilante group of miners.

Another town in the Sierra foothills, where no vigilance committee hampered merrymaking, was christened Rough and Ready.

Racial hatreds increased the violence. Indians, blacks, Chinese, and Mexicans were often ostracized, oc-casionally killed. Chinese labor, imported to build rail-roads, worked in the mines for very low wages, with the result that Americans and European immigrants feared for their jobs. In 1850 the California legislature imposed a

work tax on "foreign" labor, making it almost impossible for Chinese or Mexicans to earn their way in the mines. (Europeans and even Australian convicts were counted as "native Americans" by the mine owners.) The Mexicans were more numerous and better established than the Chinese; California, after all, had recently been theirs. Many of them reacted with ferocity, joining mounted *bandido* troops, stealing horses and cattle, holding up stagecoaches, stores, saloons, assay offices, and pay offices at the mines. They raided the camps at such places as Mariposa, Whisky Slide, Poverty Flat. Thus arose the legend of Joaquin Murieta. Most historians believe there were several Joaquins, perhaps as many as five, and one, indeed, may have been named Murieta. Another may have been Joaquin Carrillo, since the governor mentioned a bandit of that name. By the spring of 1853, so many stories of depredations had reached Sacramento that Governor John Bigler posted a $1,000 reward for the bandit Joaquin. The notice specified no last name though most Californians were talking excitedly about Murieta. Like Jesse James, he was accused of atrocities that took place simultaneously in places hundreds of miles apart. And like James he was becoming a Robin Hood figure, though only to impoverished Mexicans.

The legislature authorized a ranger patrol under Captain Harry Love, a flamboyant and ruthless Texan who boasted that he had fought Indians, soldiered in the war with Mexico, and run desperadoes to ground during an earlier stint as peace officer and Texas Ranger. At $150 a month per man, Captain Love had no trouble recruiting a paramilitary force of twenty riders, several of whom had killed men. They suffered no casualties while on duty, but at least half a dozen of them eventually died (to use the delicate phrase then current) with their boots on. Innocent Mexicans were terrified. In July, 1853, Love wrote to the governor that he had taken a prisoner who claimed to be the bandit chief's brother-in-law and who promised, as the Captain explained, "he will take and show us Joaquin, if we release him."

Two weeks later the rangers and their involuntary guide surprised a camp of Mexicans near Cantua Creek. The posse captured two and killed two. Three others escaped. Love promptly identified one of the dead as Joaquin Murieta in spite of the fact that no one had ever seen an authenticated picture of the outlaw and descriptions were scanty. The other corpse had only three fingers on one hand, so Love announced that this was Manuel Garcia, a bandit more widely known as Three-Fingered Jack, who was supposed to be Murieta's lieutenant.

As proof that he had earned the governor's reward, Love cut off the three-fingered hand of one corpse and the head of the other, pickled them in jars of whiskey at Fort Miller, and rode into Sacramento with his grisly evidence. His two captives had no opportunity to challenge the identification. One of them was somehow drowned while fording a river on the way to jail and the second was lynched at Mariposa. Love received the promised $1,000 for Murieta, an extra $500 for Three-Fingered Jack, and an additional $5,000 bestowed by a grateful legislature. The three Mexicans who had escaped the posse said afterward that their beheaded friend was an innocent man named Joaquin Valenzuela. In San Francisco, the *Alta California* printed an editorial comment:

> "It affords amusement to our citizens to read the various accounts of the capture and decapitation of 'the notorious Joaquin Murieta' .... A few weeks ago a party of native Californians and Sonorians started for the Tulare Valley for the express purpose of running mus-

Top: Broadside advertising display of alleged bandit's head at saloon in Stockton, California. Bottom: Artist's conception of Joaquin Murieta and henchmen battling miners for their gold in early 1850's. Most scholars now believe there were several "Joaquins"—perhaps as many as five—whose exploits blended into single Robin Hood legend.

WILL BE
EXHIBITED
FOR ONE DAY ONLY!

AT THE STOCKTON HOUSE!
THIS DAY, AUG. 19, FROM 9 A. M., UNTIL 6 P. M.

THE HEAD
Of the renowned Bandit!
JOAQUIN!
AND THE
HAND OF THREE FINGERED JACK!
THE NOTORIOUS ROBBER AND MURDERER.

"JOAQUIN" and "THREE-FINGERED JACK," were captured by the State Rangers, under the command of Capt. Harry Love, at the Arroyo Cantua, July 24th. No reasonable doubt can be entertained in regard to the identification of the head now on exhibition, as being that of the notorious robber, Joaquin Murietta, as it has been recognized by hundreds of persons who have formerly seen him.

tangs. Three of the party have returned and report that they were attacked by a party of Americans . . . . It is too well known that Joaquin Murieta was not the person killed by Captain Love's party at the Panoche Pass . . . and this is positively asserted by those who have seen the real Murieta and the spurious head."

Violence abated somewhat, perhaps under the menace of further such reprisals, and the rangers were disbanded. Love's most publicized exploits thereafter consisted of beating Mrs. Love until she left him. She hired a bodyguard, Christian Fred Iverson, who killed Love in a shoot-out at Santa Clara in 1868. For years the pickled head and hand made the rounds of saloons in various California towns. They disappeared in the great San Francisco earthquake and fire of 1906. Murieta might have been forgotten but for the appearance in 1854 of a paperbacked potboiler by John Rollin Ridge, a Cherokee writer who sometimes called himself Yellow Bird. His book was *The Life and Adventures of Joaquin Murieta, Celebrated California Bandit.* Next came one of the popular dime novels published by Beadle and Adams, then a fifteen-center and then a twenty-five-center, and so on. Murieta had fertilized literary imaginations for three quarters of a century when Walter Noble Burns (who also wrote glowingly of the Earps and Billy the Kid) published *The Robin Hood of El Dorado.* Hollywood foresaw new gold-rush profits in a movie adaptation with the same title, so in 1936 Metro-Goldwyn-Mayer starred Warner Baxter as a noble Murieta, with J. Carrol Naish as his quaintly rough and lovable partner, Three-Fingered Jack.

In Harry Love's time San Francisco was a metropolis, but it remained one of the wildest of boom towns. In 1852, when gold production peaked, some 67,000 immigrants landed at San Francisco and another 30,000 or so came overland to the West Coast. Even before that, the city had spawned several red-light districts, including the festering strip that came to be known as the Barbary Coast. In 1851 the *Alta California* editorially scolded rowdy drunks for riding their horses into saloons and for "careless shooting" when a bullet grazed "three gentlemen at the bar of the Hotel de Ville in Montgomery Street."

More serious were the deeds of outlaw gangs roaming through town. Robbery and murder were rampant. The small gold camps set up "miners' courts" to deal with criminals by whipping, banishment, or hanging, but San Francisco had sheriffs, a constabulary, and a civic government to maintain order. Part of the city's trouble was that so many of its elected and appointed officials were renowned for corruption, and part of the trouble was an influx of hoodlums. Those from the East (particularly New York) formed gangs known as the Hounds. Even greater numbers were released convicts from Australia, known as the Sydney Ducks or Sydney Coves, who established their own shanty enclave, Sydney Town, on the city's fringe. They robbed miners on the streets and stabbed or shot customers in saloons and gambling halls, calmly picking the pockets of fallen victims. They set fires in order to loot stores during the confusion and rob people fleeing the blaze. Whole sections of town were destroyed by their conflagrations at least four times in two years. Arrested criminals who could not bribe the police were often freed because witnesses did not dare to testify against them.

In February, 1851, a merchant named C. J. Jansen was beaten and robbed in his dry-goods store on Mont-

Great seal of San Francisco's Committee of Vigilance, whose leaders put great stock in official-looking trappings of legality. Right: Century Magazine's rendering of confrontation when Vigilantes trained cannon on doors of San Francisco jail and abducted two killers, Charles Cora and James Casey. Both prisoners were "tried" and lynched.

gomery Street. Sam Brannan, a Mormon elder who had risen to prominence as a printer, newspaper proprietor, and storekeeper, became so incensed that he formed San Francisco's first Committee of Vigilance. It began simply as a mob of businessmen who were convinced the police would refuse to act. Two Australians were caught and tentatively identified by Jansen as his assailants. One of the two was mistaken for James Stuart, a burglar and horse thief who had murdered a storekeeper in a mining camp. Preparations were under way for a hanging when a cooler-headed merchant named William Coleman persuaded the gathering to hold a formal if not legal trial. After an indecisive verdict the suspects were jailed rather than executed; they were subsequently proved innocent.

But Brannan, Coleman, Jansen, and other prominent citizens organized about two hundred men into a Commit-

tee of Vigilance which gave itself power to hold trials and executions if the sheriffs, police, and courts failed to do so. Almost immediately they caught a petty criminal named John Jenkins as he was carrying off a small safe. When the Committee hanged him, the street crowd approved, as did the newspapers. The vigilantes had established their reign.

In July they captured the real James Stuart. The hanging took place on the Market Street wharf as throngs of citizens bared their heads and ships in the harbor fired salutes and raised flags. Two other outlaws, Sam Whittaker and Robert McKenzie, were rescued from the Committee by sheriff's deputies and police. The Vigilantes invaded the jail, spirited the badmen away, and conducted another public hanging. Despite weak protests from the governor, the Committee tried eighty-nine sus-

pects, hanged four, publicly whipped one, deported twenty-eight, released forty-one, and turned fifteen over to the police before declaring San Francisco safe again and adjourning in September.

For a while the city was relatively peaceful but by 1855 residents were again furious. The administration was corrupt, several officials were believed to have been elected by the criminal element voting as a bloc, fraudulent elections had become the rule, and tensions were increased by a depression that had forced several bank failures as gold production dwindled. In November a gambler and professional ballot-box stuffer named Charles Cora shot and killed an unarmed man, William H. Richardson, outside the Cosmopolitan Saloon. Cora's mistress, a prostitute, hired lawyers who succeeded in achieving a mistrial, and Cora languished in jail while newspapers speculated about a rigged jury and citizens talked of reviving the Vigilance Committee. In the spring of 1856, editor James King of the *Evening Bulletin*, in denouncing the local political machine, pointed out that editor James P. Casey of the *Sunday Times* was an election inspector who had somehow won a ward seat on the Board of Supervisors, even though no one knew he was running for the office. King also published the known fact that Casey had served a term in Sing Sing Prison before coming west. Casey sought out King, called, "Draw and defend yourself," and before King had the slightest chance to do so shot him down at fifteen paces with a Navy Colt.

Four days later some five hundred vigilantes, led by "Chief Marshal" Charles Doan on a white horse, appeared before the jail with rifles, bayonets, and a cannon. When they threatened to blow in the doors, the jailers surrendered both Cora and Casey as the governor and mayor watched helplessly from a nearby rooftop. Two days later, after a dignified but illegal tribunal, both killers were

Above: Studio portrait of Tiburcio Vasquez, probably made after his final capture. He was hanged at Sacramento in 1875 after rampage reminiscent of James gang and Murieta bandits. Upper right: Daguerreotype of San Francisco Vigilance Committee's uniformed "Sharpshooters." Lower right: Invitation to double hanging at wild town of Helena, Montana. Spectators were disappointed because executions, scheduled for Christmas season, were postponed until spring.

1 - Capt. Smith.
2 - 1st Lieut. Bannerman
3 - 2d - Willis

3d Lieut. Hayes. - 4
Private Kone. - 5
" Shearer. - 6

San Francisco
May 15th 1856

— underneath its clouds of sin,
The heart of man retaineth yet
Gleams of its holy origin;
And half-quenched stars that never set,
Dim colors of its faded bow,
And early beauty, linger there,
And o'er its wasted desert blow
Faint breathings of its morning air,
O, never yet upon the scroll
Of the sin-stained, but priceless soul,
Hath Heaven inscribed "DESPAIR!"

Mr. *Frank Adkins*

    You are invited to witness the execution of **William Gay and William Biggerstaf**
on **Friday, December 20, 1895, at 10 o'clock A. M.,** at the Lewis and Clarke County Jail.
    Respectfully,

Henry Jurgens

Sheriff of Lewis and Clarke County.

Above: 1874 wood engraving from Harper's *shows "Vigilance court in session." Man bandaging leg at right provides visual hint that miscreants put up fight. At least one prisoner has hands tied behind back, and one vigilante, while awaiting formality of verdict, climbs telegraph pole with rope. Poles were often used as gibbets, especially on plains where large trees were scarce. Right: Unknown tramp hanged by lynch mob from telegraph pole over Northern Pacific tracks at Billings, Montana, in 1891. His crime was murder of saloon-keeper John Clancey.*

dropped from a makeshift hinged gallows extending from the second-floor windows of the committee's meeting house. Vigilante William Coleman now called for volunteers to enforce the law. More than six thousand San Franciscans responded. The governor declared this to be an insurrection and directed General William T. Sherman—who commanded the California Militia—to suppress the vigilantes. Sherman resigned. Two more murderers, Joseph Hetherington and Philander Brace, were hanged in July. By mid-August San Francisco's outlaws were so frightened that the vigilantes held a triumphal parade and then disbanded.

Seven years later the miners of Bannock and Virginia City in the Montana Territory decided to emulate San Francisco. The new outbreak of vigilantism may have been sparked when the Plummer gang killed a popular businessman in 1863. Thomas Dimsdale, a young Englishman who was trying to make a living as a singing teacher in the Territory, wrote a heartily approving account, *The Vigilantes of Montana*, in which he placed the number of hangings at an even two dozen. Later investigators have raised the figure to thirty. Masked committeemen called on suspects at midnight to issue warnings. They also tacked up warning posters—typically a drawing of a skull and crossbones, sometimes over a coffin, and sometimes over the mystic numbers 3-7-77. The symbolism of the numbers is no longer clear, but their effect was to scatter most of the remaining Plummer gang after Henry Plummer himself was lynched in 1864. During this period the Overland Company ran a stage between Virginia City and Salt Lake. The coach was held up at Pontneuf Canyon, below Rattlesnake, and five men were killed when they resisted the outlaws. One of the gunmen, Frank Williams, fled the Territory. He stopped for a while at Cherry Creek—the future Denver—thinking he was beyond the reach of vengeance. But the Montana vigilantes corresponded with a similar, though less organized, group in Colorado. The post carried a letter naming and describing the killer. He was suspended from a limb of a Cherry Creek cottonwood.

Another badman lynched by the vigilantes was Joseph A. Slade—usually called Jack Slade—a former Overland superintendent. In 1858 Slade had been shot five times by another Overland superintendent, Jules Bene, whom he had accused of stealing horses. Slade recovered and a year later, with the aid of several outlaw friends, caught Bene, tied him to a post, and used his arms and legs as pistol targets before delivering the *coup de grâce*. It was said that Slade carried Bene's ear as a watch fob. Arrested in 1861 after shooting up the Army post at Fort Halleck, he escaped and eventually settled on a small ranch at Virginia City, Montana. Because he became violent whenever he was drinking, the vigilantes ordered him to leave. Instead he embarked on a week-long spree, "hurrahing" the town with his six-gun. The vigilantes lost patience and hanged him from the crossbeam of a beef scaffold.

Patience was wearing thin elsewhere in Montana. Helena, then known as Last Chance Gulch, was so wild that not even the righteousness of the vigilante movement could subdue the revelry in the red-light district, which flourished for almost a century before a reform administration closed it down in 1953. But by 1870 the vigilantes were acquiring a semblance of legal formality—or at least due process. That was the year when more than a thousand citizens waited around Helena's courthouse square for a verdict in the trial of two thugs. As soon as the jury found them guilty, they were taken to the big cottonwood known as the hanging tree. Afterward a good many citizens, posing proudly for a photographer, grouped themselves around the tree with the two outlaws still dangling from a limb.

Robbery in that area was waning slightly but rustling thrived. In 1884, Dakota rancher Theodore Roosevelt attended a Montana stockmen's meeting at which plans were made to scour the range. The future president was among those who favored lynching parties. But it was the future U.S. Minister to Uruguay, the respected pioneer Granville Stuart, who organized and led this vigilante revival. His men came to be called Stuart's Stranglers; they executed thirty-five men.

But it was the establishment of an ordered society, with a regulated government, police, and courts—not sporadic vigilante risings or the threat of murderous posses such as Love's rangers—that gradually ended the era of western lawlessness. For years, heedless of probable retribution, many badmen tried to emulate the Murietas and the Jameses. California's Tiburcio Vasquez was such a bandit, and successful enough to inspire stories that he had ridden with Murieta. A product of the chaotic gold rush, he was released from San Quentin in 1870 after serving three prison terms. Three years later he led an outlaw band into the village of Tres Pinos. In the course of looting the hamlet, he (or possibly one of his men) shot down several unarmed residents. Large rewards were offered for his capture and a posse was led by George A. Beers, a reporter for the San Francisco *Chronicle*. Vasquez knew he was being pursued, yet he rampaged through Fresno County, first raiding the hotel and stores in Kingston, then robbing stagecoaches before retreating to a hideout at Cahuenga Pass, a place that would one day be called Hollywood. Beers wounded the outlaw and helped to bring him in. Vasquez was tried and in March, 1875, he climbed a gallows that had been erected in Sacramento especially for him.

Culprit dangles from tree branch in background of O. C. Seltzer's evocative portrayal of "Vigilante Ways." These are relatively late-vintage Montana vigilantes, perhaps some of Stuart's Stranglers who executed 35 rustlers, road agents, and gunslingers in mid-1880's.

Preceding pages: In E. C. Ward's painting,
"Enter the Law," peace officer rides into cow town
where his welcome will depend on his combining
stubborn courage with Saturday-night permissiveness.
Above: "The Trial of a Horse Thief," by Jno. Mulvany, is
circa 1877 evocation of informal frontier justice.

Wildness seldom came to western towns in cinematic style, with mounted raiders swooping down to terrorize the Saturday night square dance, the revival meeting, or the ladies' church supper, then retreating in panic before the blazing guns of the heroic marshal. More often the marshal or sheriff was primarily a tax collector, a server of foreclosures and eviction notices, a jailer of drunks, and a protector of the more influential or moneyed citizens whether or not they themselves were among the wild ones. For each of the truly heroic lawmen, like John Slaughter, Bill Tilghman, Chris Madsen, and Heck Thomas, there were others who took bribes or actually joined forces with the rustlers and the robbers. And for every posseman or vigilante who acted on sincerely noble motives, there were sadists who enjoyed lynchings and there were self-interested parties enriching themselves or engaging in private feuds. On several occasions in Montana, Wyoming, and Texas, vigilante groups were composed chiefly of cattle barons to whom every small but competitive rancher was a rustler. In Arizona, Colorado, and California, there were vigilante miners to whom every rival was a claim-jumper. And at one time in Dodge City, Kansas, it was alleged that Bat Masterson—among the West's most effective town tamers—organized a "Peace Commission" solely to protect Luke Short's Long Branch at the expense of rival emporiums. The wild towns were made wild by their own residents.

After the California gold camps came the Colorado silver and railroad towns, like Durango, which had its own vigilantes and its own renowned Hanging Tree. A similar community was Leadville, which was still being called a "shooting town" by newspapers of the 1880's. The discovery of the Comstock Lode in 1859 led to the booming of the other Virginia City, in Nevada, where the first hanging—of a murderer named John Millain, who had

killed a local madame for her jewels—was a gala public event. The region's badmen seemed irrepressible. In November, 1870, Comstock gambler E.B. Parsons and Virginia City businessman Jack Davis succumbed to fashion by robbing the Central Pacific train at Verdi, a few miles west of Reno. They took $40,000 from the Wells Fargo box but were quickly caught and jailed. However, the same train was robbed again the next day at Independence, and these were the first episodes in an epidemic of robberies throughout the region.

In 1863, while working for the *Territorial Enterprise* in Virginia City, a young reporter named Sam Clemens began using the pen name Mark Twain. Later, when he wrote a story about "The Bad Man from Bodie," he was referring to a place across the line in California. Bodie was long considered "the wickedest town in the West." The *Sacramento Union* called it a "shooter's town," even though none of the famous outlaws lived there. In 1867, when it had a population of 15,000 miners, unsung badmen, and women, J. Ross Browne, artist-correspondent for *Harper's*, confirmed that it was properly notorious for shootings and stabbings. In the 1870's another reporter calculated that shootings averaged one per evening. In the mid-eighties the *Bodie Standard* recorded a single day's events: two fatal shootings at saloons, two local stage robberies by a single pair of badmen, and the funeral of an outlaw who had killed a lawman. What finally quieted Bodie was the petering out of the local gold veins. It was a virtual ghost town in 1932 when, like many of the old wild towns, it burned to the ground.

One of the last big gold booms was the Black Hills rush, which resulted in the breaking of treaties with the Sioux and the consequent massacre at the Little Big Horn. Cheyenne was then the nearest railroad stop and supply depot for the Black Hills and it was wild, but not so wild as

Deadwood, where Wyatt Earp briefly prospected for easy money but found the competition disheartening, where Bill Hickok's corpse was only one of many, where a "suburb" was named Robbers' Roost, and where the stages were held up every few days. Deadwood burned down in 1879 and flooded out in 1883 but, like Tombstone, was said to be too tough to die.

The Kansas cow towns were no tamer. The first important ones were Abilene and Hays. Abilene was established in 1868 as the Kansas Pacific railhead, one hundred and sixty-four miles west of Kansas City. The pattern was set there for Ellsworth, Dodge, Newton, Wichita, Caldwell. Longhorns were driven up from Texas and the buyers waited at the loading pens or in the new hotels. Each sale was followed by soaring profits for the vendors of whiskey, the proprietors of casinos, and the inmates of bawdy houses. The fanciest of Abilene's score of watering places was the Alamo (soon to be emulated by another of the same name in Dodge), where two dozen bartenders and three orchestras operated around the clock.

Hays outdid Abilene. In 1867 a buffalo hunter named Matt Clarkson described Hays in his diary: "There are 22 saloons, three dance halls, one little grocery store and one clothing store. We do not think anything of having one or two dead men on the streets every morning. Some of them are soldiers from the fort. There is no law except the law of the six shooter."

When straight-laced Kansas farmers and other reformers passed a law prohibiting the loading of cattle at Abilene, the shippers switched to Hays and in 1872 put a million longhorns aboard the cattle cars. Almost as quickly, Dodge and Wichita gained ascendancy; early billboards proclaimed that "Everything Goes in Wichita." At the Long Branch Saloon in Dodge, Deputy Marshal Bat Masterson is said to have faced down the notorious

Top: Deadwood in 1876, when Black Hills gold rush turned mining camp into wild boom town. It was in '76 that Wild Bill Hickok was shot to death in one of Deadwood's saloons. Far left: Marshal Jim Courtright of Fort Worth, who was reputed to extort protection money from saloon keepers. He was killed by gunfighting gambler Luke Short in 1886. Left: Texas longhorns arriving in Dodge City, where drovers often defied lawmen.

gunfighter Clay Allison. Such episodes were common in Dodge, where gunfighters joked about "having a couple of dead men for breakfast."

A few other wild towns began as outposts, way stations, and construction camps on the railroads stretching across the continent. Fort Riley and Cheyenne were such places, and so was the tiny West Texas settlement of Eagle's Nest, where Judge Roy Bean dispensed whiskey and something he called justice. Bean was born in the 1820's in a backwoods Kentucky cabin. At the age of about sixteen he left for New Orleans with a party of slave traders, and a few years later drove an ammunition wagon for the American forces in the war with Mexico. In 1848 he and his brother Sam opened a cantina in Chihuahua, but within a year he put a bullet through an inebriated Mexican (a badman, according to Bean) and hastily joined the gold stampede to California. He tended bar for another brother, Josh, in San Diego until he was jailed for wounding a man and his horse during a drunken horseback duel. He escaped, worked in another saloon at San Gabriel, joined a posse on a futile hunt for Joaquin Murieta, and went back to tending bar until 1858. After an argument (possibly involving gunplay) for the favors of a local lady, he narrowly escaped being lynched and once again departed hastily, this time to work for Sam at a saloon in Messilla, New Mexico. During the Civil War he led a small band of guerrillas who styled themselves the Free Rovers but were labeled the Forty Thieves by disinterested observers. Following a couple of skirmishes with Federal patrols, they scattered.

Bean settled in San Antonio, where he smuggled cotton and then worked for two decades as a teamster, occasional Indian fighter, butcher, dairyman, and petty swindler. In 1882 he began following the track-laying crews of the Southern Pacific and the Atchison, Topeka &

Santa Fe, setting up tent saloons in the construction camps. At Eagle's Nest, some twenty miles west of the Pecos, he managed to get himself appointed justice of the peace. He jailed miscreants by chaining them to a tree outside his tented bar. That autumn he and the camp moved a little west, to a site named Vinegarroon in honor of the local variety of scorpions, and he put up a saloon building. He named it the Jersey Lilly, a misspelled tribute to the actress Lily Langtry, who was born on the Channel island of Jersey. He conducted trials on the saloon porch, beneath a big sign that proclaimed him to be the "Law West of the Pecos."

Soon the town of Langtry sprouted from the desert, and Mrs. Langtry graciously sent the self-styled judge a pair of silver-plated six-guns as a gesture of appreciation. He used the revolvers as gavels and perhaps for more deadly purposes. Once, during the 1890's, a man entered the saloon to tell Bean he had found a corpse in a canyon. The Judge replied that he already knew just where the corpse was. Rapping with a gun butt, he announced, "I rule that this *hombre* met his death by being shot by a person unknown who was a damn good shot."

There were Langtry residents who claimed that Bean imposed the death sentence only once and even then let the prisoner escape. Others claimed that there were twenty-three shootings during a two-year period in the 1880's and no one kept count of Bean's sometimes arbitrary hangings.

That he was feared there is no doubt, nor is there any doubt he frequently arrested men on absurd charges and extorted money by fining them or ordering them to buy drinks for everyone present at the courthouse saloon. After the post of justice became an elective office, he was once jailed by Texas Rangers for influencing votes at gunpoint. And in 1896 he was the major promoter of an

"A Row in a Cattle Town," engraved from sketch
by Frederic Remington, shows that western
communities were not yet quite civilized in
1888. Lawmen sometimes invested in saloons and
gambling houses, so they were tempted to overlook
violent incidents in certain establishments
or even shoot down competition in others.

89

illegal heavyweight championship bout (prize fights being against the law at the time) in which Bob Fitzsimmons knocked out Peter Maher after less than two minutes. By the time the Rangers galloped into Langtry to disperse the thousands of spectators, the show was over

Regardless of proved and suspected transgressions, Bean had the approval of most local residents. They cared more about keeping the peace than about how it was kept or whether a few potentially dangerous saddle tramps were exterminated in the process. He was out of office for only two years between 1882 and his last spree in 1903. That March, after returning from a binge in San Antonio, he died of pneumonia.

Equally disreputable and considerably more dangerous was Ben Thompson, who served briefly as city marshal of Austin. Born in England but raised in Texas, he rode with the Confederate cavalry. After returning home wounded, he spent two years in prison for shooting his brother-in-law in the leg because he had struck Thompson's wife. Upon his release he became a roving professional gambler. He was known in his time as an unusually honest dealer but one who was deplorably quick to reach for a pistol. In 1869 in a small Kansas cow town he reportedly discouraged the exhibitionism of a gun-spinning cowboy by shooting the revolver out of his hand. In Abilene he ran a prosperous gambling concession with Phil Coe as his partner, but after Bill Hickok shot Coe the business failed and Thompson moved to Ellsworth, where he set up his gaming tables in Joe Brennan's saloon. By then he had been the victor in a number of gunfights and Hickok seems to have avoided him.

Ellsworth was among the wildest of cattle-loading towns. The marshal was John "Brocky Jack" Norton, who had killed a man while working for Hickok in Abilene. An outlaw called Brocky Jack had been among Plummer's gunmen, and writers have speculated that he was the same man. His deputy, Happy Jack Morco, had killed four men. The sheriff was Chauncey B. Whitney, an honest peace officer, and the sheriff's deputy, Ed Hogue, was relatively reliable. But there were four additional policemen, each of whom was accused of serious crimes at one time or another. Some of the wild towns hired desperadoes as lawmen on the theory that it took a killer to deal with killers.

A feud smoldered between Thompson and Morco, possibly because Texans in general had a bad reputation in Kansas and because Morco enjoyed harrassing them. In June, 1873, after Morco evidently threatened to arrest him, Thompson turned himself over to the sheriff on his own complaint—literally arresting himself for being "drunk, disorderly, carrying deadly weapons." Ironic gestures were not enough, so in August he led a delegation of Texans who protested to Mayor James Miller that Ellsworth's bounty-hunting police were overzealous in their pursuit of the $2 fee paid for each arrest.

The tension was almost palpable one hot summer day when Thompson demanded payment of a gambling debt from a man named John Sterling. Sterling slapped Thompson, who was unarmed—having checked his rifle, pistol, and shotgun at another saloon in accordance with a town law. Morco stepped between them, drew his revolver, threatened Thompson, and then left with Sterling. Expecting more serious trouble, Thompson reclaimed his rifle and pistol. Unfortunately, his impetuous younger brother Billy was in town. Billy got the shotgun and joined him. Then Sheriff Whitney arrived and promised his protection if the Thompsons would put up their guns. They were entering a saloon to talk it over when someone shouted that Morco and Sterling were behind them, ready to shoot. As they whirled back into the street, Billy

Thompson's gun went off accidentally, mortally wounding Sheriff Whitney. Morco and Sterling leaped for cover and the only shot Thompson fired hit a door casing as Morco lunged through it.

Whitney made a dying statement that Billy's shot had been accidental. Ben persuaded his younger brother to leave town, nevertheless, then turned himself in. He was acquitted and the Mayor dismissed Morco and the entire police force of Ellsworth. Years later Wyatt Earp—horse thief, procurer, stagecoach robber, and killer—claimed to have been Ellsworth's marshal, to have personally arrested Ben Thompson, and to have tamed the town. He was not even there at the time. The facts have been verified by the police docket, as well as an account of the shooting in the *Ellsworth Reporter* on August 21, 1873, and papers in the archives of the Kansas State Historical Society. The newspaper listed the names of all Ellsworth peace officers. Earp was not among them.

Ben Thompson drifted down to Sweetwater, Texas, where in 1875 he became a friend of Bat Masterson. In later days Masterson walked with a limp and used a cane, having been shot in the hip during a brawl over a girl in a Sweetwater saloon. There is a story, probably true, that Masterson killed his adversary while Thompson drew two guns to prevent bystanders from raising the odds against his friend. A little later Thompson operated gambling concessions in Dodge while Deputy Marshal Masterson kept the peace. Later still, he and Masterson did a little railroad work for the Santa Fe, leading a small private police force during a dispute with the Denver & Rio Grande. A more official police force ended the episode without bloodshed. In 1907 Masterson wrote of Thompson that "it is very doubtful if in his time there was another man living who equalled him with the pistol in a life and death struggle." Though there is no record of how many men he bested, he was acknowledged by such experts to be the deadliest of the gunfighting gamblers.

For a while in 1880, both Thompson and Masterson dealt cards in Tombstone, Arizona. Then Thompson's reputation earned him a job as city marshal of Austin, Texas. He thoroughly enjoyed parading about in a stylish police uniform, and his biographers have claimed that Austin's crime rate slumped during his brief tenure. In 1881 he got into a gambling argument with a San Antonio saloon keeper named Jack Harris, who died forthwith of gunshot wounds. Thompson was tried for murder, and though acquitted he resigned as Austin's marshal. Some observers have inferred that official duties interfered with his gambling and drinking. In March, 1884, he went to a vaudeville theatre in San Antonio with J. K. "King" Fisher, a rancher who had once recruited his own ruthless vigilante force to expunge Rio Grande rustling and banditry, had himself been called a desperado, and had also been a lawman. The theatre was managed by two partners, Joe Foster and W. H. Sims, who had been friends of Thompson's last victim, Jack Harris. As Thompson and Fisher ordered drinks at the bar, Foster and Sims joined them. There was a brief conversation, then a crackle of shots. Foster was hit in the leg. Thompson and Fisher fell dead. Thompson was forty-one, and it may be that alcohol had finally slowed his reflexes. The coroner's inquest failed to determine who fired the first shot.

Wyatt Earp, thought by many to be the ideal town-taming western lawman, was born in Kentucky in 1848. His half brother, Newton, oldest of the six Earp boys, was the only one who stayed out of trouble. James, Virgil, Wyatt, Morgan, and Warren Earp all worked as "sporting men," gambling, tending bar, or doing whatever else opportunity offered. In 1870, farming in several states and driving a stage in California, Wyatt Earp was elected town

constable of Lamar, Missouri. There he married his first wife, Rilla. She died within a year and he wandered off to Muskogee, considered to be the worst of the Indian Territory settlements with which the Fort Smith courts had to deal. Rail lines were being pushed west from Missouri through part of Kansas, then south to the Territory. During a few weeks when a railroad terminus and stage offices were located at Muskogee and neighboring Fort Gibson, sixteen murders were committed in those two little towns.

Those who have read about Wyatt Earp or seen melodramas about the nemesis of western villains may be somewhat chagrined to learn that in April, 1871, U.S. Marshal J. G. Owen swore to a "Bill of Information" in which he stipulated that "Wyatt S. Earp, Ed Kennedy, John Shown, white men and not Indians or members of any tribe of Indians by birth or marriage or adoption on the 28th day of March AD 1871 in the Indian Country . . . did feloniously, wilfully steal take away carry away two horses each of the value of one hundred dollars the property goods and chattels of one William Keys . . . ."

Actually, the theft occurred on or about March 25 and the three men were caught with the horses on March 28. Kennedy spent time in jail but eventually was acquitted. Earp and Shown each managed to raise $500 for bail, and both fled. A Federal warrant was signed by Judge William Story, instructing Deputy Marshal John F. Clark to apprehend Earp for an appearance before the U.S. Court for the Western District of Arkansas, at Fort Smith, during its November session. But Earp got away and the matter was dropped.

During the early 1870's, Morgan and Warren Earp were helping their father with the farm chores, Virgil was driving a stage, and Jim was tending bar at Newton, Kansas. Wyatt later claimed (in autobiographical newspaper articles and in interviews with his biographer, Stuart N. Lake) that he had spent this period fighting badmen and Indians, arresting Ben Thompson in Ellsworth, and hunting buffalo for a Government surveying party. Investigators have disproved each of those claims. Evidently he spent a couple of years working with his brother Jim, tending bar, gambling, perhaps cheating a few gullible cowhands at cards and dice. According to a Kansas State census, he was living in Wichita in 1875, at which time Bessie Earp (probably Jim's wife Bessie) and Sallie Earp (possibly a woman living with Wyatt) were hauled into court more than once for prostitution. Six different girls named Earp had been fined a total of thirty times in Wichita Police Court during the period from May to December, 1874. A livestock shipper named Joe McCoy was then promoting and building Wichita as he had earlier promoted Abilene, turning a few loading pens into a rip-roaring boom town. The police permitted prostitution and pandering, but insisted that it be contained within the red-light district and conducted with Victorian decorum.

Earp did not become a deputy marshal and tame the

Above: Doc Holliday in his Dodge or Tombstone days.
Opposite: Some of Dodge City's notorious
gunslingers. From left, they are Sheriff Charlie Bassett,
Deputy Marshal Bat Masterson, Wyatt Earp, Luke Short,
Frank McLean, W. H. Harris, and Neil Brown.

town as he claimed. He began wearing the citified garb of a professional gambler and at first lived by his wits (or by various other attributes of his women), then became a bill collector and, for eight months, a Wichita policeman. Morgan joined him and was almost immediately arrested on unspecified charges. Wyatt Earp's boasts of having rid Wichita of Wes Hardin and Wild Bill Longley are suspect since neither man was in the region that year, and his story of scaring Hardin's cousin, Manning Clements, out of town is strange in view of the fact that Clements remained

there. Earp was, however, involved in a minor dispute over cattle (which he later magnified into the "Pole Cat War"). He hired on as a drover to take a herd whose rightful ownership was in question south from Wichita to the Indian Territory. The Sumner County Vigilance Committee overtook him and brought the cattle back. As a Wichita peace officer he made no important arrests but was himself arrested, fined, and dismissed from the police force after getting into a fight with a reform candidate for the post of city marshal.

Next he turned up in Dodge, where he also claimed to have been marshal. The burial ground at Dodge was the first to be called Boot Hill and in 1875, the year before Earp arrived, more than twenty homicide victims had been interred there. Dodge was slowly tamed, but not by Earp. The job was done chiefly by Deputy Marshal Bat Masterson, his brothers Ed and Jim, Marshal Larry Deger, Deputy Joe Mason, and Sheriff Charlie Bassett. Though these men occasionally feuded among themselves and not only condoned but invested in the wide-open night life of Dodge, they also reduced the degree of violence significantly. As for Earp, he was a Dodge policeman (never a marshal) for a few months in 1876, while his brother Morgan served as a deputy sheriff, and he was a deputy town marshal during the last half of '78 and the early part of '79. He made thirty-five arrests, all for minor crimes. In the pages of romanticized biographies, Virgil came to town to assist in Wyatt's town-taming, but Virgil was then a U.S. Deputy Marshal at Prescott, Arizona.

The story that Wyatt Earp faced down Clay Allison in Dodge is another garbling of the facts. Contemporary newspaper accounts show that Allison came through Dodge when Earp happened to be in Texas. It would seem to have been Bat Masterson—alone—who faced down the terror of the Southwest. When Allison came back, Jim Masterson disarmed him and briefly detained him in the Dodge jail. Earp was then in Tombstone. In 1907 Bat Masterson commented about Earp's days in Dodge: "Only once do I recall when he shot to kill, and that was at a drunken cowboy, who rode up to a variety theatre where Eddie Foy, the now famous comedian, was playing an engagement."

Earp also said he had helped to thwart a stage holdup near Deadwood in 1877. The attempted holdup was real—a foray of the Sam Bass gang—but Earp had left

Deadwood when it happened. By then, in fact, he had probably arrived at Fort Griffin, Texas, where he met a dentist named John H. Holliday and Holliday's common-law wife, Big-Nose Kate Elder, alias Kate Fisher. Doc Holliday and Wyatt Earp gambled there and at Fort Worth, and then went up to Dodge where Holliday occasionally practiced dentistry at Office No. 24 in the Dodge House. Holliday was a frail man, slowly dying of tuberculosis and alcoholism, yet he inspired fear in some of his enemies. According to tradition he had cut a man's throat during a poker game at Fort Griffin, after which Kate had saved him from a lynch mob by creating a diversion—a fire in a livery stable—and then, with a pair of revolvers, persuaded the sheriff to let the dentist check out of the hotel where he was being held.

At the end of 1879 the Brothers Earp were in Tombstone, as were Holliday, Bat Masterson, Luke Short, Ben Thompson, Johnny Ringo, and other well-known adventurers. Short, a gambling crony of Masterson, had owned an interest in the Long Branch at Dodge. He worked as a faro dealer in the Oriental at Tombstone until he shot down a gambler named Charlie Storms in an argument over cards. Though acquitted of murder, he moved on. Later he owned the White Elephant saloon in Fort Worth. The marshal there was T. I. "Long-Hair Jim" Courtright, who had himself been charged with a murder and acquitted. Courtright was hard on rustlers but amiable with gamblers, and it was rumored he extorted protection money from saloon keepers. In a confrontation over such matters, Short killed him in 1886. Having managed somehow to go free after this gunfight, too, Short died of natural causes seven years later.

John Ringgold, alias Johnny Ringo, was a drifter, cow hand, gunfighter, outlaw. He was an acquaintance of Wes Hardin and probably of Sam Bass, and he was suspected of several robberies and killings. In Tombstone he was thought to be a member of the Clanton rustling and stage-robbery conspiracy. On the basis of the scanty evidence available, it seems more likely that Wyatt Earp tried unsuccessfully to enlist him in the robbers' circle. In any event, he feuded with the Earps and Holliday, and once rode into Tombstone expressly to challenge Holliday to a duel. Holliday declined. Both men were arrested by Deputy Bill Breakenridge and fined $30 for carrying concealed weapons. In July, 1882, Ringo's body was found slumped in an oak thicket in Turkey Creek Canyon. His pistol held one empty shell and it was believed he had committed suicide, despite Wyatt Earp's claim to have slain him in a fierce duel.

The city of Tombstone materialized where a prospector named Ed Schieffelin had struck a couple of fantastically rich silver veins in 1877. Within two years, six thousand people had arrived to look for silver, work the mines, or seek other ways to profit from a new rush. Some aspects of early Tombstone history—including the Earp legend—are necessarily clouded because the *Epitaph* almost reflexively contradicted much of what was reported in the rival *Nugget*. But the town's flavor is discernible in the advertisements of a physician who offered to locate bullets lodged deep within his patients by means of a new electromagnetic device.

Wyatt Earp's second wife, Mattie, served as a seamstress while he worked for a while as a Wells Fargo shotgun messenger. Then he and the other Earp men, together with Holliday, entered into a more profitable existence gambling and occasionally tending bar at the Oriental, the Alhambra, and other places of amusement. Within a year they were suspected of cheating, pandering, rustling, and robbing stages. Tombstone reformed somewhat only after the departure of the Earps, when a stockman named John

In studio portrait made when he was city marshal of Austin, Ben Thompson proudly wears stylish new uniform. Several years later, in San Antonio, he was shot down by friends of his last victim. Revolver was used by Wyatt Earp, who favored longer-barreled "Buntline Special" for pistol-whipping his enemies but wore short-barreled six-gun for fast draw in emergencies.

Slaughter became county sheriff and led a group of determined peace officers. Wyatt Earp afterward said he had been a deputy sheriff there; actually, for a brief time he was a civil deputy sheriff empowered only to help collect taxes and the license fees of prostitutes, and he was dismissed from the post. He aspired to become sheriff but the appointment (by the Territorial governor) went to John H. Behan, who then fell under suspicion of being as active a rustler and stage robber as any of them. While he feuded with the Earps, he was astonishingly friendly to the town's other suspected outlaws, yet he rose to be superintendent of the Territorial prison at Yuma.

The Earps fared well, having convinced saloon keepers that they were quick and deadly shots who could keep the peace effectively as armed bouncers. Virgil Earp was defeated twice in elections for city marshal, but did serve for a short time as a deputy under Marhals Ben Sippy and

Fred White, and as acting marshal when Sippy took a leave of absence. Morgan and Warren Earp were listed in the county register as laborers, Virgil as a farmer, Jim and Wyatt as saloon keepers.

While Virgil was a deputy he helped Marshal White arrest some ranch hands who were shooting into the air during a spree. A gun went off accidentally, killing White. Curly Bill Brocius, who was also known as Bill Graham, was tried and released. In 1882, Wyatt Earp claimed it was Curly Bill who had killed his brother Morgan and crippled Virgil. According to one old rancher, Earp even tried to collect a reward from the Arizona Cattlemen's Association for a head he said had belonged to the "ferocious outlaw," yet Brocius was alive and well a decade later. The head, if he really brought one in, must have belonged to Florentino Cruz, a half-breed generally called Indian Charlie. Cruz was suspected of having conspired to

Judge Roy Bean in family portrait with his sons Roy
and Sam, daughters Zulema and Laura. Upper left:
Mrs. Lily Langtry, actress for whom Bean named his
saloon, The Jersey Lilly, and town of Langtry,
Texas. Lower left: Bean holding court on porch of
saloon. He is seated on keg, wearing sombrero
and six-gun, with his single law book open before him.

kill Morgan Earp, and soon afterward he was shot down by one of Earp's extra-legal posses.

In the spring of 1881, gossip insisted that the Earps, Holliday, and several of their cohorts had played some part in recent stage robberies and rustling incidents. More than one citizen also expressed the opinion that Marshall Williams, Tombstone's jovial Wells Fargo agent, was letting the gang know when a coach carried bullion, payroll money, or bank funds. Bud Philpot, the driver of a Kinnear and Company stage carrying $26,000 in specie, was killed by a rifle bullet during a bungled holdup. As the horses bolted, a passenger named Peter Roerig was mortally wounded but the guard, Bob Paul, regained control of the team and brought the coach in. A posse, led by Sheriff Behan and the Earps, rode out to track the killers. The posse split, each group taking what was afterward said to be an obviously wrong trail.

Doc Holliday had been seen in the area on a rented horse that was famous for speed, and several suspected outlaws were heard to remark that if he had not been drunk and overeager to shoot, the robbery would have succeeded. In May he was indicted for "participating in a shooting," but was released for lack of evidence. However, Big-Nose Kate strongly disapproved of his current activities and after a bitter argument she swore to an affidavit that resulted in his arrest for stage robbery and murder. Once again the charge was dropped. The fearless Doc Holliday then had her arrested for being drunk and disorderly and for threatening his life, a reasonable precaution for a man like Holliday if he was preparing to kill her and claim self-defense. As soon as she was released, Kate Elder left town to start a new and safer life running a boarding house in Globe.

Other suspects in the attempted robbery included the Earps, Luther King, Bill Leonard, Harry Head, Jim Crane, Frank and Tom McLaury (often spelled McLowry or McLowery), N. H. Clanton (known as Old Man Clanton), and Clanton's sons Ike, Finn, and Billy. Probably the worst offense of the McLaury brothers was keeping bad company. There is little doubt, however, that the Clantons were rustlers and bandits. Their close friend Sheriff Johnny Behan may well have been in league with them. Wyatt Earp was feuding with Behan over women and also because Behan had won the sheriff's badge Earp coveted. The Earp faction was also worried that the Clanton and McLaury brothers might talk too much, especially about Doc Holliday's part in the stagecoach shooting.

Old Man Clanton, who had been making a profitable sideline of waylaying Mexican smuggling trains, was ambushed and killed by a group of Mexicans in Guadalupe Canyon. Several of the other suspects were shot down by lawmen before they could do any talking. The Wells Fargo agent, Marshall Williams, left town and disappeared. But Ike and Billy Clanton and the McLaury brothers remained a danger to what Virgil Earp's widow later termed "the Earp gang." Several local diarists and memoirists noted in their journals that this was a case of thieves falling out and that a shooting was inevitable. The stage was set for the great Earp melodrama, the Gunfight at the O.K. Corral.

It was not a gunfight, of course. Two of the victims were unarmed, and not one had a chance to defend himself. On the afternoon of October 5, 1881, Ike Clanton and Tom McLaury came into town for supplies. That night Doc Holliday dared Clanton to reach for his gun and Clanton was heard to say he was unarmed. The next day witnesses saw Wyatt Earp hit Tom McLaury with his left hand while keeping his right on a holstered revolver. McLaury, too, protested that he was unarmed and not looking for a fight. Earp's response was to hit him on the head with his long-barreled revolver, knocking him down.

That night or the next morning Billy Clanton and Frank McLaury also arrived in town. At about two in the afternoon Frank and Tom McLaury, Ike and Billy Clanton, and a friend named Billy Claibourne were at the O.K. Corral—the holding pen for a livery stable—preparing to mount and leave Tombstone. There were rifles in saddle scabbards on two of the horses but no one reached for them. Only Billy Clanton and Frank McLaury were wearing revolvers. Down the street came Wyatt and Morgan Earp, their hands ready above their holsters, accompanied by Virgil Earp and Doc Holliday, each with a shotgun. Virgil Earp, wearing a badge as acting marshal, had deputized the whole crew for the occasion. According to Sheriff Behan's own testimony at a subsequent hearing, he followed them, begging them "not to make any trouble." They were on foot and they spread out as they neared the corral. Claibourne was a lucky man; at the last moment he left.

Witnesses heard someone say, "Let them have it," and heard Doc Holliday answer, "All right." A witness also heard Virgil Earp shout, "Throw up your hands!" Ike Clanton turned, saw what was coming, and grabbed Wyatt Earp's arm but was thrown aside. He escaped death by lunging into the doorway of a photographer's studio as Holliday fired both barrels at him. His brother and both McLaury boys raised their hands in surrender and fell before a fusillade.

Warrants were issued, a hearing was conducted before Judge Wells Spicer, and eyewitnesses testified to the circumstances of the murders as described here. The Earps and Holliday—who had acquired considerable town property as well as interests in saloons and other businesses—were officially absolved. Tombstone justice consisted of suspending Virgil Earp from duty and appointing a new acting marshal.

In December, Virgil Earp was shot by an unknown assailant and crippled for life. In January, 1882, there was so much shooting in Cochise County that an official call was issued for volunteer deputy marshals, and Wyatt Earp at last received a badge he had long sought. Amid much fanfare of his own making, he led posses about the countryside hunting desperadoes with such devastating effect that a few months later President Chester A. Arthur threatened to impose martial law in Arizona if lawlessness in the territory did not immediately cease.

In March, Morgan Earp was playing billiards with saloon-owner Bob Hatch. As Earp stood chalking his cue, the glass of the alley door shattered, a revolver shot echoed, and he fell dying. The bullet passed through Earp's body and smashed into the thigh of a bystander, George Berry, who died of a heart attack induced by the shock. No one knew who had fired the bullet but the surviving Earps and many others suspected that the murder had been planned by three local badmen of small repute—Pete Spence, Deputy Sheriff Frank Stilwell of Bisbee, and the half-breed Florentino Cruz.

Virgil Earp and his wife Allie left for Colton, California, the final home of old Nicholas Earp, father of the clan. Jim Earp, who had served in the Union Army and had never fully recovered from a Civil War injury, went along with his wife Bessie. The gunfighting days of the Earps were nearly at an end. Morgan's body was in the baggage car. Wyatt and Warren Earp and Doc Holliday, accompanied by Sherman McMasters and Turkey Creek Jack Johnson, went along as far as the Tucson junction.

As the train pulled out of Tucson, shots were heard, and afterward the body of Frank Stilwell was found at the side of the tracks. Following a coroner's inquest, Bob Paul—who had become sheriff of Pima County—swore out warrants for the arrest of Wyatt and Warren Earp, Holliday, McMasters, and Johnson. Before the sheriff arrived with the warrants, the Earps and their friends rode out of Tombstone, leaving word that they were traveling as a posse and intended to end all these terrible killings by cleaning the outlaws out of Arizona. The only outlaw they found was Florentino Cruz. After killing him they scattered, McMasters and Johnson to the Texas Panhandle, Holliday and the two Earps to Colorado. Riding with them for a while was another badman named Texas Jack Vermillion; he fled to Big Stone Gap, Virginia, where he became a respected citizen and a member of the school board.

Sheriff Paul came after Holliday and the Earps, but Colorado refused to honor his request for extradition and the murder charge was dropped—perhaps because Arizona's lawmen and courts had more cases than they could manage, perhaps because the Earps had influential friends in Tombstone's business community. Wyatt Earp never returned for his wife. Six years later she was buried in the little town of Pinal. Chronically drunk and reduced to prostitution, she had swallowed a lethal dose of laudanum. By then Warren Earp had foolishly bullied a drunken cowboy, who shot and killed him at their next encounter, and Doc Holliday had succumbed to the combined ravages of alcoholism and consumption. Virgil Earp became city marshal of Colton for a while, ran a small and unsuccessful detective agency, tried mining and lumbering, tended bar, and did odd jobs until he died in 1905.

Wyatt Earp went to San Francisco in search of Josephine Sarah Marcus, a former vaudevillian who had been known rather more familiarly as Sadie at Tombstone. He found her and she remained with him to the end. In 1884 the *Arizona Gazette* reported that he had been shot in the arm during a poker game at Lake City, Colorado, but he never again was involved in any serious violence. He ran saloons and gambled in various parts of the West, seldom remaining in one town long but building a reputation as an old-time lawman through interviews and the sale of "autobiographical" writings.

In 1896 he was racing rented horses near San Francisco, and that year he refereed a famous fight between Bob Fitzsimmons and Tom Sharkey at the Mechanics Pavilion. In the eighth round, with Fitzsimmons winning easily, Earp stopped the bout. He claimed Fitzsimmons had struck a foul blow and declared Sharkey the winner. The decision nearly caused a riot since the spectators had seen only Sharkey deliver foul blows. It was assumed that Earp had placed a sizable bet on the winner. The result was an indecisive court hearing, after which Earp left San Francisco to explore the possibilities of the new gold rush up in Alaska. At Nome in 1897 he opened the Dexter Saloon (possibly named for the Dexter Corral, across the street from the O.K. Corral in Tombstone). In his cups one night and basking in his notoriety, he brandished a revolver. Marshal Albert Lowe took it away, slapped his face, and told him to go home to bed. Earp ran the saloon for about four years, then opened another in Tonopah, Nevada, and finally settled in Los Angeles, where he was charged with vagrancy and conducting a bunco operation in 1911. As usual, he somehow managed to stay out of prison.

He was almost eighty-one when he met the writer Stuart N. Lake and began collaborating on a heroic biography. He died on January 3, 1929, two years before it was finally published under the title, *Wyatt Earp: Frontier Marshal*. The San Francisco *Chronicle* had appraised him more accurately when, in reporting the Fitzsimmons-Sharkey bout, it had sardonically labeled him the Tombstone Terror.

William M. Harnett's famous and magnificently
realistic still life, "The Fateful Colt," memorializing
percussion six-shooter that was of vast importance
in Civil War and was favored for years afterward
by lawmen and badmen. Rust-flecked specimen portrayed
by Harnett, with weathered brass frame and cracked,
yellowed ivory stock, shows ravages of long, hard use.

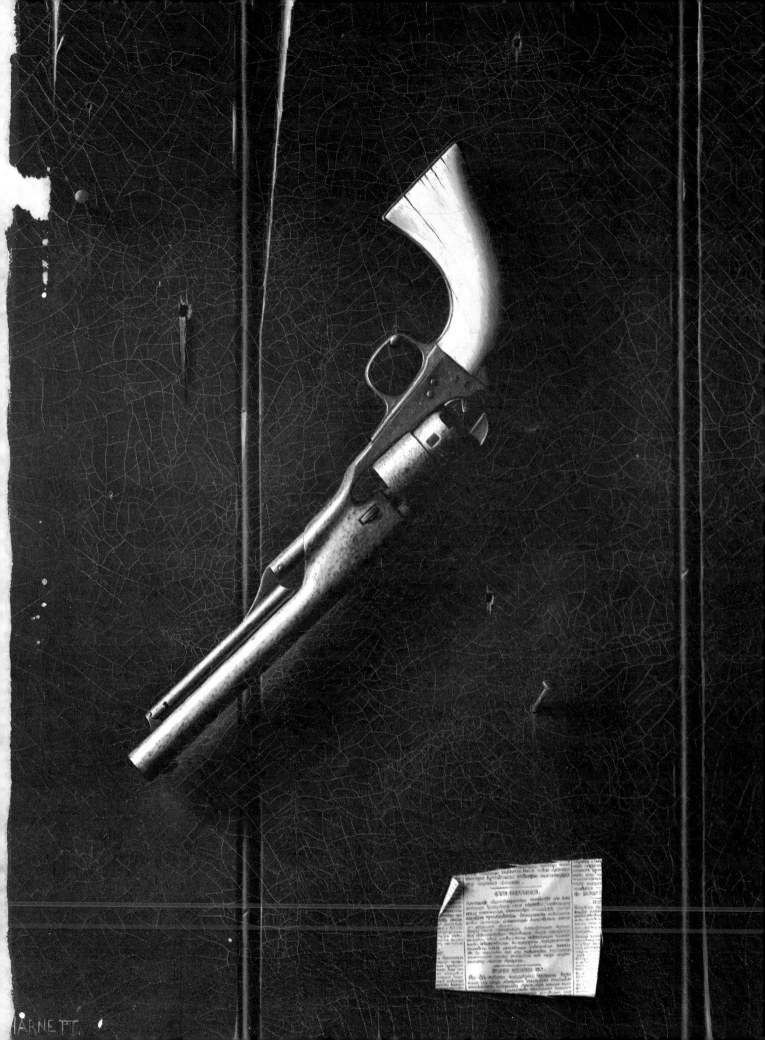

Preceding pages: "The Faro Layout at the Mint Hotel,"
by O. C. Seltzer, typifies frontier scenes of relaxation that
hid extreme tension, turning violent if a bad-tempered
drinker like Clay Allison (opposite) or Wes Hardin suspected
cheating, or simply resented some casual remark.
Above: "Indian Encampment in the Rockies," by Albert Bierstadt,
is reminiscent of Ute villages where Indian-hating
Bill Longley lived for months to avoid lawmen and soldiers.

In the years following the Civil War, violence rose to a crescendo of gunfire in the Southwest. Raids by and against Comanches and Apaches had continued since the time of the Texas Republic, as had the bloody enmity between "Anglo" and Mexican settlers. Mexican-Americans who owned property, spoke English well, and had been born north of the Rio Grande sometimes achieved positions of influence, yet the poor among them were regarded almost as a pestilence. Reconstruction added new hatred—for carpetbaggers, for Northern authority, for those who collaborated with that authority, and for the freed blacks.

Out of this background came men like Clay Allison, Wild Bill Longley, and John Wesley Hardin. In the environment of the brutal frontier and the boom towns, the barbarous code duello had by then eroded into something still more barbarous, which condoned the killing of a man for virtually no reason as long as he was armed and had been warned an instant before the trigger was pulled. Allison, Longley, and Hardin ceaselessly claimed to have done no wrong in such "fights."

One historian attributes fifteen killings to Allison, another raises the estimate to eighteen, another to twenty-six. Allison objected vociferously when newspapers published such estimates. He obviously enjoyed his reputation, but wished his admirers to know that he had "never killed a man who didn't need it" and was only "protecting the property holders and substantial men of the country from thieves, outlaws, and murderers." In his own system of addition he probably did not count the slaying of the Mexican Francisco Griego and almost surely not the three Negro soldiers he had gunned down.

William Preston Longley's murderous career began with the shooting of an "upstart Nigra." Contemporary newspapers charged him with more than thirty killings;

one writer of western history reduced that toll to a vague number that "exceeded twenty," another set the figure at twenty-six, another at thirty-two "counting Negroes and Mexicans." Longley and Hardin both seemed to take pride in the nickname "nigger killer."

The popular western chronicler James D. Horan has noted that Hardin's last victim, Charles Webb, was probably his fortieth if the count includes "anonymous Negroes, Yankee soldier-police, and Indians and Mexicans." A black or Mexican cow hand, teamster, or lawman might become a formidable gunfighter if he lived long enough, but minorities were generally easy prey. Another historical writer, Mark Sufrin, estimating Hardin's killings at forty-three, noted that "approximately two-thirds of his victims were Mexicans, Negroes, and Indians, men who had had little opportunity to develop gunfighters' skills, and at least twelve of those shootings were outright murder. It is estimated that only six of his kills were quick-draw contests against qualified foes."

Clay Allison was born in 1840 in Wayne County,

Tennessee. While still in his adolescence he shot himself in the right foot, evidently while practicing his draw. It was this hazard of accidental discharge that prompted most westerners of his era to load their six-guns with only five cartridges, letting the hammer down on an empty chamber. Allison was a big, handsome, muscular man, but he had unusually small hands and a limp. It was said that these physical peculiarities made him murderously resentful of any remark that could be taken as a slight. Perhaps. There is little doubt that he was an alcoholic who simply became dangerous when drunk.

Serving in the Confederate forces during the Civil War, he was captured and condemned as a spy. His small hands enabled him to slip out of his manacles and he escaped, killing a guard or two guards according to various accounts. After the war he drifted about New Mexico, Colorado, Texas, Kansas, Wyoming. He became a foreman on a ranch north of Cimarron, New Mexico, and later ran his own herds in the northeastern part of the territory, near the borders of Texas, Oklahoma, and Colorado. He was accused of grazing his cattle on other men's pastures, far beyond the boundaries of his small ranch on the Washita River, even as far as Las Animas County in Colorado. And yet, in the early seventies, he made extra money as a hired gun enforcing boundary claims of larger ranches. Some of his shootings resulted from disputes over grazing and water rights and accusations of rustling—the chief causes of range wars—but perhaps just as often Allison's fights originated in grudge-settling, boasting, or trading jocular insults over drinks.

One night he met a little-known gunfighter named Chunk Colbert for dinner in the Clifton House at Red River Station, Texas. Colbert supposedly had shot down a friend of a friend of Allison, and Allison supposedly had killed an uncle of Colbert in a knife fight. Each of the

In caption for one of Frederic Remington's 1895 illustrations, man holding six-gun cautions his colleagues, "Don't nobody hurt anybody." In this instance, cool heads perhaps prevailed, but often such gatherings–involving disputes over land rights, cattle, or gambling debts– ended in feuds. Clay Allison, Bill Longley, and John Wesley Hardin all participated in fights of this kind.

dining partners had let it be known that he could best the other in a shoot-out. Afterward, Allison claimed that he had heard Colbert's gun touch the underside of the table in an attempted sneak-draw, whereupon he had no choice but to tip his chair back to duck the expected shot, simultaneously drawing his own gun and sending a bullet through Colbert's head. He finished his dinner while onlookers carried the corpse away for burial.

In 1875, after the Federal Government had rejected the claim of the Maxwell Land Grant and Railway Company to a tremendous strip of acreage in Allison's vicinity, local cattlemen felt threatened more than ever by an invasion of small competitors and homesteaders. The newcomers, probably fearful of being lynched for rustling, drove strange livestock off their lands and killed many strays. Allison was a member of the Stockgrowers' Association and was expected to go gunning for the homesteaders. Instead, he championed their cause and ran one vindictive rancher out of Cimarron to stave off gunplay. On this occasion, as no blood was shed, his actions may have averted a range war. His motives are puzzling until one considers that Allison himself had grazed cattle on land considered to be the exclusive domain of larger competitors, and he may have felt a kinship with squatters.

Not long afterward, a belligerent young cowboy named Buck Bowman arrived in Cimarron during a Mexican fiesta whose chief attraction seems to have been the flow of spirits. Displaying twelve notches on his pistol butt, he made some remarks about Rebels and particularly about Allison. Inevitably the two men met. Allison drawled an observation regarding the size of Bowman's mouth, Bowman dropped into a crouch, guns flashed, and Allison walked away from another dead man. There is a story, possibly true, that Bowman's uncle soon arrived to investigate the boy's death and beat Allison to the draw to

prove he could not be mocked or ignored, after which he accepted Allison's explanation.

In autumn of 1875 the Reverend F. J. Tolby was ambushed and killed as he rode back to Cimarron after holding a prayer meeting at a mining camp. Tolby had written letters to newspapers, attacking a territorial political machine. Many citizens, including Allison, suspected that the killer had been hired by a group of politicians known as the Santa Fe Ring. A man named Cruz Vega was implicated. Before hanging him from a telegraph pole a lynch mob forced him to confess. He insisted that the fatal shot had been fired by Manuel Cardenas. As Cardenas was being led to jail he was shot down by vigilantes. Word spread that Allison had led the men who killed Vega and Cardenas. Their close friend "Pancho"—Francisco Griego—rode into Cimarron to avenge their deaths. In the saloon of the St. James Hotel he announced that he was looking for Clay Allison, who was standing at the bar. The two men sat down to talk. Suddenly three shots were heard. Someone extinguished the lights, and Griego's body was left there until morning.

In March, 1876, Allison was drinking in the same saloon when three Negro soldiers appeared on the wide threshold. The swinging doors were still in motion when all three slumped to the floor in a roar of gunfire. Clay Allison did not deem it suitable for Negroes, even if they were American soldiers, to drink in a white man's establishment. Black troopers under Captain Francis Dodge clamored for Allison's arrest. Though he permitted them to take him from his ranch, in compliance with a warrant, he defied them to disarm him. Finally he was escorted to Taos by a sheriff and a detachment of soldiers, but returned almost immediately. The lawman in charge claimed that the soldiers had scattered when Allison dove behind a boulder and leveled a gun. It seems more likely that the local peace officers, having made a small gesture to appease the Army, saw no reason to incarcerate a man for killing blacks.

But in December, Clay Allison and his brother John committed a more serious offense. The trouble began when they refused to remove their guns while in the Olympic Dance Hall at Las Animas. Constable Charles Faber withdrew to the American Hotel to borrow a 10-gauge shotgun and deputize two reluctant citizens. Faber led the way to the Olympic, and as he came through the entrance he pointed the shotgun at John Allison. Before Faber could step inside, Clay Allison's pistol went off. As Faber fell he shot and wounded John Allison and then died on the doorstep.

The brothers surrendered without resistance to Sheriff John Spear. John Allison was removed to a hospital. When he had recuperated sufficiently to stand trial, Justice of the Peace John M. Jay released him for lack of evidence. Clay Allison had been brought before District Judge John W. Henry in Pueblo and had been charged with manslaughter. He immediately raised $10,000 bail, was released, and later persuaded a grand jury to dismiss the charge. His plea, as usual, was self-defense.

There are conflicting accounts regarding the date of his death, but it was not very long after that and it was an ignominious end for a man who took pride in handling horses as well as he handled guns. Evidently drunk and in a reckless mood, he jumped aboard a friend's wagon, emitted a Rebel yell, and cracked the whip. The team pitched forward, the heavily loaded wagon lurched into a hole, and Allison fell beneath the wheels.

Younger Rebels—those too young to have served the Confederacy—seemed to feel so guilty for having missed the conflict that they fought a private civil war. Bill Longley was raised on a little ranch at Evergreen, Texas. He was fourteen when Lee surrendered and the first carpetbaggers arrived. The thoroughly southern Texas Rangers were replaced by the Texas State Police, whose leaders were corrupt opportunists. Some of the policemen were blacks, assisted by Negro soldiers who were understandably quick to level bayonets at unruly young whites. The policemen themselves proved to be so trigger-tempered that they were relieved of their guns and equipped with an archaic form of billy club—a lead ball on a leather thong. In 1866 young Longley found himself facing a blue-uniformed Negro who was swinging such a mace and intent on redressing humiliations he had suffered at the hands of whites. Longley had ridden a freight into Houston to shop for a cheap gun. There he met a boy who, like him, had no place to spend the night. They were about to bed down in an alley when the policeman demanded to know what they were doing there. According to Longley, instead of trying to search them for weapons, he swung the mace and ordered them to undress. Longley's anonymous companion pulled a knife from under his shirt and killed the policeman.

The next day Longley was back in Evergreen carrying a Dance Brothers revolver, a gun that had been in great demand among Rebel soldiers. Soon afterward a black man came riding along the Camino Real, past the Longley place. Perhaps he had been drinking. He had a rifle across his saddle and was cursing all white men. Catching sight of Longley's father he loudly damned him. Young Bill Longley, by his own account, ordered the Negro to drop his rifle, was answered by a shot, and promptly put a ball through the rider's head. According to some writers it was then that Longley became a fugitive, yet it appears that he buried the body and the crime went undetected until he confessed it, almost twelve years later, while awaiting execution.

But Longley's first known killings also occurred in 1866. He and a comrade, Johnson McKowen, had entered a horse in a race at Lexington, Texas. They withdrew in a rage when several black men also entered horses. That night Bill Longley galloped into the midst of a Negro street dance, firing as he charged and killing two men.

Longley and others claimed that during these early years of Reconstruction the law so favored blacks that a white man had to defend himself with a gun. It was a curious claim, considering that no one arrested him for double murder, and within two years he had a statewide reputation as a fanatical bigot who would kill any black on the slightest pretext. He was not quite eighteen when three heavily armed black men entered an Evergreen saloon, demanded drinks, and expressed a doubt that anyone in town was tough enough to make trouble about

their color. Someone got word to Longley. When he arrived the three men had ridden away, but he followed and found them encamped for the night ten miles from Evergreen. In the exchange of shots two of the men escaped. The third lay dead.

Warned by friends that this time lawmen were coming to arrest him, Longley rode off to Karnes County, where he herded cattle for a rancher. This general region was the scene of the famous Sutton-Taylor feud in which John Wesley Hardin participated. The Suttons declared it began when Bill Sutton and a band of vigilantes killed Charley Taylor for rustling. The Taylors claimed it began when Buck Taylor was ambushed by Bill Sutton and some rifle-carrying henchmen. Actually the families had been antagonistic for years and the latest trouble, like many other range wars, had begun as a dispute over the owner-

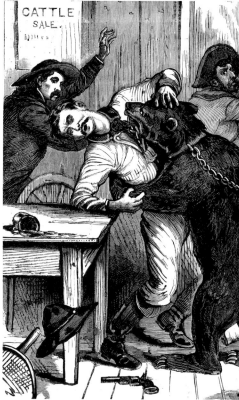

ship of longhorns. It continued intermittently for almost fifteen years until Captain Lee Hall of the restored Texas Rangers put an end to it one night in 1876. He and seventeen Rangers, though outnumbered four to one by celebrants at a Sutton wedding dance, arrested seven members of the clan, disarmed all the others, and enforced a truce until both factions at last calmed down.

But in 1867, when Longley herded cattle there, the Suttons had revived the concept and the name of "Regulators," with a band of two hundred riders, and Army troops were sent to restore peace. Longley was a friend of the Taylors and often visited their holdings near Yorktown. Some soldiers saw him ride through the village and, mistaking him for one of the Taylors, approached to question him. He thought they had come to arrest him for his latest murder, and so he spurred his horse. One pursuer

overtook him. As the soldier came up with him, close enough to reach for the reins, Longley rammed a gun into his side and killed him with one shot. He then fled to Bowie County, where he planned to join Cullen Baker's renegades—an outlaw band that specialized in looting Government trains, robbing carpetbaggers and tax collectors, and protecting die-hard Confederate sympathizers.

Waiting for Baker to return from a foray into Arkansas, Longley stayed one night at the home of Tom Johnson, a horse thief. Before dawn, vigilantes dragged both boys into the yard and hanged them from a tree. As the vigilantes rode off they fired several shots at the swaying bodies. According to tradition, one bullet glanced off Longley's belt buckle and another frayed the rope so badly that it snapped, dropping him to the ground still alive. Tom Johnson was dead, but Johnson's younger

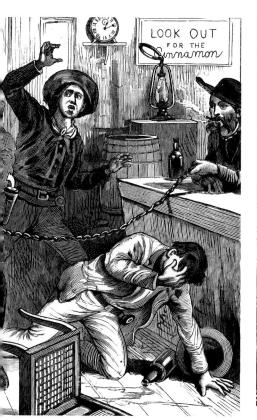

Police Gazette *illustrations in 1886 were variations
on theme of how easily horseplay could become ugly where politics,
prejudice, or absence of law excused killing. Left:
Members of Anti-Chinese League in Arizona show "Celestial . . . error
of his ways in refusing to 'move on.' " Center: New Mexico
editor's pet bear attacks would-be lynchers. Right:
Montana ruffians demand drink for skeleton of lynched comrade
while black employee of saloon wisely hides under bar.*

brother ran up to save Longley by loosening the noose.

Longley rode with the Baker gang for almost a year before Baker was killed in 1869. During that time, it is believed that Longley killed seven men, not including several blacks who were murdered by Longley and other gang members firing together. Then he returned to Evergreen for a while, killed several more blacks, and escaped again. Heading for Utah, where he had kinsmen, he joined a trail drive but quickly changed his plans after a gunfight in which he killed the herd boss. He went to Abilene, Kansas, where his background was unknown. After over-hearing two saddle tramps discussing a pair of horses they had stolen, the fugitive murderer arrested the thieves at gunpoint and collected a reward. However, he was ordered to comply with the town's no-guns ordinance, whereupon he rode away to Leavenworth. There he shot a soldier dead for making a slurring remark about Texans, then boarded a freight for St. Louis. Intercepted at St. Joseph he was brought back to Leavenworth military prison. He bribed a guard, escaped, drifted out to Cheyenne, joined a mining party, and killed several Indians who were trying to halt the treaty-breaking invasion

Top: Miners and businessmen refresh themselves
in saloon at Virginia City, Nevada. Above: Stagecoach rolls
at Cripple Creek, Colorado. Such scenes were familiar
to gunfighters like Clay Allison and Wes Hardin, who roamed
Southwest like bewildered knights seeking battle.

of the Big Horn Mountains and Black Hills by prospectors. An Army detachment forced the miners to return to Camp Brown. Seeing an unusual opportunity there, Longley overcame his loathing of Federal soldiers and hired on as an Army teamster so he could develop a partnership with the quartermaster to embezzle Government horses and mules. After a disagreement about the proceeds, he was arrested for the murder of the quartermaster.

He escaped, was recaptured, and was sentenced to death. The sentence was commuted to thirty years in the Iowa State Prison, however, and before he could be transferred he broke out of the stockade. When he headed into Indian country the Army gave up pursuit. Longley, who supposedly had little more use for Indians than for blacks and Mexicans, lived for months with a band of Utes before daring to set foot again in white man's country. Next he showed up in Parkersville, Kansas, using the name Tom Jones. There he became involved in a disagreement over cards with a young man named Charles Stuart and shot him down. Stuart's father offered a reward for his son's killer. Longley arranged with two outlaws to turn him in, collect the reward, help him escape, then split the reward with him.

He returned to his father's farm, killed another Negro

over a fancied slight, and once more fled. Governor E. J. Davis had offered $1,000 for his capture, but now Richard Coke was elected governor, and Coke was not eager to prosecute a man for killing insolent blacks. Longley, using the alias William Henry, was apprehended but released when the state refused to pay a reward to the arresting officer. The reward offer was revived after Longley shot down a Mexican, however, because his conduct was becoming a scandal to Texas. He then discovered that a new acquaintance, Will Scrier, was really a bounty hunter named Lew Sawyer. The result, of course, was another shoot-out, another victim for Longley.

Finally, in 1875, he committed the crime for which he would pay. A cousin, Cale Longley, had been killed in a fall from a horse, but some members of the family believed he had been slain by an old friend named Wilson Anderson. Bill rode to the Anderson farm and cut Wilson down with a shotgun.

Within the next year the fugitive killed a farm hand named George Thomas with a revolver and a preacher named Roland Lay with a shotgun. Using the name Jim Patterson and then William Black, he continued to evade the law for a while even after Governor Coke began raising the reward bids. But in the summer of 1876, with

the state police disbanded, the Texas Rangers reinstated, and rewards mounting, he fled to Keatchie, Louisiana, about ten miles from the Texas line. There he rented land from the sheriff, began courting the sheriff's daughter, and worked at farming until, for unknown reasons, he revealed his identity to the girl. Soon Sheriff Milton Mast of Nacogdoches County, Texas, was on his way. He and Deputy W. M. Burroughs, holding cocked shotguns that were far more persuasive than any extradition papers, surprised Longley and took him without a fight. He was tried for the murder of Wilson Anderson, and at about one-thirty on the afternoon of October 11, 1878, was led to the hangman's scaffold. There were more than four thousand spectators, many of them Negroes. Eleven minutes after the trap was sprung three doctors pronounced the gunman dead and the crowd slowly began to disperse.

There were people who refused to believe he died that day. They were convinced he had bribed lawmen and doctors to rig a harness under his shirt to prevent the noose from strangling him or breaking his neck, and that they had placed him alive in a coffin and helped him escape to South America. Legends like that are persistent. When the *Lusitania* sank in 1915, writers noted that its passenger list included one W. P. Longley, a South American

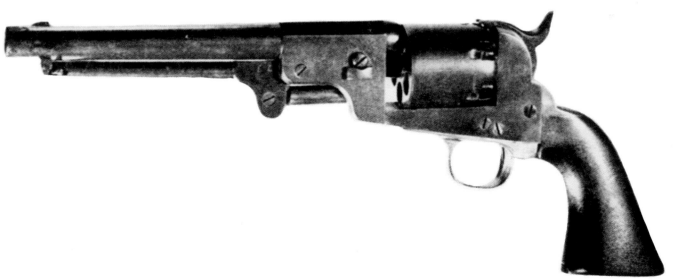

Wild Bill Longley, handcuffed at last, stands between Deputy W. M. Burroughs (left) and Sheriff Milton Mast. Gun is Dance Brothers percussion revolver with which Longley reportedly killed his first man. Charles M. Russell painting— "When Guns Speak Death Settles the Dispute"—exemplifies Texas and Kansas shoot-outs involving men like Longley and Hardin.

cattleman. But legends notwithstanding, Wild Bill Longley had died by hanging at the age of twenty-seven.

The average life span of the West's two hundred and fifty most notorious gunmen was thirty-two years. John Wesley Hardin lived to be forty-two, but he spent nearly sixteen of those years safely in prison. The second son of a Methodist circuit rider who also taught school and practiced law, he was born in Bonham County, Texas, in 1853. When the war ended he was only twelve years old but he had learned to hate, and early lessons were reinforced under state police and carpetbag rule. By the time he was fifteen, having decided to tolerate no insolence from any black, Indian, Mexican, or Yankee-lover, he committed his first murder. Years later he wrote a self-vindicating memoir (as did many nineteenth-century badmen), and in it he explained that a Negro "came at me with a big stick." He felt no need to explain why at that moment he was carrying a loaded Colt revolver. His parents were "nearly distracted," he recalled mildly. To be tried for the killing "meant certain death," he declared, "at the hands of a court backed by Northern bayonets . . . . I became a fugitive not from justice, be it known, but from the injustice and misrule of the people who had subjugated the South."

The righteous young fugitive then ambushed and killed three soldiers who came after him. Hardin probably could have escaped without shooting his pursuers, but two of them were Negroes. He briefly joined an unsavory cousin, Simp Dixon. When a second group of soldiers overtook them, he and Dixon each killed another man, then escaped and went separate ways. Hardin got a job as a ranch hand at Navarro but was soon on the run again, this time for killing a gambler named Amos Bradley, who accused him of cheating at cards. The sixteen-year-old killer stopped at Horn Hill, Texas, to attend the Robinson Brothers' Circus. Unwilling to pay admission, he crawled

under the canvas, and when he was caught he shot down the roustabout who tried to evict him. The spectators were too stunned to prevent his escape.

A hundred miles away, in the town of Kosse, he tried to make a living as a gambler. However, he began to monopolize the services of a prostitute who was considered the property of a pimp named Alan Comstock. According to Hardin, Comstock burst into the girl's room, threatened to kill him, and demanded $100. Pretending he would pay, Hardin dropped some of the money on the floor. Comstock stooped to retrieve it and as he straightened up Hardin shot him through the head. According to other chroniclers, Comstock was shot as he came through the door, before he could have made demands of any kind. Whatever the truth was in this affair, Wes Hardin had killed eight men by the time he was eighteen years old.

At Waco he soon killed yet another in a gambling dispute. He was captured near Longview, but pulled out a concealed gun and shot down a half-breed posseman who was guarding him. The incident may have inspired him to devise the unique vest he soon began wearing. It had two big inner pockets which served as hidden cross-draw holsters for short-barreled guns. Contrary to romantic legend, most outlaws wore only one sidearm. Two would be heavy and awkward, and few men could fire accurately with both hands. But when Hardin was seen with a gun on his hip he frequently had two more ready in his vest.

Again he was captured, this time by three state policemen as he rode for Mexico. How he managed to kill all three has been a subject of surmise. Deciding against flight to Mexico, he rode to Gonzales, where four cousins operated a ranch. They were the Clements—Manning, Jim, Gyp, and Joe—all reputed to be hard-working stockmen but dangerous gunfighters as well. Hardin joined them in a cattle drive to Abilene, reportedly after killing a Mexican monte dealer in Gonzales. En route, it is said, he shot down two Indians and a Mexican trail boss. Later he claimed that in Abilene Ben Thompson tried to persuade him to kill Wild Bill Hickok, but he told Thompson to do it himself if he felt it needed to be done. He also claimed that Hickok tried to disarm him and that he embarrassed the marshal by executing the "road agent's spin"—presenting his gun, butt forward but with his index finger in the trigger guard, then spinning it around so that his finger was on the trigger and his thumb on the hammer. However, most gunfighters used trick spins, ambidextrous "border shifts," and the like only for practice, to limber up their fingers and gain dexterity. A trick could too easily go wrong in a hostile encounter. Moreover, Hickok would never have been so innocent as to let Wes Hardin keep his finger in the trigger guard while surrendering his gun. There is some evidence that Hardin used the road agent's spin to kill Green Paramoor, an inexperienced Negro state policeman who tried to arrest him near Gonzales, but that was probably the only time he ever tried it against anyone.

During his stay in Abilene it appears that Hickok ignored or avoided him, even when Hardin killed another man in a poker game. And after that shooting, Hardin avoided Hickok, leaving town temporarily and joining a posse to track a Mexican bandit named Pablo Gutierrez. At Bluff, Kansas, he shot down Gutierrez, then returned to Abilene, expecting to enjoy new popularity as a result of this deed. But he was awakened in his hotel room one night by a prowler, and after shooting the intruder he looked out the window and saw Hickok stepping out of a hack. Guns were prohibited in town, even for the purpose of self-defense. By his own admission, he avoided a showdown by fleeing in his night clothes on a borrowed pony. He headed back to Gonzales, along the way killing Green Paramoor and then (probably with some help from one or more of the Clements) three possemen.

He married a Gonzales girl named Jane Bowen and apparently tried for a while to make a peaceful living as a horse trader. But in the summer of '72 he killed another Mexican, who may have been trying to rob him, and then was wounded for the first time in a gunfight with a gambler. Hardin was causing too much bloodshed even for the callous residents of the unruly Central Texas communities. After another posse came for him and he was wounded again, he surrendered to Cherokee County Sheriff Dick Reagan, remaining in jail for some months before sawing through the bars and riding off to DeWitt County to visit some distant relations named Taylor—the Taylors of the Sutton-Taylor feud. Very little time elapsed before Hardin shot a member of the Sutton faction, Pat Morgan, in a Cuero saloon. Morgan was a deputy of Sheriff Jack Helm, who led the Sutton Regulators. After both sides committed several more homicides, Hardin and Jim Taylor went to a blacksmith shop for a peace conference with Helm. When the negotiations deteriorated into violence, Hardin and Taylor defended themselves by killing the sheriff, "whose name," Hardin proclaimed, "was a horror to all law-abiding citizens."

Deputy Sheriff Charley Webb of Brown County was a Sutton supporter. In the spring of 1874 he rode into Comanche looking for Hardin. He found him in a saloon with Jim Taylor and Bud Dixon. What can be gleaned from conflicting versions of the meeting is that Webb may have told Hardin he had no warrant and only wanted to talk, after which he may have reached for his gun. The established facts are that Hardin was wounded but killed Webb, and that Taylor and Dixon also fired at the dying lawman.

A $4,000 reward was posted for Hardin. Posses, lynch mobs, and peace officers searched for him. Using

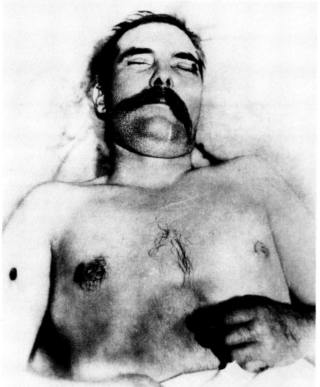

*Gun is Colt Single Action Army .45, one of two
John Wesley Hardin was wearing when he was shot down by
Constable John Selman at El Paso in 1895. His
corpse reveals multiple gunshot wounds. Frederic Remington's
1896 illustration for Harper's Monthly shows "Texas
Rangers on the Scout" in 1870's, when Rangers and other
peace officers were relentlessly pursuing Hardin.*

aliases—first John Adams, then J. H. Swain—Hardin hid for three years in Louisiana, Georgia, Alabama, and Florida, working as a farmer, timber man, stock buyer, and saloon owner. Texas Ranger John Duncan masqueraded as a farmer in Gonzales County, where Hardin's friends and kinsmen were bound to reveal something sooner or later. Finally he intercepted a letter, and Ranger Lieutenant John B. Armstrong tracked Hardin to Pensacola Junction. There Armstrong and two deputies boarded a railroad car in which Hardin and four henchmen were passengers. One of Hardin's cohorts was killed, the others were arrested, and Hardin himself was knocked senseless by a blow of Armstrong's gun barrel.

The outlaw was tried in Gonzales for killing Webb and was sentenced to twenty-five years in the Huntsville Penitentiary for second-degree murder. In prison he studied law and became superintendent of the inmates' Sunday school. When he had served almost sixteen years, Governor Jim Hogg granted him a full pardon. He went home to Gonzales, but his wife had died two years earlier and, after supporting a losing candidate for the sheriff's office, Hardin packed and left.

He practiced law very briefly in Pecos, married and soon abandoned a girl in a nearby town, then opened a law office in El Paso. Though quieter than he had been in his youth, he still wore his guns and spent most of his time in gambling halls and saloons. In the spring of 1895 a couple of cattle rustlers named Vic Queen and Martin Morose (whose name is sometimes rendered as M'Rose or McRose) were living across the river in Juarez because rewards had been posted for them in El Paso. A blonde El Paso Cyprian named Beulah was calling herself Mrs. Morose but consorting with Hardin while Mr. Morose languished in Juarez. There has been speculation that Hardin, covetous not only of Beulah but of reward money

plus funds the lady held for Morose, helped to negotiate a surrender meeting between the outlaws and three lawmen—Deputy Marshals Jeff Milton and George Scarborough and Ranger Frank McMahon. The meeting took place late one night on a trestle spanning the Rio Grande. When it was over Morose lay dead with eight gunshot wounds in his body.

There has also been speculation that the Constables Selman—Old John and Young John, father and son—had a hand in the Morose affair. The elder Selman had himself been a rustler and a deadly gunfighter in his youth, and his record as a policeman was marred by suspicions of corruption. Hardin had lately been arrested by the constables for minor breaches of the peace but seemed to be on friendly terms with them. In August, 1895, Young John arrested Beulah for being drunk and disorderly. The following morning she paid a $50 fine on a charge of vagrancy. Although the romance between Hardin and Beulah was by then foundering, Hardin reportedly warned the elder Selman that his son, "that son of a bitch," had better keep away.

Shortly before midnight on an evening later in the month, Wes Hardin was at the bar of the Acme Saloon tossing dice with H. S. Brown, when Old John Selman stepped through the door and began shooting. His first bullet would have been enough; it struck Hardin behind the right ear. Apparently in a fury, Selman fired several more shots at the prostrate body. Having killed Hardin by shooting him in the back of the head, he was duly acquitted on grounds of self-defense.

Less than a year later Constable Selman was gunned down in an alley by Deputy Scarborough, who in turn was killed by Bill Carver and Kid Curry, members of Butch Cassidy's Wild Bunch. The rogues of the Southwest were killing each other as well as the innocent.

7/The Range Wars

In the 1870's railroads were extended to shipping centers nearer and nearer the rich grasslands, while Army posts and growing settlements provided new local markets for beef. Ranchers no longer saw the prairies as limitless pasture, and competition sharpened for desirable stretches of range. Even before many fences were strung, Clay Allison had hired his gun to feuding stockmen, Bill Longley had barely escaped capture by troops enforcing a precarious range truce, and after the truce was broken Wes Hardin had killed men in the same range war. When Hardin went to prison, Billy the Kid was terrorizing New Mexico—not as a typical outlaw robbing banks or stages, but as both pawn and avenger in one of the spreading range wars.

Some writers have charged the Kid with twenty-one slayings by the time he was twenty-one years old. It is possible he may have killed as many as a dozen men—eight is a more likely estimate—but the story of his short, violent life has been warped by purveyors of ersatz Americana, beginning with *The Authentic Life of Billy the Kid*, a hair-raising collaborative effort by Ash Upson and Sheriff Pat Garrett. Garrett had once been a drinking and gambling companion of the Kid, and the sheriff's ghost-writer, Upson, had once rented a room from the outlaw's mother, yet their saga was in error even about Billy's real name. He was not called William H. Bonney until he chose to be, at about the time he arrived in Lincoln County, New Mexico. The facts to be set down here will be in disagreement with many earlier accounts, for much of the information was unearthed only within the last ten or fifteen years by such historians as W. E. Koop, R. N. Mullin, and M. G. Fulton, who searched long-forgotten records, depositions, warrants, and court proceedings.

There is an old tradition among New York City policemen that "Billy Bonney" was first arrested as a juvenile delinquent in Brooklyn. He was probably born in New York in 1859, but his mother took him west when he was an infant and he never returned. His name was Henry McCarty. His mother was Mrs. Catherine McCarty, the widow of a man, probably named Michael McCarty, who may have been killed while fighting for the Union. Henry had a younger brother, Joe McCarty, who later took his stepfather's name, Antrim; evidently Joe died in the late 1920's or early '30's, after a nondescript life of odd jobs and faro dealing. Mrs. McCarty moved to Indianapolis with her sons in the early 1860's. There she met William H. Antrim, an express driver and clerk. He and the McCartys moved to Wichita when Henry was eleven. Catherine took in washing while Antrim tried to establish a homestead preparatory to marrying her. But she developed tuberculosis and in an effort to save her Antrim took her and the boys out to Santa Fe, where he married her in 1873.

They were settled in Silver City, New Mexico, when Catherine died less than a year later. Antrim remained there and raised the boys. Billy the Kid did not commit his first murder at the age of twelve while the family was living in Coffeyville, Kansas, as stated by some biographers; the family never lived there, and the Kid was eighteen when he shot his first man.

The worst trouble young Henry McCarty had in Silver City was when Sheriff Harvey Whitehall caught him with a bag of stolen laundry and locked him up to scare him. Henry liked his stepfather, but was so afraid of punishment for stealing that he clawed his way up the jail's chimney and ran away to Graham County, Arizona. There he called himself Billy Antrim, after his stepfather, and there, in allusion to his extremely youthful appearance, accentuated by buckteeth, he was first called Kid Antrim and Billy the Kid. He worked in Arizona as a

Preceding pages: "Sheep raid in Colorado," illustration for 1877 report in Harper's Weekley *on range wars between cattlemen and sheepherders. Two cow hands hold sheepmen at gunpoint while comrades ride through flock slaughtering animals—common practice until after turn of the century. Upper right: Photograph, probably authentic, of Henry McCarty, alias William H. Bonney—Billy the Kid. Lower right: Bonney shooting foe in saloon. Artist inadvertently injected element of humor by giving Kid two right hands.*

teamster for a couple of years. Then, in 1877, near Fort Grant in Pima County, he began quarreling with "Windy" Frank Cahill, an Irish blacksmith (not a Negro, as legend has it). Cahill taunted him, probably about his appearance, and reportedly called him a pimp. The Kid shot Cahill and the blacksmith died the next day. It is not known whether Billy the Kid even owned a gun at that time. In one account of the shooting, he snatched the pistol from Cahill's holster.

Jailed for murder, he escaped and rode for New Mexico, traveling for a while with a trail acquaintance named Tom O'Keefe. When they lost their horses in a skirmish with some larcenous Indians, they separated and the Kid arrived at Seven Rivers, New Mexico, after a two-day walk without food or water. He introduced himself as William H. Bonney, a combination of his stepfather's Christian names and possibly his mother's maiden name. But he was never shrewd enough in the ways of outlawry even to maintain an alias. He was still occasionally called Antrim, and the *Grant County Herald* informed readers at one point that "Kid Antrim's real name is W. H. McCarty."

Billy Bonney, as he called himself, went to work as a cowboy for an English merchant-rancher named John H. Tunstall, unaware at first that rival cattle interests had employed rustlers who would touch off the Lincoln County War. The trouble had begun when a friend of Tunstall, John S. Chisum, was accused by small ranchers and nesters of monopolizing a vast expanse of range. James J. Dolan and Major L. G. Murphy, partners in storekeeping, banking, and ranching, wanted to ruin Tunstall and his partner, Alexander A. McSween, so they could monopolize an equal or larger stretch of Lincoln County range. The Dolan-Murphy faction, claiming to speak for "independent stockmen" (meaning the Jesse

THE FIVE CENT
WIDE AWAKE
LIBRARY

Entered according to Act of Congress, in the year 1881, by FRANK TOUSEY, in the office of the Librarian of Congress, at Washington, D. C.

Entered at the Post Office at New York, N. Y., as Second Class Matter.

No. 451. { COMPLETE. } FRANK TOUSEY, Publisher, 20 Rose Street, N. Y. { PRICE } Vol. I.
NEW YORK, August 29, 1881. ISSUED EVERY MONDAY. { 5 CENTS. }

THE TRUE LIFE OF BILLY THE KID

Left: Famous and probably real likeness of Billy the Kid in days when he rode for rancher John Tunstall, before Lincoln County Range War erupted. Far left: Cover of "five-center" novel published in 1881. This fictionalized "True Life" has 17-year-old Billy kill his first man, "a young miner named Frank Douglass," when Douglass wins affections of "a Mexican senorita named Quiseta," whom Billy loves.

Evans gang of rustlers), was backed by U.S. Attorney Thomas B. Catron and the Santa Fe Ring. The Tunstall-McSween faction was supported only by Chisum and a few other friendly cattlemen.

Sheriff Bill Brady took orders from Dolan, and Deputy Billy Mathews was a silent partner of Dolan. Jesse Evans and his gang, though caught with Tunstall stock and that of neighboring ranchers, were at first immune to arrest in the vicinity and when finally jailed were allowed to escape. They were not pursued.

The Dolan group then claimed ownership of a number of Tunstall longhorns, horses, and mules. While the case was in litigation, Sheriff Brady received an order to "attach" the animals. In February, 1878, Tunstall rode toward Lincoln to negotiate with his adversaries in the lawsuit. He was accompanied by his foreman, Dick Brewer, and by Bonney and two other employees. At the same time two posses deputized by Brady and led by Mathews and Buck Morton were riding toward the Tunstall place. Brewer and one of his men left the trail to chase a flock of wild turkeys, while Bonney and the other hand rode at a leisurely pace several hundred yards to the rear, leaving Tunstall by himself. Suddenly the two posses, totaling some two dozen men, came galloping into view. When they sighted Tunstall alone they charged like attacking cavalry, shot him down and rode away. Later they claimed

Above: J. N. Marchand's painting of Sheriff Pat Garrett bringing in Billy the Kid and "his gang"—three companions trapped with him at Stinking Springs in 1880. Right: Garrett as he actually looked at that time.

he had fired first, resisting "lawful attachment" of stock which was nowhere near the scene.

Bonney felt a fierce loyalty to the murdered Tunstall, who had treated him with kindness and trust. The Kid and Brewer swore affidavits against several possemen they recognized. Brady retaliated with arrests on false or petty charges. Brewer then formed a vigilante group of ten men who revived the name Regulators. Bonney and some of the others joined for reasons of loyalty, but at least one recruit, Frank Macnab, was a cattle detective hired by a stockmen's association to expose Sheriff Brady and halt rustling by the Evans gang. To gain a semblance of legality Brewer managed to have himself appointed a constable by a justice of the peace, and he deputized the others. In March they caught Buck Morton and another posseman, Frank Baker, at a cow camp. There they were joined by Bill McCloskey, who was suspected of being a Dolan-Brady spy. The story they told later was that Morton and Baker, aided by McCloskey, tried to escape lawful arrest, making it necessary to shoot all three. Now there was small chance that the legal battle over cattle ownership would end the shooting war, but both factions came to Lincoln for the district court session.

At nine a.m. on April 1, Brady, Deputy George Hindman, and three of Dolan's "warriors" walked from the courthouse toward Dolan's store—past the Tunstall store. In the gateway of an adobe corral next to Tunstall's, the Kid and five Regulators waited, intent on ambush.

Brady and Hindman fell before a barrage, and while Dolan's men opened fire the Regulators rode away—all but Billy the Kid, who walked across the dusty street and picked up a rifle Brady had confiscated from him. As he stooped to retrieve it, either Billy Mathews or Jack Long put a bullet through his thigh. Unable to mount a horse, he ran through alleys and back streets. Dolan's men followed

the blood trail but failed to find him. Dr. Taylor Ealy had given him shelter and then another Tunstall partisan, Sam Corbett, took him in, sawed a hole in the flooring under a bed, and hid him there with a gun until he could ride.

Bonney was indicted *in absentia* for Brady's murder, and a new sheriff, Dad Peppin, sent a posse looking for him. The search was a travesty but in July, 1878, Billy the Kid returned to Lincoln voluntarily with thirteen or fourteen armed men. By then Dick Brewer and a couple of other friends had been killed by a Dolan gunfighter known as Buckshot Roberts, who also died in the encounter. Billy and his men barricaded themselves in the McSween house and traded shots with Peppin, Deputy Marion Turner, and a large Dolan contingent in the Murphy-Dolan store across the street.

After three days of noisy stalemate, Lieutenant Colonel Nathan A. M. Dudley arrived with troops from Fort Stanton, trained a cannon on the McSween house, and ordered both sides to cease fire. Billy's force, vastly outnumbered and facing the cannon, obeyed the order. The soldiers permitted the Dolan men to slip behind the McSween place and put torches to it. As a result of Colonel Dudley's flagrantly partisan conduct, he was afterward court-martialed and, inevitably, acquitted.

With the building in flames Bonney and his men ran for whatever horses they could find. McSween, like poor Tunstall, had tried to discourage his men from committing violence and had relied on the courts to end the conflict. But he was in the house when the fighting began, and as the flames spread he walked out unarmed. Bob Beckwith shot him down. Bonney, more furious than ever, turned back and killed Beckwith before escaping.

Only one other Dolan man was shot. Five of the Tunstall-McSween men died in the battle. And that really

Top: Modern photo of Lincoln County Courthouse after extensive restoration. Lower left: In scene from 1930 MGM movie, "Billy the Kid," Bonney escapes from fairly accurate reconstruction of same edifice, built to look as it did in 1881. Far right: In another scene from same film, Sheriff Garrett (Wallace Beery) confronts handsome, sartorially splendid Billy (Johnny Mack Brown).

ended the Lincoln County War, because President Rutherford B. Hayes was sufficiently outraged to strip Territorial Governor Samuel B. Axtell of authority and send General Lew Wallace—an adequate soldier though better remembered as the author of *Ben-Hur*—to replace him and restore order. Governor Wallace simply ordered all hostilities ended and declared amnesty for all partisans except those under indictment. Bonney was excluded because of the Brady killing, and he made his position still worse by raiding the Mescalero Reservation for horses and killing Morris Bernstein, a Government clerk.

However, Billy had been learning about devious tactics and he sent Wallace a note, offering to testify against Dolan, Mathews, and Bill Campbell; he had seen them shoot a McSween attorney named Huston I. Chapman, who had only one arm and could scarcely defend himself. A meeting was arranged. In March, 1879, Billy the Kid came calling on General Lew Wallace.

He was held in rather relaxed custody long enough to give some testimony before a grand jury, but then lost faith in Wallace's promise of extreme leniency and simply rode away to Fort Sumner, where he had staunch friends. Wallace offered a $500 reward to anyone who would "capture William Bonny, alias The Kid, and deliver him to any sheriff of New Mexico." In 1880 Lincoln County elected Pat Garrett sheriff. Born in Alabama and raised in Louisiana, Garrett was a tall, mustachioed southerner who had punched cattle, hunted buffalo, wrangled horses at Fort Sumner, and gambled often enough with Bonney so that the two were jokingly called Big Casino and Little Casino. No matter. It was reported that Bonney had killed at least two more men, and had become a common thief after McSween's death ended all hope of winning the range war.

One of his victims was Joe Grant, a Texas badman who announced he would rid Fort Sumner of Billy the Kid. There is no way to prove or disprove the traditional story that Grant was drinking heavily in a Fort Sumner saloon when an innocuous-looking youngster came up, admired Grant's elegant single-action .45, and asked if he could examine it. Grant handed it over and the boy inspected it closely, surreptitiously turning the cylinder so that the hammer, when cocked, would fall on the empty sixth chamber. Then he handed the gun back, informed Grant that he was Bill Bonney, and inquired about Grant's immediate plans. Grant cocked the gun and pulled the trigger, but the only shot heard was that of Bonney's new, very fast double-action revolver—the Lightning Model.

Garrett and a posse trapped the Kid and four companions in an abandoned sheepherder's hut at Stinking Springs. One of Bonney's men, Charley Bowdre, was killed. The others withstood the siege for three days without food, and they could smell beef frying over Garrett's fire. Two days before Christmas, 1880, they surrendered. The Kid was imprisoned at Las Vegas and then at Santa Fe. In the spring he was taken to Mesilla for trial in the Brady killing and was sentenced to be hanged in Lincoln. He arrived there, manacled, in April and Garrett locked him in a second-story room of a makeshift adobe courthouse, guarded by Deputies J. W. Bell and Bob Ollinger. A week later Bell was on duty while Ollinger was across the street at La Rue's Bar. Bell unlocked Bonney's left handcuff so the prisoner could eat supper. Bonney swung the dangling handcuff, felled the guard, snatched his revolver, and killed him. Ollinger heard the shot and came running. Bonney picked up a shotgun with which Ollinger had previously taunted him. He killed the second guard, too, and rode away.

Garrett felt that his newly acquired reputation was tarnished. For three months he tracked his former friend, while observers wagered that future escapes would be forestalled by bringing the Kid in dead. Upon hearing that Bonney visited a girl at Pete Maxwell's Fort Sumner place, Garrett set out with two deputies. Maxwell ran an adobe roadhouse for ranch hands. The three lawmen arrived at midnight. While the deputies stationed themselves on the porch, watching the door and windows, Garrett quietly entered, awakened Maxwell, and sat on his bed. Maxwell, terrified, shouted no warning, but Bonney heard some noise and appeared in the doorway. He was holding a pistol but did not appear to be greatly alarmed. "*Quien es?*" he whispered. He may not have heard the two shots that came in answer, for the first bullet struck just above his heart. The coroner's jury called it justifiable homicide, but Garrett lost the next election to one of his deputies.

Years later he served one more term as sheriff in another county, and for a while a customs collector at El Paso, but he spent most of his remaining years as a not-very-prosperous cattleman. Eventually, he tried to evict a young tenant rancher named Wayne Brazil, who shot him dead and was speedily acquitted on a plea of self-defense.

By then the name of Henry McCarty was only vaguely remembered, while the legend of Billy the Kid and Pat Garrett was assuming a mantle of nostalgic pathos. Southwesterners, many of them, have forgotten the causes of the Lincoln County War but remember the Ballad of Billy the Kid: "Come gather around and I'll sing you a song,/ A tale of Pat Garrett, and the Kid, who went wrong,/ Way down in New Mexico long, long ago,/ Where a man's only law was his own forty-four."

Range wars were kindled periodically for generations, like the yearly prairie fires. As they spread slowly north, they involved some unlikely incidents and personalities. Even among aficionados of western Americana it is not widely known that Frank M. Canton, revered lawman of Wyoming and Oklahoma and controversial hero or villain of the Johnson County Range War, began his shooting career as a Texas badman. Canton had little education but he was articulate and a natural writer. After his death in 1927 his widow deposited his private papers in the Frank Phillips Collection of the University of Oklahoma Library. The historian Edward Everett Dale, curator of the collection, discovered among the papers five thick writing tablets on which Canton had recorded the story of his life. He covered in considerable detail his years as a hunter of outlaws in Wyoming, the Indian Nations, and the Oklahoma Territory, and later in Alaska during the Yukon gold rush, but said very little about his life in Texas from 1871 to 1878. Dale investigated and discovered that at that time the famous deputy marshal had been a minor outlaw and a fugitive from justice. His real name was Joe Horner; he may have changed it in 1878, when he joined a cattle drive to Nebraska and decided to stay in the North, where he was not wanted by the law—where, in fact, he could switch from the role of fugitive to that of detective and man hunter.

Canton's autobiography, *Frontier Trails*, reveals much about the attitudes and motives of western adventurers, as well as about eruptions of violence like the Johnson County War. He was born in 1849 in Virginia but brought up in northern Texas. "In the late sixties," he noted, Texas was "in a fierce struggle with the various elements of outlawry," and its rolling prairie region was "the natural home of the cow, the land of the cowboy, and the paradise of the desperado." In the spring of 1869 he helped to take fifteen hundred head of cattle from Denton up to Abilene. Despite swollen rivers and storms the drovers brought their herd almost all the way through the

131

Indian Territory without serious incident. Then, only twenty miles from the Kansas line, a war party of Osages demanded a tribute in cattle for the privilege of crossing their land. When the Texans refused, the Osages killed six steers, stampeded the herd, and ran off almost all the saddle horses. The stampede was headed off but the cowboys, all wearing tight, high-heeled riding boots, were forced to walk the herd the rest of the way. "We decided in our own minds," Canton remarked, "that the proper thing to do in the future was to kill and scalp every Indian we met."

Later, as a peace officer, Canton dealt impartially with the Indians but he was quick to arrest those who broke laws they could not understand and had no compunction about shooting any who resisted arrest. In 1884 he sent two young braves to prison for a year for slaughtering a white man's calf. To him they were rustlers. To them, cattle were the white man's buffalo, replacement for the herds their conquerors had slaughtered and on which the life of the Indian depended.

On that first drive Canton forded the Arkansas at Wichita, which then consisted of two shacks: a saloon and a grocery. After a week in Abilene he joined a larger drive to North Platte, Nebraska. On the Blue River, almost at their destination, three hundred head were run off one night in September, 1869. Canton and three other men tracked and recovered the cattle. When one of his companions accidentally fired a revolver, the three thieves fled, unaware that only four cow hands were pursuing them. Canton and his men then helped themselves to the rustler's provisions, equipment, and a splendid mule as well as their own cattle. That was frontier justice. They did not complain when a scouting party from Fort McPherson confiscated the mule. It had been stolen from the fort.

Near Platte, Canton and his friends came upon seven or eight white men living in dugouts near an adobe corral large enough to hold several hundred cattle or horses. Later they were told it was a rustlers' rendezvous called Robbers' Roost. There must have been Robbers' Roosts sprinkled all over the plains. A Utah stronghold of Butch Cassidy's gang went by that name, as did a settlement near Deadwood in the Dakota Territory. And yet on the trail of almost a thousand miles from Denton, Frank Canton saw only two real communities, the railroad towns of Abilene and North Platte. Unhampered by any organized police force, countless desperadoes sought refuge as well as prey in this immense wilderness where the only law was enforced by an individual's conscience, wits, gun, and fists. The undermanned and widely scattered Army posts as a rule had no authority to pursue criminals.

In 1878, after helping to drive another large herd up from Texas to Ogallala, Nebraska, Canton became a "field inspector" for the Wyoming Stockgrowers Association. At first he ran down Crow Indians who were killing cattle and selling beef as "elk meat." More serious trouble was developing, and in Canton's opinion the chief reason was

Deputy Marshal Frank M. Canton as he looked in early 1890's, when he participated in Johnson County, Wyoming, range war. Far right: Barn at TA Ranch, near Buffalo, where Canton's faction withstood siege by alleged rustlers.

that the Northen Pacific railroad had furnished free transportation to laborers who would extend the tracks. "The loose criminal element in New York, Chicago, and other cities took advantage of this opportunity to leave the Eastern States," he explained:

"The country west of Miles City, Montana, was soon overrun with the most desperate gang of cutthroats that ever went unhung . . . . At one time we had seventy-five prisoners in the old stockade. . . . Miners and ranchmen organized vigilance committees. . . . If the first warning was not obeyed, you would probably find several dead bodies hanging to telegraph poles. . . . Granville Stuart, president of the Montana Stock Association, at the head of fifty cowboys, commenced a war of extermination. . . The criminals who were fortunate enough to get out of Montana alive all came south into Wyoming and Idaho."

Canton continued to work as a range detective while he served as sheriff of Johnson County, Wyoming, for two terms, from 1882 to 1886. During this period he captured a number of road agents and horse thieves, including the murderous rustler Teton Jackson, for whom Jackson Hole, Wyoming, was named. Jackson belonged to an outlaw band of Mormons known as the Destroying Angels. Except with regard to polygamy, the Mormons obeyed the laws of the land at least as strictly as other westerners. But their neighbors in parts of Utah, Idaho, and Wyoming had about as much use for them as for Indians. Some of the Mormons, for their part, regarded "Gentiles" as having most of the rattlesnake's virtues. Jackson was taken to Blackfoot, Idaho, where he was tried and sentenced for stealing horses. He was wanted for several murders, but it would have taken time to gather the evidence and witnesses, and the peace officers at Blackfoot feared that the Destroying Angels would arrive at any moment to rescue him. He was rushed to the penitentiary at Boise. Though he soon broke out he was never seen again. His gang disintegrated after several more members were shot or captured. Canton also helped to catch Bill Booth, a horse thief and murderer who sold stolen ponies at Deadwood. Since the Territory of Wyoming offered $250 for every horse or cattle rustler, and much higher rewards for killers, Canton must have made a comfortable living.

Johnson County Cattle Raiders . Prisoners at Ft. D. A. Russell - 1892

B. Clark, E. W. Whitcomb, A. D. Adamson, C. S. Ford, W. H. Tabor, G. R. Tucker, A. R. Po

E. Booke, B. M. Morrison, W. A. Wilson, M. A. McNally, Bob Barlin, W. S. Davis, Sutherland

x Lowther, W. J. Clarke, J. A. Garrett, Wm. Armstrong, Buck Garrett, F. H. Labertraux,

nson, Alex Hamilton, F. M. Canton, W. C. Irvine, J. N. Tisdale, W. B. Wallace, F. De Billeir, H. Te

k ., W. E. Guthrie, F. G. S. Hesse, Phil DuFran, Wm Little, D. R. Tisdale, J. D. Mynatt, M. Shonsey

s Elliott, C. A. Campbell, J. Borlings, L. H. Parker, S. S. Tucker, B. Wiley, J. M. Bedford, k. Ricka

nk Walcott, B. Schultz, — Names not in order. Copied from "Longest Rope" by Baber.

By - A. B. Daniels

red to the Wyoming Pioneer Assn. 8-31-56 Wonewoc. Wis.

Made 30 April on R. to Hno
In Johnson Co. Ter.

In 1886 he left office to run a small ranch, but within a couple of years rustlers again infested the county. He went back to work for the stockgrowers' association, and this time also obtained a commission as U.S. Deputy Marshal. While some of the absentee owners of large ranches hired excellent foremen (who subsequently were deputized), others hired drifters fleeing from Texas Rangers, Stuart's Stranglers, or other police and vigilante groups. Cattle barons occasionally sought cheap labor in order to crush demands for higher wages. The first big labor strike among cowboys had involved seven large Texas ranches in 1883, and Texas Rangers were summoned as strike-breakers. A Wyoming strike three years later was more successful, but its leaders were blacklisted.

Some of the disreputable foremen hired only hands who were willing to help with a bit of rustling. Some of the cowboys carried small iron rods called running irons, with which to blotch and change a brand either for themselves or a foreman. A rustling cowboy would register a brand in his own name, then use his running iron on unmarked calves and on cattle whose brands could be disguised. A new industry was in the making and it required no capital. In Rawlins, Wyoming, even a prostitute, Cattle Kate Watson, soon acquired a nice herd by taking beef in trade. The furious stockgrowers fired many men, blacklisted suspected foremen, and pushed the 1884 Maverick Bill through the territorial legislature, making every un-branded calf on open range the property of the Association. Any nonmember who came into the possession of cattle was blacklisted as a rustler. Lynchings were threatened. A range war was building between the Association and Johnson County's small, independent farmers and cow hands who owned livestock.

In 1891, near Buffalo, two men named John Tisdale and Ranger Jones—rustlers, according to Canton—were ambushed. As no attempt was made to find the murderers, the independent faction decided Canton must be the killer. He was tried and acquitted. Rustlers then attempted to ambush Canton but failed. There seems to be little doubt that on occasion both sides resorted to assassination. And by this time some anonymous cattlemen had perhaps made overtures to a most efficient man-killer, Tom Horn, though there is no indication that he was the one who eliminated Tisdale and Jones for the stockgrowers. His viciousness would not be exposed for another decade.

In the spring of 1892, warrants were secured for about a dozen suspected rustlers, and Frank Canton joined a posse of forty-two men under the leadership of Major Frank Wolcott, a prominent cattleman. At the KC Ranch on the Powder River they trapped two suspects in a fortified cabin. Both men, Nate Champion and Nick Ray, refused to surrender and were shot dead.

During the siege Jack Flag, a leading opponent of the stockgrowers, approached in a wagon. As he had been accused of rustling, the posse called to him to surrender. The raiders fired without effect when he turned and fled. After unhitching and mounting one of the wagon horses he outdistanced pursuers and spread word of the raid. The possemen intended to ride into Buffalo to make several arrests, but they received a message from the townspeople begging them to avoid a pitched battle where women and children might be hurt. Over Canton's protests they stopped at a ranch fourteen miles south of town, and this gave the opposition time to organize. A force of eighty men soon surrounded the ranch house. Reinforcements nearly tripled that number before the fight ended. Trenches and breastworks were dug and sporadic firing continued for two days and two nights. On the third day a group of Flag's men, aboard a fortified wagon, bore down on the trenches with dynamite and homemade grenades.

Top: Major Frank Wolcott's 42-man rustler-arresting posse after posse itself was arrested by mounted troops from Fort McKinney who enforced truce between Wolcott's faction, representing Wyoming Stockgrowers Association, and independent ranchers accused of rustling. Wolcott's name is inked above his head but Frank Canton—badman turned lawman—cannot be positively identified. Names were added years after picture was taken and are not in proper order. Bottom: Battering ram mounted on wagon chassis, charged with dynamite, and used by Jack Flag against Canton's defenders.

According to Canton, a black flag and a red flag were nailed to the wagon, the black one signifying "no quarter," the red one symbolizing the political views of those who opposed the cattle barons, especially Arapaho Brown, allegedly a rustler, an anarchist, and the man who directed the fortification of the wagon. With unintended irony, some chroniclers have written of "gunslinger Frank Canton" and his "Red Sash Gang"—so named for sashes they supposedly wore to proclaim political sentiments which, in reality, would have infuriated them. It was an age of bungled journalism as well as the rise of red-bannered labor movements rebelling against inhuman working conditions and subsistence wages.

The wagon withdrew under heavy fire before the explosives could be used. Meanwhile, in Buffalo and Cheyenne, supporters of the Wolcott raid wired a plea for help to President Benjamin Harrison. Several of Flag's men were shot and two of Canton's men lay dying, but before more carnage could be inflicted a mounted column arrived from Fort McKinney, enforced a truce, arrested all participants on both sides, and thereby moved the Johnson County War off the range and into the courts.

Some of the smaller ranchers on both sides, including Canton, lost everything they owned in the legal battle. While litigation continued, rustlers murdered George Wellman, foreman of the Hoe Ranch; Arapaho Brown was killed by some of his own men; rustling increased; and martial law was declared. With troops stationed at Gillette and on the Lower Powder River, theft and murder finally dwindled. The Johnson County Range War was over. Canton moved on to serve as a U.S. Deputy Marshal in the Oklahoma Territory and the Indian Territory, where he helped to capture or kill a number of vicious killers (including some members of the Dalton-Doolin gang) and then to the Yukon, and then back to the new State of Oklahoma, where he was appointed adjutant general of the National Guard.

Frank Canton was a badman who became an outstanding lawman; Tom Horn was a lawman who became a hired assassin during the range-war era. Born in Missouri in 1861, he left the family farm at the age of fourteen and drifted out to Arizona to become a mule skinner, cowboy, and Overland Mail driver. (He never rode for the Pony Express, as some writers have averred, since that enterprise failed while he was still an infant.) Wandering about the Southwest he learned Spanish and enough of the Chiricahua dialect to converse with Apaches. He scouted for Generals Nelson A. Miles and George Crook, serving

Innocent and necessary work of catching and branding calves on open range, as depicted in 1887, sometimes led to shooting incidents and even full-scale range wars. Disputes were inevitable because cow hands became greedy and used "running irons" to counterfeit brands.

as the Army's intermediary in peace talks with Geronimo.

In the 1880's he became a Pinkerton agent, specializing in the tracking down of train robbers. One such bandit was Peg Leg Watson, alias Peg Leg McCoy, a former member of Butch Cassidy's Wild Bunch who had recruited a small gang of his own. J. P. McParland, chief of Pinkerton's Denver office, reported that Horn trailed Watson to a cabin, called to the outlaw that he was coming for him, and calmly walked across the open yard to the door with his rifle cradled. He displayed the same coolness in arresting several rustlers in the vicinity of Hole in the Wall and near Buffalo, where Canton was operating. But in the early 1890's, having informed the Pinkerton agency

that he had "no more stomach" for that kind of life, he moved to Cheyenne to work for unidentified cattle barons, ostensibly as a range detective.

Writers of semifictional western history have charged him with killing "dozens of men." The true number is unknown, but he did earn a reputation as a cold-blooded killer. He left several corpses on the trails around Hole in the Wall, and he also left a trademark, or signature—a rock placed beneath each victim's head—as a warning, perhaps, to would-be rustlers. Some of his victims certainly were rustlers or road agents, but they were executed without a trial. Moreover, since bandits like the Wild Bunch were then operating far away from that area,

the motives of Horn's employers were thought to be mere vengeance in a range-war vendetta. Testimony at his subsequent murder trial revealed that he preferred to ambush those marked for death, waiting in the rain for hours on one occasion, chewing raw bacon, until he had the chance for one sure rifle shot.

By 1902 most of the big ranchers had resigned themselves to nesters and small cattle outfits but were still warring with sheepherders. Horn ambushed and killed fourteen-year-old Willie Nickell, reportedly while lying in wait for the boy's father, a sheep raiser who had angered local cattlemen. U.S. Deputy Marshal Joe Lefors, one of the possemen who had kept Butch Cassidy and the Sundance Kid on the move, became friendly with Horn and got him drunk enough to admit the killing while hidden witnesses listened and a secretary took meticulous notes.

When Horn was convicted of murder, cattlemen wagered that he would never hang. Horn himself brooded in jail, hurriedly writing brief memoirs but never naming his employers. With the aid of unidentified friends he devised a plot to blow out the wall of the Cheyenne jail with dynamite. The plot was discovered. Then he and another prisoner tried to escape. He wrested a Luger pistol from one of his guards but was unable to operate the strange new semiautomatic weapon and was recaptured. He mounted the gallows in November, 1903, and was hanged with a rope he had braided himself.

That, however, did not end the wars between cattlemen and sheepmen. Sheep crop their grass much more closely than cattle, and when many sheep are held too long on a relatively small pasture they overgraze and trample it so badly that in dry weather it may require months to recover. For generations, moreover, range lore included the false gospel that "woollies" muddied waterholes so terribly as to prevent cattle from drinking. Eventually,

ranchers discovered that sheep can be grazed where cattle cannot and that the two species, properly managed, can share a range and increase a stockman's profits considerably. But for nearly half a century, until after the First World War, bloody clashes erupted between cattlemen and sheepherders.

The feuding was exacerbated by racial hatreds. Especially in the Southwest, many sheepherders were Mexican or Indian. The cowboys, utterly accepting their own aristocratic images as presented in dime novels, held that "sheepherding is no job for a white man" and "a sheepman is lower than a thief." Later, when sheep raising spread through the North, many herders were Basques who regarded Americans with suspicion or contempt and were regarded with equal scorn by Americans.

Range warfare often began when cattlemen established a "deadline" beyond which sheepherders were warned not to trespass on the range. The edict was inevitably violated as the sheep moved to new pastures or were herded down from the high country for winter. Cattlemen dynamited herds of sheep, or set them afire, shot them, knifed them, clubbed them, poisoned them, drowned them, or "rimrocked" them—drove them over cliffs. Saltpeter was popular as it was deadly to sheep but not to cattle, and poisoning sometimes got rid of the animals without the need for a confrontation.

Cattlemen in San Saba County, Texas, slashed the throats of two hundred and forty sheep in January, 1880. Seven years later at Tie Siding, Wyoming, twenty-six hundred sheep in Charles Herbert's corrals were burned alive. That was the first year of the Tonto Basin War between the Tewksbury and Graham clans in Arizona. It erupted when the Tewksburys hired on as armed guards for sheepherders who crossed a deadline into Pleasant Valley. It ended in 1892, when no able-bodied men were

Tom Horn obliges photographer by posing with rope he braided for his own hanging. Picture evidently was taken in 1902, after he was convicted of killing sheep rancher's 14-year-old son. Horn had once been reliable Army scout and Pinkerton detective, but he became professional assassin for Wyoming cattlemen in vendetta against sheepmen.

left to fight. The corpses were listed as four of the Tewksbury group, twelve of the Graham group, and eleven noncombatants caught in the line of fire. Six victims were unidentified.

Every state in the Rockies and the Great Plains suffered similar atrocities. In 1909, near Tensleep, in Wyoming's Big Horn Basin, masked cattlemen stole up to the wagons of sheepmen Joseph Allemand, Joseph Emge, Pierre Cafferal, Charles Helmer, and Jules Lazair. Cafferal and Helmer were taken from one wagon and held under guard while raiders fired their guns into another. Emge and Lazair were killed in their bedrolls. Allemand staggered out as the marauders piled up sagebrush to burn the wagon. He raised his hands, as he was ordered to. "It's a hell of a time of night to come out with your hands up," a cattleman said, and killed him.

One of the raiders left a distinctive boot print at the scene of the Tensleep Murders, and when cattlemen converged there to gloat over the bodies of the slain, alert lawmen noticed that Herb Brink's boot left a matching print. He went to prison for life. Six accomplices received terms ranging from three to twenty-six years.

Range warfare had almost flickered out at last in 1920, when Colorado cattlemen killed a hundred and fifty sheep for the crime of grazing in the White River National Forest. By then many cattlemen were showing affection for "woollies." The decline of open rangeland and changes in ranching practices removed the causes for hostilities. But a more immediate corrective has been pointed out by such western scholars as Lowell H. Harrison: "the development of law and order that accompanied the passing of the frontier."

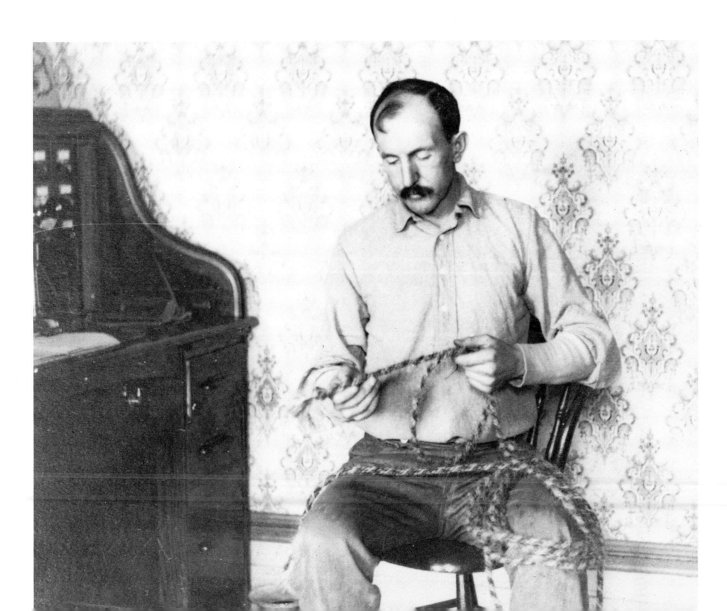

*Preceding pages: Group of Deputy U. S. Marshals who
helped patrol more than 70,000 square miles of
Indian Territory in early 1890's, bringing many hundreds
of desperadoes to Fort Smith court. From left, they
are Wess Bowman, Dave Rusk, Miller (first name uncertain),
Heck Bruner, John Tolbert, Paden Tolbert, Bill Smith,
Charley Copeland, Tom Johnson, and G. S. White. Above: Building
that served as officers' quarters and then courthouse. Its
specially converted basement was used for many years as jail.*

In scarcely more than two decades, from 1875 to 1896, the Honorable Isaac Charles Parker, judge of the United States Court for the Western District of Arkansas at Fort Smith, sentenced one hundred and sixty men to die. During the first fourteen of those years, the convicted could seek no appeal from the decisions of "the Hanging Judge," and even after 1889, when the Supreme Court began reviewing some of Parker's cases, the expected retrials sometimes only led to a confirmation of verdict and sentence. Despite reversals, commutations, and presidential pardons, seventy-nine of the hundred and sixty condemned outlaws plummeted through the trap of the Fort Smith gallows, an oversized structure built for multiple executions.

In September, 1875, six men dangled from the gibbet simultaneously. One was an Indian who bore the prophetic name of Smoker Mankiller; like the others, he was a murderer. Murder and rape were the offenses for which Judge Parker imposed the death penalty. In April, 1876, five more murderers died together as the trap was released, and another four in September. The following year Dr. Henri Stewart, who had studied medicine at Harvard and Yale, abandoned his wife and four children and drifted into the Indian Territory. For a while he rode with the Sam Bass gang of Texas train robbers. In 1879 he killed a man during an attempted train holdup at Caddo in the Choctaw Nation. Captured in Missouri and brought to Fort Smith, he stood on the gallows platform with Colorado Bill Elliott, who had been wanted for murder in four states when he killed his fifth victim and was overtaken by deputy marshals in the Choctaw Nation. The last multiple hanging took place in 1896, when five bloodthirsty renegades comprising Rufus Buck's gang died together. All had been convicted of murder, but they were hanged for the rape of Rosetta Hassan in the Creek Nation.

Most executions—sixty of the seventy-nine—were performed by George Maledon, a former Fort Smith policeman and deputy sheriff of Sebastian County. Almost as expert with pistols as with rope, he shot four prisoners who attempted to escape. He considered himself humane, taking pride in his ability to adjust a noose so that the fall through the trap would almost always break a man's neck, bringing quick death rather than slow strangulation. After his retirement he carried several of his ropes with him on a profitable tour, lecturing on the evils of crime and the badmen of the Indian country.

Judge Parker was often vilified in the press and in Congress during his last years, when his court gradually was stripped of power. By today's standards, unquestionably, he was a harsh arbiter of justice. It is also true that his instructions to juries occasionally bordered on the directing of verdicts. Yet he generally found support in the Fort Smith newspapers and among the tribal councils in the adjoining Indian Territory, where most of the condemned men were captured. An ordinary frontier town, Fort Smith had four outspoken newspapers (and thirty saloons) before it had sidewalks, paved streets, or 2,500 people. When Colorado Bill Elliott was convicted, the Fort Smith *Elevator* rejoiced: "He will hardly be wanted by any other state after they get through with him here."

In the late 1870's the Indian country regulated by the Fort Smith court had a population of some 85,000, of whom perhaps 20,000 were white, some 7,000 Negroes (including freed slaves of the Cherokees), and the rest Indians or of mixed blood. By the end of Parker's tenure the population had grown to 250,000 people, of whom all but 50,000 were whites. It was a genocidal invasion, which Parker recognized and fought. He was noted for his impartial treatment of defendants, whether they were Indians, blacks, or whites. The Indians admired his impartiality,

saw his stern policies as the only way to reduce outlawry in the lands assigned to them, and appreciated his public statements defending their treaties and opposing the steady robbery of their lands. They hoped he would rid the Territory of Indian criminals and of fugitive white outlaws who seemed to regard it as their own sovereign state.

When Parker, a former Missouri Senator, was appointed by President Grant to the district bench, the Fort Smith court was in low repute because of scandal involving his predecessor, Judge William Story, who had resigned to avoid impeachment for bribery after serving fourteen months. Court costs had totaled a fabulous $400,000 during that period, while arrests had been few and trials fewer. The name Robbers' Roost was being applied to the entire Indian country instead of individual hamlets or enclaves. It was said that Story's deputies neglected to arrest suspects in at least fifty murder cases. At first the people of western Arkansas and the Indian Nations worried that Parker might bring carpetbag rule. Within a few years they were saying that only the Hanging Judge and his deputy marshals prevented outright rule by the badmen. Opponents still declared that outlawry continued to rise. In 1896 he replied that crime was rising faster in other parts of the country, that "in the past five years forty-three thousand persons, more than are in the regular army, have been murdered in the United States," and in those five years the nation counted "seven hundred and twenty-three legal executions and one thousand one hundred and eighteen lynchings," whereas within his jurisdiction only three cases of mob violence had occurred during his two decades on the bench.

To speculative historians the Hanging Judge has remained a controversial figure, a saver of lives in some accounts, "the butcher of the Fort Smith Slaughter

Left: Isaac C. Parker—the Hanging Judge—as he looked in his thirties, when he came to Fort Smith. In two decades he sentenced 160 badmen to die. Above: Chief executioner George Maledon—"Prince of Hangmen"—who performed 60 hangings for Western District of Arkansas during Parker's long campaign to reduce outlawry. Pictured with two revolvers in cross-draw holsters, he was as expert with pistols as with rope. He shot down four condemned men who tried to escape.

145

House" in others. There has been less controversy over the intractable lawlessness in the Indian Nations, for hindsight has bared its causes.

Beginning in 1832 the "Five Civilized Tribes" (Cherokees, Choctaws, Chickasaws, Creeks, and part of that branch of Creeks known as Seminoles) were driven from their southeastern homelands over the Trail of Tears into what is now Oklahoma. In 1834 Congress designated as "Indian country" the general area of exile and subjected it to the judicial authority of the Arkansas Territory's Western District, except with regard to crimes committed by an Indian against the person or property of another Indian. Each of the major tribes established its own council and courts, local constabularies, and a militia known as the Light Horse. Indian authorities, powerless to arrest or prosecute whites, tried hard to curb their own outlaws. On occasion they meted out severe punishment, but in the vast wilderness innumerable desperadoes evaded the ill-equipped, largely self-trained Indian police. Moreover, in addition to the Five Civilized Tribes, nearly thirty other tribes or tribal branches inhabited or recurrently penetrated the region. Some had difficulty accepting regulation. Some had unconventional traditions as to what constituted crime. To those who felt admiration for a daring horse thief or a man eager to avenge a friend's death, morality might consist of sending a posse in the wrong direction.

At first there were no white lawmen within the vaguely defined borders, and even in Parker's time a marshal could not go in and bring back a prisoner if both felon and victim were Indians. This is why arrest warrants described an outlaw or his victim or both as "A white man and not an Indian by birth or marriage or adoption into any tribe." There were white outlaws who detested Indians and yet claimed to be half-breeds so that they could

safely hide in the Indian country. Others married Indian women or lived in Indian settlements as "adopted tribesmen." Many more felt no need of such subterfuge in a remote territory where people relied on their own defenses, had very slow means of communication, and were casual about notifying white authorities of fugitives among them.

The first significant white invasion was of troops patrolling and building forts to pacify the Osages, who preyed upon the more sedentary Cherokees and their allies. Forts Gibson and Towson were erected in the Indian country and Fort Smith on the border. Then came the cowboys, driving cattle north to Kansas and Nebraska, northeast to Arkansas and Missouri. There were traders and trappers, prospectors, railroaders, lease-holding white ranchers and farmers on the tribal lands, as well as nesters and speculators on the so-called Unassigned Lands to which no tribe held title. The Indians made their situation worse by their eagerness to sell off lands whenever the Government permitted or encouraged them to do so.

The northern part of their Territory embraced the lands of the Creek and Cherokee Nations, as well as some concentrations of plains Indians around the Quapaw Agency. The central portion encompassed the Choctaw Nation, and the southern portion held the Chickasaw and Seminole Nations. Though there was commerce among the groups and districts, ethnic rivalry sometimes hindered cooperative police work. And among some individuals, families, even whole communities, a resentment of white authority smoldered as hotly after the Civil War as when thousands had died along the Trail of Tears. To some of these people the only whites worth befriending were outlaws who, like themselves, had been driven into exile by white law.

As there was no extradition, a road agent or gunfight-

Top: Paddle-wheel ferry on Arkansas River. In 1870's and early '80's, before bridge was built, this boat and others like it brought lawmen and their prisoners across river from Indian Territory to Fort Smith. Bottom: Waterfront street at Fort Smith in '70's, when Judge Parker arrived to extend justice from busy trade center into badman's domain.

er who was wanted anywhere but in Arkansas or the Indian country was safe in the tribal lands until he committed another crime there and was caught in the act or identified as the culprit. There were few witnesses on the lonely roads or at the scattered way stations and supply stores. Even when a man was caught red-handed, he had a good chance of evading the few available lawmen.

The slaveholding Southeastern tribes had fought for the British and later for the Confederacy against "Federal oppression." The Reconstruction treaties of 1866 were land robberies in the guise of reparation. They were also chaotic, for they failed to grant clear legal status to the freed slaves of the Cherokees and their allies. Many Indians had treated their slaves as tenant farmers or indentured servants. Intermarriage and tribal adoption were not uncommon. In either event the black man legally became an Indian, immune to white law if he committed a crime against another Indian or "Indianized" black within the Territory. Thus, black as well as white outlaws sought refuge in the Indian country, and black as well as Indian residents offered refuge to fellow outcasts.

The sale of spirits was illegal in the Indian country and whiskey peddling was the most widespread, easily proved offense. Before Judge Parker's arrival, it was fairly common for a deputy marshal to follow an innocent hunting party across the line, confiscate a pint of whiskey, and collect mileage and arrest fees for delivering the miscreants to court to be fined. Real whiskey peddlers, jailed repeatedly, became fugitives regardless of whether they committed other offenses, and they tended to experiment with more serious crimes. An astonishing percentage of bank, store, and train robbers, highwaymen, and murderers began as whiskey peddlers.

Another deplorable practice among deputies was that of bringing in trial "witnesses" by the wagonload, also for

Upper left: Deputies Wess Bowman, Bill Ellis, and John Tolbert posing with their Winchester carbines and single-action Colts. Holsters are typical of late 19th century. Note that Ellis is carrying rifle ammunition in cartridge loops on his gunbelt. Center: Law booklet issued to every deputy to govern his conduct. Territory lawmen had reputation for toughness, but Judge Parker jailed them for excessive violence or other serious infractions. Above: One of his most famous deputies, Heck Thomas, in 1886. Lower left: One of several commissions Thomas held during his long career as Federal lawman.

the purpose of collecting fees. Many of these witnesses had no knowledge of the crimes about which they were called to testify. They had difficulty obtaining subsistence allowances in Fort Smith and were paid no expenses for their return trips. In towns that had suffered wholesale roundups of witnesses, residents had some justification for public statements that they would rather harbor outlaws than deal with U.S. Deputy Marshals.

Judge Parker reduced such impositions by refusing to authorize payment of questionable fees. He fined one deputy for misconduct. And he condoned no unnecessary violence. In one instance he sent a deputy to prison for using excessive force during an arrest. But he excused a degree of force and even chicanery as necessary, asserting that men engaged in such work were not likely to be angels. He also increased his force of deputies until he had two hundred. The number is misleading. Two hundred deputy marshals were trailing countless outlaws through seventy-four thousand square miles, and a wagonload of captives, ranging from sodden whiskey peddlers to seasoned gunfighters, scalp-collecting renegades, and crazed mass murderers, might have to be carted five hundred miles along a hostile trail to Fort Smith. Sixty-five marshals were killed. A few lawmen, like Grat and Bob Dalton, soured and became dangerous outlaws. But their brother, Frank Dalton, was more typical. He remained a brave, effective deputy marshal until he was slain by whiskey peddlers. And there were survivors like Chris Madsen, Bill Tilghman, and Heck Thomas, remembered as heroes in the battle to bring peace to the American frontier. Thomas and several possemen once arrived at Fort Smith with a wagon caravan and unloaded thirty-two prisoners; nine were convicted of capital offenses.

Fiction has made much of posters that advertised rewards for outlaws "wanted, dead or alive." The deputies endangered themselves to bring in desperate killers alive. A deputy who killed his prisoner, even during an attempted escape, usually forfeited his fees and expenses, and if the corpse was unclaimed he had to provide for its burial. Deputy H. D. Fannin was out of pocket $60 for the burial of Jason Labreu, a gunfighter, rapist, and murderer wanted in Texas, Louisiana, and the Indian Nations.

Ordinarily a deputy received six cents a mile for expenses while trailing an outlaw, a $2 arrest fee, and ten cents a mile to feed and transport himself and his prisoner to Fort Smith. (Expenses were the same when he was sent to bring in witnesses. He got a fifty-cent fee for serving the first subpoena and thirty-seven cents for each additional one.) In cases of mail robbery or the murder of Federal employees, the United States Government posted rewards—to which U. S. Deputy Marshals were not entitled as Federal officers already being paid by the Government to apprehend criminals. Thus a deputy risked his life in the Nations for an average income of perhaps $500 a year, plus an occasional reward offered by railroads, express companies, individuals, local authorities, or state governors.

Fort Smith's jurisdiction was larger than that of any other court in history, and its deputy marshals killed or captured more murderous outlaws than any similar group in a comparable span of time, yet few of the desperadoes were famous. The first of Judge Parker's multiple executions disposed of six killers: Daniel Evans, William Whittington, James Moore, Smoker Mankiller, Samuel Fooy, Edmund Campbell. Though all were as vicious as the Daltons, in romantic modern accounts none is remembered—not even Jim Moore, who rode with a band of horse thieves through Missouri, Kansas, and Texas, and killed his eighth man, Deputy William Spivey, in a gunfight with the posse that captured him near Red River.

Similarly, the brothers Pink and Jim Lee have been almost forgotten, though they inflicted perhaps the heaviest casualties ever sustained by a Fort Smith posse in a single gun battle. In 1885 the Lees and their gang of rustlers, road agents, and casual murderers fought off a pursuing force, killing Marshal Jim Guy and three of his men. The Lees also slew Jim and Andy Roff, brothers who operated a ranch in the Chickasaw Nation. A third brother, Alva Roff, had become sufficiently wealthy as a Texas cattleman to offer a bounty of $2,500 for the capture or death of the Lees, and the State of Texas offered an additional $1,000 reward. Deputies Heck Thomas and Jim Taylor began tracking the Lees in June, 1885, and caught up with them in September. Declining the opportunity to surrender, both of the Lees raised their rifles. Pink Lee was killed instantly. Jim Lee managed to fire three wild shots before he died. Deputies Thomas and Taylor had the good sense to forego their fees and, instead of returning immediately to Fort Smith, they loaded the corpses in a buggy and drove to Gainesville for the reward money.

A more familiar outlaw name is that of Ned Christie, the full-blooded Cherokee who fought more skirmishes with lawmen than any other badman in the history of the Fort Smith court. He was a tribal councilor until he turned to whiskey peddling. Soon he became a horse thief and a murderous bandit. In 1889 Deputies Heck Thomas and L. P. Isabel located him and wounded him, but Christie escaped after shooting Isabel in the shoulder. During a subsequent gunfight Christie wounded three more deputies. Then he ambushed and killed Deputy Dan Maples. In November, 1892, sixteen men led by Deputies Heck Bruner and G. S. White surrounded a log fortress in which Christie and a friend named Arch Wolf were hiding. After hours of shooting without effect, the posse obtained a small cannon—hauled from Coffeyville aboard a wagon—and put thirty balls into the fort, still without effect. Finally they used dynamite to blow down part of a wall and set the building on fire. Christie came out shooting. He fell, with a dozen bullets in him, and his body was carted to Fort Smith. Somehow Wolf got away in the confusion of the fire and battle, but eventually was caught and sent to the penitentiary.

Another well-recorded outlaw—more notorious for his association with Belle Starr than for his own deeds—was a white man, a horse thief known only as Blue Duck. While on a drunken spree in 1886 he rode into a field near Fort Smith and shot down a young farmer, evidently for no reason other than the urge to kill. Belle Starr (nee Myra Belle Shirley) was at that time married to a Cherokee horse thief named Sam Starr, but she openly consorted with several lovers, including Blue Duck. Ranching, rustling, and horse trading earned her a comfortable living, and she hired Fort Smith's best lawyers for Blue Duck.

He was sentenced to hang but twice reprieved, and President Grover Cleveland finally commuted his penalty to life imprisonment. Among Belle Starr's several profitable activities was that of bribing and otherwise influencing juries, prosecutors, and various court officials. She enjoyed being called "the Fixer." A stubborn popular belief insists that somehow she obtained a pardon for Blue Duck when he had been in prison only a short time. There is a conflicting story that he was ambushed in the Indian Nations by an unknown killer. Actually, he remained in prison almost nine years and was dying of tuberculosis when President Cleveland issued a pardon so he could "die among friends."

The Daltons, of course, were the era's most famous gang. Grat, Emmett, Bob, and Bill Dalton were the four wild ones among Lewis and Adeline Dalton's fifteen children. Whereas Myra Belle Shirley Starr boasted of having been secretly married to Cole Younger (and evidently did bear his child, whom she named Pearl Younger), Adeline Younger Dalton was understandably reticent about being Cole Younger's aunt. She did not, however, disavow her kin. Lewis Dalton, a hard-drinking, light-working former tavern keeper, moved his family around Kansas and Missouri in gypsy fashion before settling on an Osage Reservation adjoining the Indian Territory. When the Civil War ended, the land was seized from the Osages and the town of Coffeyville was built there, three miles from the Indian border. Dalton stayed on, farming, selling horses obtained from the Osages, and perhaps doing a bit of illicit whiskey dispensing. Later, in the 1880's, he leased land in the Cherokee Nation, near Vinita. He would not have been reluctant to boast of a connection with the Youngers. Somehow it grew to be fairly common knowledge, to the detriment of his sons. When several of them became outlaws, a kind of reputation by association preceded them, sometimes causing them to be blamed for other men's crimes and goading three of them to attempt exploits worthy of the Younger name.

Five Dalton brothers led respectable lives and one of them, Frank Dalton, served Judge Parker for three years as a trustworthy deputy marshal. He was shot and killed in 1887, while attempting to arrest three whiskey hawkers west of Fort Smith. Bill Dalton established a ranch in California, married, and entered politics; he might have remained the sixth respectable Dalton if Bob and Grat had not come visiting while Fort Smith deputies were combing the Nations for them—and if Bill Dalton himself had not become embroiled in a Populist fight with a railroad-backed political machine.

Marshal John Carroll appointed Grat Dalton as one of his deputies to replace his slain brother Frank. Soon Bob

Dalton also received a deputy's badge under Marshal Jacob Yoes. Young Emmett was working on the Bar X B Ranch, near the Pawnee Agency, and occasionally doing unofficial posse duty for Grat and Bob. From some of the older hands at the Bar X B, Emmett learned the refinements of horse rustling. In 1888 Bob Dalton killed Charlie Montgomery, a rival for the affections of a local girl. He and Emmett brought the corpse to Coffeyville and claimed they had shot Montgomery for resisting arrest when they caught him stealing riding equipment from a stable. Grat, meanwhile, was suspected of selling other people's livestock. He and Bob lost their badges for stealing horses at Baxter Springs, Kansas.

A Federal warrant was issued for their apprehension. Grat disappeared into the Nations for a while. Bob and Emmett rode to Silver City, New Mexico, where they formed a gang with Bitter Creek George Newcomb, Blackface Charley Bryant, and Bill McElhanie. Together the five rode to a Mexican mining camp halfway between Silver City and Santa Rosa, held up a gambling hall there,

Crawford Goldsby, far more famous as Cherokee Bill, half-breed member of Bill Cook's bandit gang. Picture was taken when he was in custody at Fort Smith after killing at least three men, but before he shot down guard in crazed attempt to shoot his way out of jail. Far right: Goldsby, in 1896, standing alone on long gallows trap built for multiple executions. Such hangings drew large crowds.

and fled toward the Nations. Along the way they scattered a posse, but Emmett was shot in the arm. Deciding it would be best to separate, Emmett Dalton and Bitter Creek Newcomb went back to the Indian Territory. Bob Dalton and Bill McElhanie went to California, where they were joined at brother Bill's ranch by Grat.

While ranching at Clovis, near Paso Robles, Bill Dalton was campaigning to become assemblyman on a ticket opposing the machine supported by the Southern Pacific Railroad. Many of the area's ranchers hated the Southern Pacific for its enormous land grabs. In the midst of this bitter conflict, in 1891, three men robbed a Southern Pacific express train as it passed through Tulare County. Railroad detective William Smith informed his employers that their enemy, Bill Dalton, was related to Cole Younger and that Bob and Grat Dalton were desperadoes from the Indian Territory. When Bob Dalton and Bill McElhanie astutely left for home on a pair of fast horses, a Tulare County grand jury obliged the railroad by indicting Bill and Grat Dalton for the holdup. The Daltons also were charged with a second California train robbery that took place in September. Grat decided that railroaders' politics and his past record made his chance of acquittal poor, so he broke out of the county jail with two other prisoners. Until spring he lived in a cave with another escapee, subsisting on game and on food brought by ranchers. Then, feeling somewhat threatened by railroad and express company rewards totaling $6,000, he rode home, stealing fresh horses as he went.

He was convicted *in absentia*. Bill Dalton proved his innocence and was acquitted, making his brother's innocence obvious, since the accusation was that they had been seen together committing the robberies. Nonetheless, tales of western outlaws still commemorate the "two California train robberies by the Daltons." Bill Dalton, though absolved, was ruined financially and politically. He went back to the Indian country where for some time he tried again to make an honest living.

Railroad traffic had increased considerably since 1889, when the Unassigned Lands in the Indian Territory

Rufus Buck's astoundingly savage gang of young renegades,
who flourished for only thirteen days in Creek Nation.
From left, shackled together and in leg irons: Maoma July,
Sam Sampson, Rufus Buck himself, Lucky Davis,
and Lewis Davis. They were known to have committed
at least two murders, two rapes, and four robberies before
their capture by posse of over 100 Indian police,
deputies, and Creek citizens. Their execution for rape
in 1896 was Fort Smith's last multiple hanging.

were named Oklahoma and opened to white settlement. In May, 1891, at Wharton in the Cherokee Strip leading into Oklahoma, Bob, Grat, and Emmett Dalton robbed the Santa Fe express. They robbed another train at Lillietta and another at Red Rock in the Strip. Their gang now included Dick Broadwell and Bill Powers, ordinary badmen of the Territory with a chronic thirst for plunder. But the Daltons had an additional motive besides greed—revenge against the railroads. They were already known as the most desperate train robbers in the West when they held up another train near Adair in the Cherokee Nation. This one was guarded by a force of Indian police and railroad detectives. A withering exchange of fire kept up while they broke into the express car and looted it. Several policemen and passengers were wounded. A stray bullet killed Dr. W. L. Goff as he sat in a drugstore near the depot.

After the Wharton robbery, which had brought the gang $14,000, Blackface Charley Bryant took his share and rode away to Hennessey, Oklahoma, where he was recognized and arrested by Marshal Ed Short. En route to court Bryant somehow got his hand on a gun, and he and the marshal were both killed in the fight. But replacing casualties was not yet a problem for the Daltons.

Though the Lillietta robbery alone netted the gang $19,000 in currency and silver, and they could afford to rest for long periods at hideouts on the Canadian River and in the Creek Nation, Bob Dalton insisted on maintaining the frequency of raids. He persuaded some of his colleagues that they could "retire rich" within a year and leave the country. Bitter Creek Newcomb and Charlie Pierce were again riding with them, but protesting the division of spoils and opposing grandiose plans for a vengeful "homecoming" at Coffeyville, Kansas. Bill Dalton, still wearing a mantle of virtue, arranged for hiding places and gave tactical advice; he, too, opposed a raid on Coffeyville, especially since one of the bandits or their friends had talked too much and people all over the region now spoke of Coffeyville as the next target. The town's citizens and peace officers would be prepared and eager to trap the Daltons.

At a ranch on Cowboy Flat, fifteen miles from Guthrie, the bandits planned and argued. Another of those voting against Coffeyville was Bill Doolin, a jovial Arkansas cow hand who had ridden for the Bar X B, done a little rustling with Emmett, and been in minor scrapes with the law. Deputy Marshal Bill Tilghman, believing Doolin's early escapades to be a matter of mere youthful exuberance, had been lenient with him. There was a story, possibly true, that Doolin once dissuaded another badman from ambushing Tilghman. He was an outlaw with an insistent conscience. He had participated in the holdups at Lillietta and Red Rock, but always he had opposed wanton shooting. Now he foresaw a pitched battle. The gang split up.

In October, 1892, Bill Powers, Dick Broadwell, Bob, Grat, and Emmett Dalton rode into Coffeyville, wearing new clothes and new guns. The Daltons also wore false whiskers. They were determined to test the assumption that banks could provide more cash than express cars, and that with sufficient manpower Coffeyville's two banks could be robbed simultaneously. Bob Dalton, having convinced himself that he really was another Cole Younger, boasted that this raid would eclipse anything the James-Younger coalition had done. At half past nine in the morning Bob and Emmett Dalton strode into the First National Bank. At the same time Grat Dalton and two masked companions, Powers and Broadwell, entered the Condon Bank. None of the gang members realized that the Daltons, who had often been in Coffeyville, would have needed a better disguise than false whiskers to prevent recognition as they rode into town.

The citizens were quick to organize and the robbers in the Condon Bank were slow. Their companions left the First National but rode only a short distance before returning to investigate the delay. As Grat Dalton and his two henchmen finally prepared to leave the Condon Bank they heard a volley of shots. The Battle of Coffeyville had begun.

The outlaws ran for their horses. Bill Powers fell dead in the street. City Marshal Charles Connelly mortally wounded Grat Dalton, whose last act was to lift his revolver and kill the lawman. He might have found yet another target before expiring, had not John Kloehr, owner of a livery stable and president of a local rifle club, put a final shot through his neck. Dick Broadwell killed one of the defending citizens, George Cubine, and Bob Dalton killed two others, Lucius Baldwin and Charles Brown.

Broadwell was hit twice but reached his horse. A mile from town he fell from the saddle, dead. Bob Dalton, wounded by sniper fire from a hardware store, supported himself against a barn and kept shooting. Kloehr ended the crimes of this outlaw, too, with a bullet in the chest. Emmett Dalton, though severely wounded, remounted a horse and reached down for his dying brother but was knocked to the ground by another shot. He was bleeding from sixteen wounds, yet he recovered. Four citizens had been injured, four killed. Of the five bandits Emmett was the lone survivor. Sentenced to life in the Kansas State Penitentiary at Lansing, he was pardoned after fourteen years and died in California in 1937.

Bill Dalton, while probably helping to plan robberies for his more reckless brothers, had tried to earn his living by horse trading and land speculation. Now he was ruined

Henry Starr, sometimes called Territory's "Last Bad Indian,"
in 1915, when he went to jail for robbing bank at Stroud,
Oklahoma. Related to Sam and Belle Starr, he was clan's quiet
member, disdaining tobacco, alcohol, and wild celebrations.
But he had record of bootlegging, horse theft, banditry,
and murder. He died in 1921 of gunshot wound received during
attempted holdup of People's National Bank in Harrison, Arkansas

in Kansas and Oklahoma as he had been ruined in California. A financial panic was sweeping the country, money was scarce, and no bank would deal with any Dalton. And so he and Bill Doolin recruited a big new bandit gang. Its members included Bitter Creek Newcomb, Charlie Pierce, Ole Yountis, Tulsa Jack Blake, Little Dick West, Little Bill Raidler, Red Buck Weightman, Roy Dougherty (alias Arkansas Tom Jones), a pyrotechnical psychopath named Dan Clifton (far better known as Dynamite Dick), Bob Grounds, Alf Sohn, and several hangers-on who could dispose of surplus livestock or furnish hiding places and fresh horses.

Most of the gunmen gathered in Mary Pierce's "hotel," a brothel and saloon at Ingalls, Oklahoma, near Stillwater. It was a crossroads township gaining a reputation as a new Robbers' Roost. Early in 1893 the gang robbed a train at Wharton, where the original Dalton gang had struck two years before. Temporarily driven out of Oklahoma by posses, they robbed trains at Spearville and Cimarron, Kansas, then regrouped at Mrs. Pierce's.

In September, fourteen marshals arrived at Ingalls in a covered wagon. A young boy named Dell Simmons pointed out Newcomb, evidently near the entrance to the saloon. When Newcomb spotted lawmen emerging from the wagon he shouted a warning to his comrades in the saloon and the Battle of Ingalls erupted. Probably the first to die was young Dell Simmons, shot by the outlaws. They also killed Deputy Marshals Dick Speed, Tom Houston, and Lafe Shadley. Bill Dalton himself was identified as the man who killed Shadley. The outlaws ran through a blistering barrage to the Pierce stable, where they were pinned for several hours—all but Arkansas Tom. Perhaps he was in the brothel when the shooting started. Unable to get out of the building, he began firing from Mrs. Pierce's attic. Marshal Jim Masterson, Bat Masterson's brother, then resorted to the kind of tactics Dynamite Dick would have favored. Displaying two sticks of dynamite he threatened to blow the house "into the middle of next week," whereupon Arkansas Tom surrendered. The outlaw served seventeen years in the penitentiary, robbed a bank after his release, and was killed by lawmen in 1924.

Newcomb's recent bride, Rose Dunn—Rose of the Cimarron—ran into the stable with the outlaws, carrying extra guns and helping to keep them loaded. Newcomb was badly wounded but when darkness came he and the others managed to escape. Rose went with them. She nursed her husband until he was fit, and remained ferociously loyal until he was killed by trusted friends. Then she married an obscure blacksmith and vanished.

The gang hid for a while in the Creek Nation, uncomfortably aware that the most famous trio of deputy marshals—Chris Madsen, Heck Thomas, and Bill Tilghman—had been assigned to track them down. Needing funds, the bandits held up the depot at Woodward, Oklahoma, and took $6,500. Dalton and Newcomb robbed a general store at the edge of the Seminole Nation and escaped after wounding a part-time lawman named T. H. Carr. Meanwhile, the three peace officers in charge of the pursuit were organizing an unprecedented manhunt, having prevailed on Oklahoma's Chief Marshal, E. D. Nix, to recruit a force of one hundred and fifty men to exterminate or capture the desperadoes. Again the gang split up.

One of the officers trailing them was Deputy Frank Canton, formerly of Wyoming. He contacted Dal, John, and Bill Dunn, suspected rustlers who had furnished hiding places for the Doolin-Dalton gang. Bill Doolin was one of the very few badmen who ever practiced the Robin Hood ethic ascribed to so many western outlaws. According to Canton, Doolin had friends who protected him because he "furnished many of them money to buy

groceries to live upon when they first settled in that country." But to the Dunns, the possibility of amnesty and a cash reward outweighed any obligation to Bill Doolin. In 1895, after the Rock Island train was robbed at Dover, Oklahoma, they expected some of the gang to rendezvous at their place. They were not disappointed. In due course they brought the bodies of Newcomb and Pierce into Guthrie for identification by Canton, Marshal John Hale, and Sheriff Frank Lake.

After the Spearville robbery Ole Yountis was trailed to his home near Orlando, Oklahoma. When he refused to surrender, Chris Madsen killed him in an exchange of shots. Then Madsen and a posse killed Tulsa Jack Blake. Bill Dalton fled to Texas, probably in the winter of 1894, and the gang began to disintegrate in panic. Dan Clifton—Dynamite Dick—fled to Arizona, where he murdered two Mexican sheep ranchers and then hid in the Chickasaw Nation. He was captured by a posse of deputies from Paris, Texas, and brought back to Oklahoma by Canton. Bill Tilghman, catching up with Little Bill Raidler in the Osage country, wounded and captured him. In 1895 a posse killed Red Buck Weightman and at Eureka Springs, Kansas, Tilghman captured Bill Doolin, who had now robbed at least two Texas banks and killed at least two men.

Clifton and Doolin were held in the jail at Guthrie. Dynamite Dick soon overpowered a jailer and escaped with a dozen other prisoners, including Doolin. All were killed or recaptured. In the Creek Nation, Deputy Bud Ledbetter shot down Dynamite Dick. The Dunns informed Heck Thomas of Doolin's hiding place, and the deputy marshal surrounded the house with nine or ten possemen, including Bill Dunn. Marshal Thomas is usually credited with killing Doolin, and he may have, although Frank Canton said it was Dunn's shotgun that cut

Left: America's first popular semiautomatic deer rifle, recoil-operated Remington Model 8, designed by John Browning and introduced in 1906. Specimen shown was not used to hunt deer. It was taken from Henry Starr when he was captured after Stroud bank robbery. Right: Bank of C. M. Condon & Co. in Coffeyville, Kansas, where bloody 1892 battle erupted between citizens and Dalton gang. Gunfight took lives of four citizens, four bandits.

the outlaw down as he came out of a house into a cornfield. Afterward Dunn apparently became concerned that his activities on both sides of the law would not bear scrutiny by certain officers. He threatened Canton's life, then made the mistake of trying to draw his pistol. Canton killed him.

Bill Dalton was in Texas now with a new but drastically reduced cortege: a cowboy named George Bennett, Jim Wallace, an idler from the farm country near Ardmore, and an anonymity who may have been named Bill Jones. In May, 1894, they robbed the First National Bank in Longview of $2,000. In a battle reminiscent of Coffeyville, Bennett was killed, as were two citizens and a lawman. Marshals traced some of the stolen currency to the town of Duncan in the Chickasaw Nation, where Deputy Marshal T. S. Lindsay captured Wallace and found out that the last Dalton at large was hiding near Ardmore.

In June a nine-man posse surrounded the house where he was staying. He jumped from a window, and as he ran toward a ravine, Marshal Loss Hart cut him down with a .44 bullet. In 1936 Emmett Dalton, an ailing old man with a year to live, collaborated with a ghost writer named Jack Jungmeyer on a book entitled, *When the Daltons Rode*. He claimed, among other falsities, that his brother Bill was shot in the back while playing with his young daughter on the porch of his farm. Another largely false biography, Marshal Ransom Payne's *Eyewitness*, stoked a legend that Payne had been instrumental in breaking up the gang, work that was accomplished chiefly by the "Three Guardsmen" as they were called— Marshals Tilghman, Thomas, and Madsen. Perhaps the last of the Doolin-Dalton outlaws to be tracked down was Little Dick West. Bill Tilghman and Heck Thomas surprised him at a ranch near Guthrie in 1898. He tried to shoot his way free and was killed.

Corpse of Cherokee outlaw Ned Christie, propped upright with hands cradling rifle used in last battle after posse flushed him from log fortress with dynamite and carted his body to Fort Smith. Upper right: Shotgun-blasted body of Bill Doolin after he was killed by Deputy Heck Thomas or (according to Deputy Frank Canton) by Bill Dunn, rustler turned informer. Lower right: Poster offering reward for Doolin after he and Dynamite Dick escaped Guthrie jail.

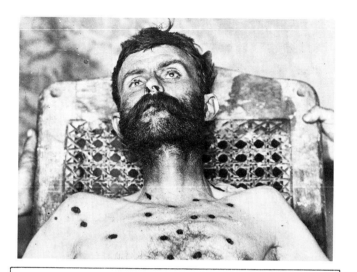

$5,000.00 REWARD

FOR CAPTURE

DEAD OR ALIVE

OF

BILL DOOLIN

NOTORIOUS ROBBER OF TRAINS AND BANKS

ABOUT 6 FOOT 2 INCHES TALL, LT. BROWN HAIR, DANGEROUS, ALWAYS HEAVILY ARMED.

IMMEDIATELY CONTACT THE

U.S. MARSHAL'S OFFICE, GUTHRIE, OKLAHOMA TER.

But other desperadoes had replaced the Daltons before the decade was half over. Bill Cook's gang, for example, included the half-breed Crawford Goldsby, known in the territory as Cherokee Bill. The gang became so troublesome that the railroad line between Fort Smith and Coffeyville repeatedly changed its schedule to foil robbery attempts during the last half of 1894. Cook's marauders also robbed the Muskogee-Fort Gibson stage, the Lincoln County Bank at Chandler, Oklahoma, and the J. A. Parkinson & Company store at Okmulgee, among other depredations. A citizen was killed during the bank robbery. After several more raids, Cook and some of his men fled to Texas. Three were intercepted by Texas Rangers and sent to prison. Cook headed into New Mexico, where two deputies surprised and captured him in a sod house near the place where Pat Garrett had killed Billy the Kid. He was sentenced to forty-five years in prison. Before he left for the penitentiary he saw three cohorts carried into Fort Smith, all killed while resisting arrest.

Crawford Goldsby, born in Texas in 1876, was raised at Fort Gibson. There, when he was eighteen, he killed a black man named Jack Lewis, evidently in a fight over a girl. Then either he or Cook shot down a Cherokee lawman, Sequoyah Houston. During a holdup of the general store at Lenapah, he noticed a man watching him through a restaurant window. The man, Ernest Melton, could do nothing to prevent his escape, yet Goldsby took careful aim with a rifle and murdered him, seemingly for the love of killing. During a robbery of the depot at Nowata he killed yet another man, and another while looting a freight train at Fort Gibson.

Isaac Rogers, a Cherokee who had worked as a lawman, lured Goldsby to his home to visit a girl. Rogers overpowered the outlaw and brought him in. While

Solemn young man in studio portrait is Bob Dalton.
Woman's identification is disputed, but Emmett Dalton claimed she was Eugenia Moore, his brother's "faithful sweetheart." Eugenia Moore was really Florence Quick, Bob Dalton's mistress and scout, who rustled horses and helped rob trains.
Right: Bodies of Bill Powers (labeled Tim Evans), Bob and Grat Dalton, and Dick Broadwell after Coffeyville raid. Visible through break in board fence is face of curious child, peeping at corpses. Inset: Woodcut version of Bill Dalton's death.

TIM, EVANS

BOB DALTON

GROT DALTON

DICK BROADWEL

Goldsby awaited execution, an unknown accomplice smuggled a gun to him. In his attempted break from the Fort Smith jail in 1895, he never got beyond the door of his cell, but he traded many shots with the guards. Each time he fired he uttered a sound like a turkey's gobble —the Cherokee death cry. And yet, unaccountably, having killed guard Lawrence Keating and tried to kill others, he abruptly surrendered. According to some reports he handed his gun to a fellow prisoner, Henry Starr, who passed it to a jailer. Cherokee Bill was hanged in 1896.

Henry Starr was another Indian, one of the last to be brought to court by Judge Parker's marshals. He was the grandson of Old Tom Starr, who operated a bandit hideaway in the Cherokee Nation. And he was the son of George "Hop" Starr and the brother of Sam Starr, and therefore brother-in-law of Belle Starr—every one of whom was an outlaw. Henry was born near Fort Gibson in 1873. He attended an Indian school for a couple of years, then became a cowboy at the Open A Ranch near Nowata, about twenty-five miles from Coffeyville.

Hardly an ordinary criminal, he disdained coffee, tobacco, and liquor, yet in 1891 he paid a $100 fine for introducing whiskey into the Nations. He always claimed the deputies knew he was only bringing a bottle to a friend, but they got their $2 arrest fee. A lawyer recommended by one of them also got Henry Starr's last $22. After that he spoke openly of his hatred for what he called "the white man's government." Arrested for horse theft, he had his case dismissed, but in August he was arrested on the same charge. He was released on a bond furnished by a kinsman and the chief of the Cherokee Nation. When he failed to appear for trial his bondsmen offered a reward for his capture.

Already a fugitive, he decided on a course of defiant rebellion. With a white outlaw named Jesse Jackson and a half-breed Delaware named Ed Newcome, he held up the Missouri Pacific depot at Nowata, taking $1,700. Then he robbed the Schufeldt & Son store at Sequoyah and fled in the direction of Albert Dodge's XU Ranch near Lenapah. When Dodge reported seeing him, Deputy Marshal Floyd Wilson rode out to investigate. He came upon Starr in a clearing on Wolf Creek. The Indian fired at him. Wilson fired back once, but then a shell jammed in his rifle. Starr kept shooting. He stood over the wounded lawman, who could no longer defend himself, and delivered a *coup de grâce*.

Following the murder he quickly organized a gang and by the summer of 1893 had robbed the People's Bank at Bentonville, Arkansas, the Chelsea railroad depot, a train at Pryor Creek, stores at Nowata and Choteau, and the banks of Aldrich, Missouri, and Caney, Kansas. A lawman and several citizens were wounded. Some of the gunmen were killed or captured. But Starr and John Wilson, alias Kid Wilson, got away and did some celebrating at Colorado Springs, where they were arrested by detectives. Wilson was sentenced by Judge Parker to twenty-five years for armed robbery. Starr was sentenced to die for the crime of murder but won a new trial on the ground that the judge's charge to the jury verged on directing a guilty verdict.

His second trial took place in the fall of 1895, shortly after Cherokee Bill's celebrated attempt to escape. Starr confessed in court that he had stood over Deputy Floyd Wilson's prostrate body to deliver a final shot when he could have ridden away unpursued. Again he was sentenced to hang and again he won an appeal. Eventually he drew five years for manslaughter and twelve for robbery, to be served in the penitentiary at Columbus, Ohio. While there, with the help of newspaper reporters, he wrote an account of his life. Starr and the journalists repeated the story that it was he who approached Cherokee Bill and passed the renegade's gun to a jailer, perhaps averting more bloodshed after the guard was killed. Readers who recalled the details of Floyd Wilson's death still regarded Starr as a vicious murderer, but there were others who called him heroic and many who saw him as the embodiment of the noble savage oppressed by white tyranny. The Cherokee Council petitioned President Theodore Roosevelt to pardon him. He was released in 1903.

He settled near Tulsa, married, and worked at farming until Arkansas attempted to extradite him on old robbery charges. He fled and rejoined Kid Wilson, who had just been paroled and who now assisted Starr in robbing several banks. Wilson then disappeared forever. Starr was captured near Phoenix, Arizona, and imprisoned again until 1913 for the robbery of a bank in Amity, Colorado. Between early September, 1914, and mid-January he and an unknown accomplice robbed fourteen Oklahoma banks. In March, 1915, he and six other men held up the State Bank of Stroud, Oklahoma. A seventeen-year-old boy named Paul Curry grabbed up a hog-slaughtering rifle in a butcher shop and wounded Starr and one henchman, Lewis Estes. Though the others got away, all but one were eventually caught. After nearly four years in the Oklahoma State Penitentiary, Starr was paroled again in 1919. He rewrote his memoirs for the Wichita *Eagle* and in Tulsa portrayed himself in a silent film, *A Debtor to the Law*. He was penniless when he borrowed $20 from a woman acquaintance who was active in prison reform and convict rehabilitation.

He probably used the money to buy the double-action .45 revolver with which he attempted his last hold-up. In 1921, he and three companions, now traveling by automobile rather than horseback, crossed from Oklahoma into Arkansas and pulled up at the People's Na-

tional Bank in Harrison. "Thumbs up and stand steady!" Starr shouted.

As he prodded cashier Cleve Coffman to open a safe, a bank stockholder named W. J. Meyers picked up a rifle kept in an alcove and shot the bandit. His accomplices fled, empty handed, and were never apprehended. Starr died of his wound. He knew he was dying when he made a final statement, a claim that he had "robbed more banks than any man in America."

In this instance as perhaps in many, Judge Parker would have felt that justice—in the form of the gallows—had been thwarted by governmental leniency. In the 1890's, more and more criticism had been directed against him by the press and the Supreme Court. His jurisdiction was eradicated in 1896, replaced by new Federal courts within the remaining Indian Territory. He was fifty-eight years old. For several months he had been showing signs of illness and exhaustion. In November the Hanging Judge died. Eleven years later Oklahoma devoured the Indian Territory and became the forty-sixth state.

Rose Dunn—Rose of the Cimarron—bride of Bitter Creek George Newcomb, who rode with Daltons and then with Doolin gang. At Ingalls, Oklahoma, in 1893 she helped her husband and his comrades fight off posse, but after Newcomb was shot down by trusted outlaw friends she adopted peaceful, anonymous existence as law-abiding blacksmith's wife.

9/Some Badwomen

The female role in western outlawry is commonly described in terms of prostitution, pandering, petty thievery, occasional crimes of passion, and the harboring of kinsmen, lovers, or husbands fleeing the law. There is some truth in this view of feminine crime as a mere adjunct of male chauvinism, but it fails to take into account women's unusually high status on the frontier.

Women were scarce in the newer cow towns, mining camps, supply depots, railroads, and Army villages, and they were able to exercise greater power than in the East. Further, the division of labor and responsibility was blurred by frontier living conditions, which often allotted the hardest physical and mental tasks to anyone who was available and capable, regardless of sex or traditional caste systems. A strong, resourceful ranchwoman, store proprietress, or lady poker dealer could forge her own matriarchy. So could a woman who maintained a bandit hideaway, directed rustling operations, or disposed of contraband livestock. Finally, rugged individualism was not a chosen attitude but a frontier necessity where there were no guidelines, no restraints, no social order, no governmental aids to survival and prosperity. Distinctions of gender and class were sometimes regarded as luxuries.

It was in the West, where spinsters and widows had to operate their own isolated homesteads, that women won the right to vote. In 1869 Wyoming became the first territory to grant them the ballot; Utah followed in 1870. The first eleven states to establish female suffrage all were west of the Mississippi.

This does not imply that the western tradition of protective chivalry toward the "weaker," or "gentler," sex was an afterthought of romantic writers. In Miles City, Montana, in 1883 saloon-keeper Charlie Brown (who was normally cordial to hell-raising outlaws) cracked the skull of a hoodlum named Bill Rigney for insulting a respectable citizen's wife and daughter. Thereupon Rigney, apparently dying, was lynched by a hastily formed vigilante committee intent on avoiding the embarrassment of trying Brown for manslaughter. The townspeople regarded Brown's act as justifiable homicide, necessitated by the code of chivalry. If Rigney had insulted one of the "girls on the line," Brown and his friends and the girl herself probably would have laughed, unless the girl were under the protection of a more or less exclusive "sweetheart."

Yet even the attitude toward prostitutes differed significantly from that in the East. When a local ranch hand was dismissed by his employer for failing to pay a popular slut called Cowboy Annie, the other hands took up a collection for her. A man might be in danger of losing more than his job if he tried to cheat one of the tougher prostitutes or female gamblers. Some took pride in their speed and ruthlessness with a "purse pistol" or "garter pistol,"

Preceding pages: Girl at right is Pearl Starr,
daughter of Belle Starr and Cole Younger, posing with two
colleagues who helped her entertain Dalton gang and
other badmen at her Territory bawdy house. Left: Roaming lady
gambler, perhaps modeled on Poker Nell or Madame Moustache,
fleeces passenger in palace-car stateroom. Right:
Helena, Montana, harlot who was known to callers as Billie.

and a few carried full-sized revolvers in conventional holsters slung at the waist. To boom-town merchants striving for the dollars of miners and drovers, a red-light district was a civic attraction and every bawd a valued asset. The sudden death of some anomymous welsher was a matter for consignment to boot hill, not presentation to a sheriff or grand jury.

In the absence of reliable statistics, frontier accounts lead to the conclusion that surprisingly large numbers of prostitutes became wives and mothers, respectable and respected. Once a harlot reformed and wed, erstwhile customers treated her with the same deference accorded all "decent" women. The deference seemed to be sincere, though any other behavior would have incurred the wrath of her husband and neighbors. In an era that spawned mail-order brides and public announcements regarding shipments of unattached females, wifely qualifications included hardiness, self-reliance, and probable fecundity, but not necessarily an unblemished past.

While some prostitutes descended to working the cribs where violence was commonplace, a few became prosperous entrepreneurs. Prosperity occasionally bred social acceptance. A brewer named Bill Bullard, one of Miles City's early sheriffs and considered a leading citizen, lived with his common-law wife, Maggie Burns, who supervised the area's fanciest sporting house. It was of the kind known as a parlor house because, in addition to the girls' rooms, it featured a dancing parlor, complete with piano. In the larger boom towns some of the madams made and spent fortunes in their baroquely splendid establishments. When Omaha was a rip-roaring cattle center in the nineties, the renowned Everleigh sisters, Ada and Minna, opened a plush bordello there and enhanced the decor with a gold-plated piano.

In this lurid sisterhood, the examplar of female rebellion was Belle Starr, who began her adventures as a Missouri tart and probably added to her income in the Indian Territory through at least occasional service as a madam. She was christened Myra Belle (or Myra Maebelle) Shirley in 1848, near Carthage, Missouri, where her father farmed, operated a livery stable and blacksmith shop, and dabbled in politics. She took piano lessons and attended the Carthage Female Academy through the eighth grade. In 1863 Union troops killed her brother Ed, who was leading a band of bushwhackers, and twice razed the town. After the Shirley home was burned in the second attack, the family moved to a farm east of Dallas, Texas, between Scyene and Mesquite. Before leaving Missouri,

Top: Tough, cigarette-smoking female gambler deals cards at Leadville, Colorado, as dance-hall girls and prostitutes look on. Such women often concealed derringers in their voluminous dresses. Bottom: In 1877 photograph of Leadville, two women ride sidesaddle down center of street.
Perhaps they were respectable and peaceable, but men's wives more often drove wagons or sedate buggies when in town.

Myra Belle had attempted a grandiose gesture of revenge, strapping on a pair of revolvers and joining the Confederate guerrillas as an informant. In Texas her father and her older brother Preston put her in school again and tried to dampen her defiant impulses, but the Shirley place became a refuge for guerrillas whose boldness enthralled her.

In 1866 four of the Younger brothers rode in with Frank and Jesse James after robbing the bank at Liberty, Missouri. The eighteen-year-old girl perceived little difference between guerrilla exploits and banditry. When the gang rode back to Missouri a few months later she was pregnant. She never again saw the father, Cole Younger, but in later years she claimed to have been secretly married to him. For his part, Younger sometimes denied he had even known her. She left the child, named Pearl Younger, in the care of her parents while she went off to Dallas, where she fared well financially dealing cards,

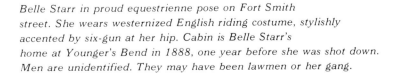

Belle Starr in proud equestrienne pose on Fort Smith street. She wears westernized English riding costume, stylishly accented by six-gun at her hip. Cabin is Belle Starr's home at Younger's Bend in 1888, one year before she was shot down. Men are unidentified. They may have been lawmen or her gang.

singing in dance halls, and probably whoring. She occasionally wore masculine clothing, and she may have been the unidentified desperado who, with John Younger, shot down Dallas Deputy Sheriff Charles H. Nichols in 1871. About a year later she met a young Missouri horse thief named Jim Reed. According to some accounts she married him; according to others there was only a mock ceremony on horseback.

The couple took young Pearl to live with Reed's parents at Rich Hill, Missouri, where Jim Reed joined a consortium of horse thieves led by a Texas outlaw, John Fischer. By then Belle Reed habitually wore a revolver and was an accomplished horsewoman. She aided and advised the thieves and probably rode with them on occasion. Then Jim Reed's brother Scott was killed by a rival gang, two of whose members Jim shot in revenge. Murder warrants were issued and the Reeds fled to California. A second child, Ed Reed, was born in Los Angeles. Almost

immediately afterward they had to flee again, partly because suspicion arose that they had some part in a stage robbery near San Diego, and partly because a local constable learned of a reward for Jim Reed. After that, the children were raised chiefly by Belle's parents. She stayed with them for a time, but Reed hid in the Indian Territory on the ranch of Tom Starr, a Cherokee renegade who was still fighting for the Southern cause in guerrilla fashion, and who had encouraged so much bloodshed and pillage that the tribal council signed a treaty with him. It granted him tribute money, as well as amnesty for past crimes, in return for lawful behavior. His ranch, on a bend of the Canadian River between Briartown and Eufaula, was becoming a celebrated outlaw retreat. Here Belle Reed met two of her future lovers, Blue Duck and Tom Starr's son Sam, as well as dozens of other badmen.

In 1873, three men accompanied by a woman dressed as a man raided the home of a wealthy Creek named Watt Grayson. They tortured the Indian and his wife until Grayson revealed the hiding place of more than $30,000 in gold coins. One of the men was later identified as Jim Reed. There is little doubt that the disguised

Left: With characteristic bravado, Belle Starr wears
one revolver and holds another in 1887 Fort Smith photograph.
Her private guerrilla war and horse rustling earned
Army's wrath, but Major Crail's dead-or-alive reward offer
proved ineffectual. Right: Martha Canary—Calamity
Jane—in life and in one of her dime-novel incarnations.
In photograph she is dressed as scout for Crook's
Sioux-fighting cavalry and holding civilian buggy rifle.

woman was his wife Belle. Jim Reed, named in warrants for two murders and a Texas stagecoach robbery, was finally shot down near Paris, Texas, by Deputy Sheriff John T. Morris.

Belle sent her son Ed to Rich Hill and her daughter Pearl to relatives in Arkansas, then joined the Reed-Starr gang in the Territory. They burglarized stores, sold whiskey to the Indians, robbed tribal treasuries, and rustled cattle and horses. Belle was arrested on suspicion of arson during a drunken celebration in 1875 (and was bailed out by an amorous stockman), but as a rule during her early years in the Indian country she avoided scrapes with the law. She did not participate in the gang's raids. Instead she planned the robberies, found buyers for stolen livestock, disposed of other loot, and became mysteriously successful in arranging fast release for gang members brought to Fort Smith on various charges. In her photographs—made at Fort Smith and during sprees in Tulsa, Claremore, and Catoosa—she appears dashing (especially when brandishing a revolver), but distinctly unattractive, even homely. Yet she seems to have been esteemed for her erotic expertise as well as her gang leadership.

Eventually she married Sam Starr and then had the temerity to rename Sam's place Younger's Bend in memory of her first lover. In 1882 she and Sam were caught stealing horses from a neighbor's corral, and a year later they faced Judge Isaac Parker at Fort Smith. Both received short sentences. Nine months later, after celebrating at Catoosa—reviled in some newspapers as "the hellhole of the Territory"—they were back at Younger's Bend. Belle Starr then took a new lover, John Middleton, a cousin of Jim Reed who was wanted for arson, robbery, and murder. After killing Sheriff J. H. Black of Lamar County, Middleton dallied with Belle while Sam Starr and Felix Griffin held up the Creek Nation's treasury. Griffin was captured. Sam returned to find that Belle had ridden off with Middleton. At Keota she and Middleton separated to allay suspicion, agreeing to meet near Dardanelle. But Starr caught up with Middleton and left his body on the bank of the Poteau River. He then permitted Belle to return to his bed and board, though he must have known he shared her with other outlaws, including Blue Duck before he was sent to prison for murder.

Belle was arrested again, in 1886, for robbing an old man named N. H. Farrell and his three sons. Leading three men on that raid, she had once more worn male attire and could not be positively identified. A few weeks later she was arrested for rustling and acquitted.

That fall Sam was captured in a gunfight but was almost immediately rescued by henchmen. Because the tribal council was dangerously enraged, Belle Starr persuaded Sam to surrender to U. S. marshals on a robbery charge rather than face an Indian tribunal. He was arraigned and released on bail to await trial. At a dance near Younger's Bend a week before Christmas, Starr recognized an Indian policeman, Frank West, who had helped to capture him a few months before. Starr drew his gun and two minutes later both men lay dead.

After the demise of her irascible husband, Belle Starr sent for her children, Pearl Younger and Ed Reed. Within two years Ed was at the Columbus, Ohio, penitentiary for bootlegging, and Pearl, having sent an illegitimate daughter off to the Arkansas relatives, was working as both madam and inmate of a Territory bawdy house. Far better looking than her mother, she did a thriving business. Her clientele included the Daltons.

Having seen to her children's prospects, Belle Starr married an educated young Creek horse thief named Jim July. In 1889 she rode with him part of the way to Fort Smith, where he was to answer a larceny charge. On the way back to Younger's Bend she stopped at a friend's cabin, and there she argued with E. A. Watson, a man who had been trying to rent land from her. Watson taunted her about the frequency with which Federal marshals investigated her activities. She replied with a remark about a rumor that he was wanted in Florida for murder. That afternoon two men heard shots close to the bank of the Canadian, saw Belle's horse trot past with an empty saddle, and found the woman who had come to be known as Queen of the Bandits, face down in the mud, killed by a charge of buckshot in the back and a second charge of smaller shot in the face and neck.

July himself arrested Watson, who was not wanted in Florida and was cleared of suspicion in Belle Starr's killing. Then it was learned that July had offered a man named Milo Hoyt $200 to kill his wife, because she had caught him philandering and threatened to withhold help in the pending larceny case. July jumped bail. In January, 1890, Deputy Marshal Heck Thomas brought him, weak and bleeding, to Fort Smith. The outlaw had been shot by Deputy J. R. Hutchins and knew he was dying. He said he wished to make a confession to Hutchins, presumably

Prostitute in Creede, Colorado, in 1890's. By then gambling- and vice-lord Soapy Smith had left Creede and ore deposits were dwindling, but boom-town atmosphere lingered, as did wanted gunmen and their consorts-for-hire.

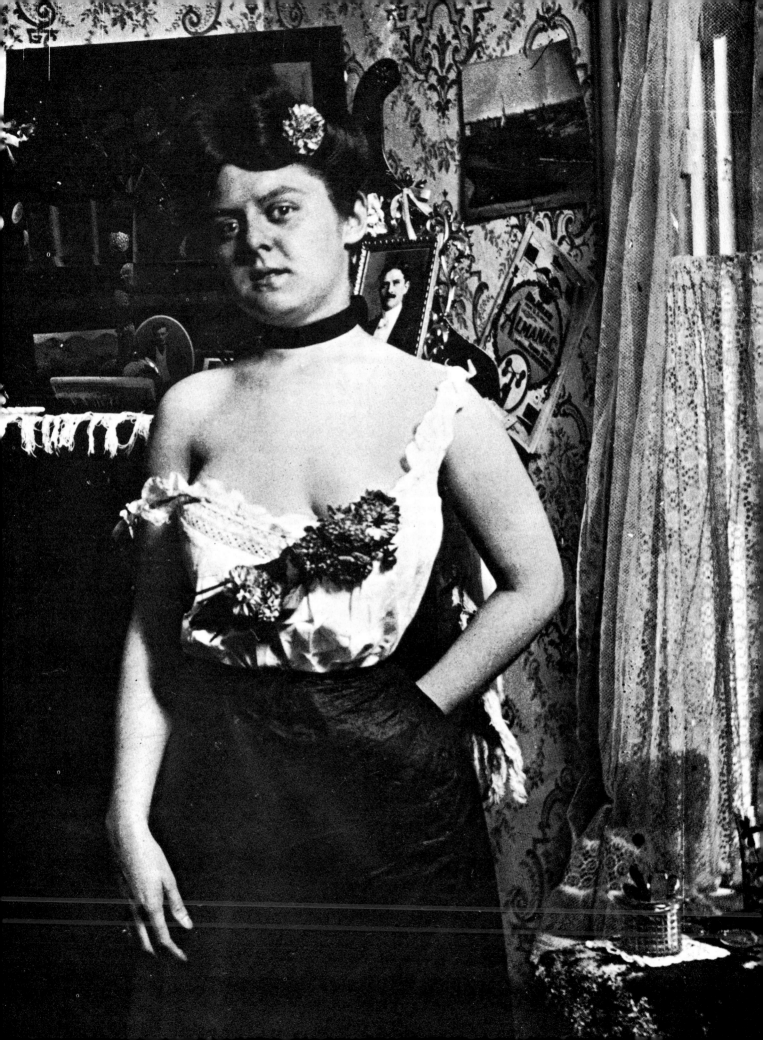

Inmates of parlor house in Creede pose with
recently invented Gramophone, which was probably emporium's
greatest attraction. Right: In one of San Francisco's
infamous Barbary Coast tavern-brothels, customer sleeps off
effects of knockout drops while "waiter girl"
searches his clothing and passes his money to proprietor.

about Belle Starr's murder. But July was dead when Hutchins arrived.

Pearl Younger, thriving on the attentions of local badmen and cowboys, had more than enough money to bury her mother at Younger's Bend beneath an elaborately chiseled gravestone inscribed with her name, birth and death dates, a bell, a star, the B-S brand, Belle Starr's favorite horse Venus, and a verse in remembrance of the Queen of Bandits: "Shed not for her the bitter tear/Nor give the heart to vain regret;/'Tis but the casket that lies here,/The gem that filled it sparkles yet."

Sometimes in accordance with the western custom of slapstick hyperbole, sometimes because an alias was desirable—and sometimes because it paid to advertise one's wares—flamboyant sobriquets flourished among strumpets, female gamblers, and other adventuresses, from Missouri to California's Barbary Coast and the

shacks of the Yukon. Drovers bringing their herds to eastern Montana felt lustily confident of the welcome they could expect from two regionally celebrated "entertainers" who publicized themselves as Cowboy Annie and Connie the Cowboy Queen.

Poker Nell was the title used by Nellie Bruce, who presided over the card tables in the Miles City saloon of her common-law husband, Harry Bruce.

A drifting lady gambler, hailed for her masculine toughness as well as her honesty, and perhaps endowed with a shadow of down on her lip, was addressed only as Madame Moustache in the Colorado mining towns and then in Nevada City and Bodie. Few men dared bully Madame Moustache, especially after the night in Bodie when two footpads tried to take the house winnings from her. She drew her derringer and instantly killed one of them. His partner fled.

In Butte, Montana, Molly Demruska abdicated as queen of local Cyprians when she wed the town marshal, Jack Jolly, in the Clipper Shades Saloon. After the ceremony she and her groom paraded about on the town's fire engine. Though marriage withdrew her from the ranks of ribaldry, admirers must have delighted in referring to her as Jolly Molly, at least until her husband was killed several years later. He was shot down by Soapy Smith, an infamous confidence artist, gunman, gambler, and autocrat of vice, who was en route from the dwindling silver veins at Creede, Colorado, to the shanty boom towns of the opening Klondike gold fields. Caring nothing for Jolly Molly, Smith left Butte in haste for the domain of Yukon *femmes fatales* like Diamond Tooth Lil and Sad Story Mary, over whose fortunes he would reign until he lost a gunfight with a Skagway vigilante.

Among the crib girls of the Klondike there were also such male-chauvinist designations as Nellie the Pig, Flora the Ton, Muckland Maud, Spanish Jeanette, Glass Eye Annie, and The Oregon Mare. Among the "pretty waiter girls" who were renowned for their rapacity in the neighborhood of San Francisco's Jackson and Kearny streets —"Murderer's Corner"—picturesque names included Lady Jane Gray, The Roaring Gimlet, and The Waddling Duck. In the Sweetwater Valley of Wyoming and as far off as Rawlins, Cheyenne, Casper, even up in Johnson County, "Fat Ella" Watson became Cattle Kate after she began taking rustled stock in trade. When Annie McDougal, an adolescent girl from the Osage Nation, graduated from whiskey peddling to rustling, she was dubbed Cattle Annie; her partner, Jennie Stevens, dressed herself as a cowboy and earned the name Little Britches.

Best known of all was Calamity Jane, who never really qualified as a badwoman. The accounts of how she got that name are many and conflicting. At one time Calamity herself claimed she had joined the Army to fight Indians in the early 1870's and her comrades wished to commemorate her prevention of a calamity when she saved a young cavalryman from hostile warriors. In other versions she fended off Indian attack, road agents, runaway horses, and assorted calamities while working as a shotgun messenger on a stagecoach. In still others she rode about the vicinity of Deadwood like a latter-day Paul Revere or the boy who cried "Wolf!"—habitually warning the citizenry of real or imagined raids by Indians and bandits. The truth seems to be that the name was a barroom joke, an allusion to her effect on glassware and fragile decorations when she was on a roaring binge. For although she was the incarnation of the proverbial whore with the heart of gold, she was a very reckless drunk.

She was born on a Missouri farm, probably in about 1848, and her real name evidently was Martha E. Canary, or perhaps Martha Jane Canary or Martha Jane Canarray. In 1863 she began drifting. She was known in Alder Gulch, Virginia City, Abilene, Hays, Livingston in the Montana Territory, and the Cheyenne region of Wyoming. She often wore men's clothing and at one time worked as a laborer on the Union Pacific.

Her tales of Army life were based on a flyspeck of truth. In 1875, disguised as a man, she became a mule skinner with General George Crook's expedition to pacify the Sioux. Captain John G. Bourke, who rode with Crook against Sitting Bull the following year, entered her in his journal: "It was whispered that one of our teamsters was a woman, and no other than 'Calamity Jane,' a character famed in border story." A little later, while driving for a Government wagon train, she was caught swimming nude with the other drivers. Officers summarily halted the gleeful dip and "drummed her out of camp."

But she probably experienced not one of the hair-raising adventures she boasted about. The guns with which she liked to be photographed were part of her swaggering pose. The only shooting she did was at bottles, chandeliers, streetlights, top hats on saloon pegs. As a badwoman she was a fraud.

In 1876, when Dead Tree Gulch had suddenly become the Dakota boom town of Deadwood, she worked there in a bawdy house. She was mannish-looking but popular because of her hilarious sprees and her fabled generosity. Once she gave a destitute woman her shoes. And after she persuaded Wild Bill Hickok to let her tag about as part of his colorful entourage, her fame was assured. A little later, like many prostitutes, she began visiting cow towns when cattle drives were due to arrive, periodically showing up in Miles City. The town had been founded in 1876, when camp-following bullwhackers, whiskey hawkers, food-and-clothing peddlers, and the like were evicted by Colonel Nelson A. Miles from the nearby Tongue River cantonment. It became a freighting and cattle center, known for its wildness, yet almost unique in the rarity of its shooting incidents. The worst scrape Calamity Jane had there was when she was arrested for drunken brawling in 1895 and jumped bail to avoid paying a $100 fine. She lived with several frontiersmen and married several, the last of them a Texan named Clinton Burke. She had a dilapidated cabin near Deadwood and was calling herself Mary E. Burke when she died of pneumonia and alcoholism in 1903.

Though Cattle Annie McDougal and Jennie "Little Britches" Stevens (alias Jennie Metcalf) were called "Oklahoma's Girl Bandits," they were thrill-seeking amateurs of the kind who believed the dime-novel tall tales about Calamity Jane. Their brief career began when sixteen-year-old Jennie and seventeen-year-old Annie,

respectable farm girls, nearly swooned at the sight of Bill Doolin and a couple of his men at a dance. The girls rode off to the gang's headquarters at Ingalls to join the dashing desperadoes. "Soon," according to the *Guthrie Daily Leader,* "they were eating with [the gang] and in the corral they shook out oats and fodder for their horses." It appears that the bandits took the girls seriously only to the extent of letting them do some barnyard and kitchen chores, but Annie and Jennie did some whiskey peddling and rustling on their own initiative.

In 1894, after most of the gang had been killed or captured, Deputies Steve Burke and Bill Tilghman located the girls in a farmhouse near Pawnee. Little Britches leaped from a window and rode away, with Tilghman in pursuit. Burke grabbed a rifle Cattle Annie was trying to level at him and subdued her when she had exhausted herself clawing, kicking, and biting. Little Britches fired over her shoulder at Tilghman. He could not bring himself to aim at her, so he shot her horse and captured her after a struggle. Then he spanked her. The young women served two years at the Federal reformatory in Farmington, Massachusetts. Annie married and settled respectably near Pawnee. Jennie labored briefly as a domestic in Boston, then did "settlement work" in New York, where she died of consumption two years later.

Less famous but more wicked was Florence Quick, alias Eugenia Moore, alias Mrs. Bryant, alias Mrs. Mundy, alias Tom King, described by the usually mild-tongued Deputy Chris Madsen as a "hard-bitten bitch." She may have been a schoolteacher at one time, but when she was in her early twenties she was known in the Indian Territory as a rustler and then as Bob Dalton's mistress. Since she dressed and rode like a man and enjoyed being called Tom King, perhaps she had a lesbian tendency. However, she was sufficiently feminine to become the "belle of the Daltons." Arrested more often than Belle Starr, she disappeared from jails at Guthrie, Oklahoma City, and El Reno. "She was the greatest jailbreaker I have ever known," Madsen said of her. "She would be on the streets at Guthrie, dressed in a fancy buckskin suit, and after dark you would find her out in the country dressed up in a pair of overalls spotting horses for the rustlers."

She located and maintained hideouts for the Daltons in the Indian country, served as a courier when they were separated, posed as a telegrapher to get information about the schedules of trains they planned to rob, and before the Wharton train holdup in 1891 obtained the information that the baggage car would contain a money-laden express vault. By bedding with a railroader or express agent, a clever woman could sometimes learn much that was of value in planning train robberies. Before the Lillietta holdup in the autumn of 1891, Flo Quick taught the Dalton brothers the flash code used by locomotive engineers to signal station agents. That winter she and Bob Dalton hid on a ranch in Greer County, Texas, where she stole and resold enough horses to keep groceries on the table without significantly depleting the railroad loot. In preparation for the Coffeeville raid in 1892 she rustled five fast ponies. After Bob Dalton was killed in that ill-conceived raid, she organized her own small band of train robbers, but within a year she vanished and a report reached the marshals that she had died in a gunfight.

Her independent forays notwithstanding, Flo Quick was essentially a gang moll, a precursor of the defeated "flappers" and Depression victims who cooked, copulated, and opened automobile doors for twentieth-century bank robbers. Even more closely akin to the latter-day hangers-on were Fannie Porter, Annie Rogers, Laura Bullion, and Etta Place, pictured in the glamorized myths of female outlawry as hard-riding consorts of Butch Cassidy, the Sundance Kid, and Kid Curry, mainstays of the Wild Bunch. Actually, Fannie Porter was only their procuress. The other three were handsome but low-priced whores who became their mistresses. Laura Bullion was wanted for forgery, and she and Etta Place sometimes rode with the gang, but they lacked the initiative, the cunning, the ruthlessness of the frontier's Flo Quicks and Ella Watsons.

Fat Ella Watson—Cattle Kate—must have been amused by her reputation as a cattle rustler. She was a rifle-brandishing merchant of stolen cattle who probably never learned to handle a rope or a running iron, despite the fanciful journalism of a reporter for the *Cheyenne Mail Leader* who described her as "a dark devil in the saddle, handy with a six-shooter and a Winchester, and an expert with a branding iron." She was a strapping Kansas farm girl, born in 1862, a toiler in the bawdy houses of Denver, Cheyenne, and Rawlins. Her father described her as "a little girl, between one hundred and sixty and one hundred and eighty pounds." In 1888 she was hired by Jim Averill, who operated a post office and saloon on the Sweetwater range. He was eagerly acquiring cattle and promoting himself as spokesman for the small ranchers—honest homesteaders and rustlers alike—in a feud with the cattle barons that would eventually grow into the Johnson County War. To provide female companionship for cowboys who stopped at his saloon, he sent to Rawlins for Ella Watson and established her in her own little log-cabin bagnio adjoining his corral.

Major stockmen in the vicinity were angry at Averill about letters he wrote to the editor of the *Casper Daily Mail*, championing the independent ranchers against the stockgrowers' association. They grew angrier when unbranded cattle and even cattle bearing their brands appeared in Averill's corral, angrier still when Ella

Top: Cattle Kate, drastically slenderized by artist, is lynched with her employer, Jim Averill, by Wyoming stockmen. She had bartered her portly charms for rustled beef and had threatened a protesting rancher with a rifle. Right: Cattle Annie holds rifle and Little Britches wears revolver in forlorn attempt to match their description as "Oklahoma's girl bandits."

Watson—now known as Cattle Kate—enlarged the herd by bartering her favors for beef of dubious ownership. Severe blizzards in the winter of 1888 depleted the herds on the range, while Kate's cattle continued to increase.

In June of 1889 a stockman demanded to know how animals bearing his brand came to be in Kate's corral. Leveling a rifle at him, she replied that she had bought them. A few weeks later another stockman trailed some missing steers to her corral. On a scorching July day, a self-appointed posse of seven rode to her cabin and forced her and Averill into a wagon. Averill's foreman, Frank Buchanan, caught up with the vigilantes on the bank of the Sweetwater and tried to scatter them with rifle fire but a fusillade drove him away. Jim Averill and Cattle Kate Watson were then hanged from a large cottonwood.

Earlier that year a shotgun had blasted Belle Starr from her saddle, yet she retained a perverse posthumous influence as heroine to frontier drabs who yearned for rebellion. Pearl Hart decided to attempt the kind of exploits Belle Starr had gloried in and Calamity Jane still dreamed about. In legend Mrs. Hart became Miss Hart, a daring young lady from an Eastern boarding school, gone west to find adventure. In reality she was a mining-camp cook. She was born in Ontario in 1871 and her maiden name was Pearl Taylor. At seventeen she married a man named Hart and emigrated with him to the Southwest before their marriage foundered. She was working in an Arizona mining camp in 1898 when Joe Boot, a miner generally too drunk to dig, persuaded her to help him rob the Globe stage.

After donning britches and galluses, buckling on a cartridge belt with a revolver in a typical cowboy's cross-draw holster, and laying a lever-action rifle across her saddle, she waited in the road with Joe Boot. The stage driver, seeing the way blocked as he rounded the bend,

hauled back on the reins and slammed the brake with his foot. As the team skidded and reared, the three passengers were thrown to the coach floor. When they disentangled themselves they were staring into the muzzles of two six-guns.

The road agents, richer by $431, galloped away, immediately got lost, and were captured without a fight three nights later, drenched and trembling with cold, huddled in a barn to wait out a storm. Boot drew a thirty-five-year term, Pearl Hart drew five years. She was pardoned after about half that time, to the relief of officials at the

Yuma Territorial Prison who were having difficulty maintaining proper accommodations for a young lady. After three years of freedom she was arrested again at Deming, New Mexico, on suspicion of complicity in a train robbery, but was released for lack of evidence.

She lapsed into obscurity, her whereabouts unknown for long periods. She was last seen in 1924, when she visited the Pima County jail to reminisce. Though she was a dismal failure as an outlaw, she achieved a hazy immortality, for the holdup at Globe was this country's last stagecoach robbery.

Left: Pearl Hart poses demurely after her arrest
for committing America's last stagecoach holdup at Globe,
Arizona. Center: Same girl, in working attire
and carrying road agent's tools that she never had time
to master. Right: Charles M. Russell's wry
portrayal of more typical badwoman's modus operandi.

10/ Border Clashes

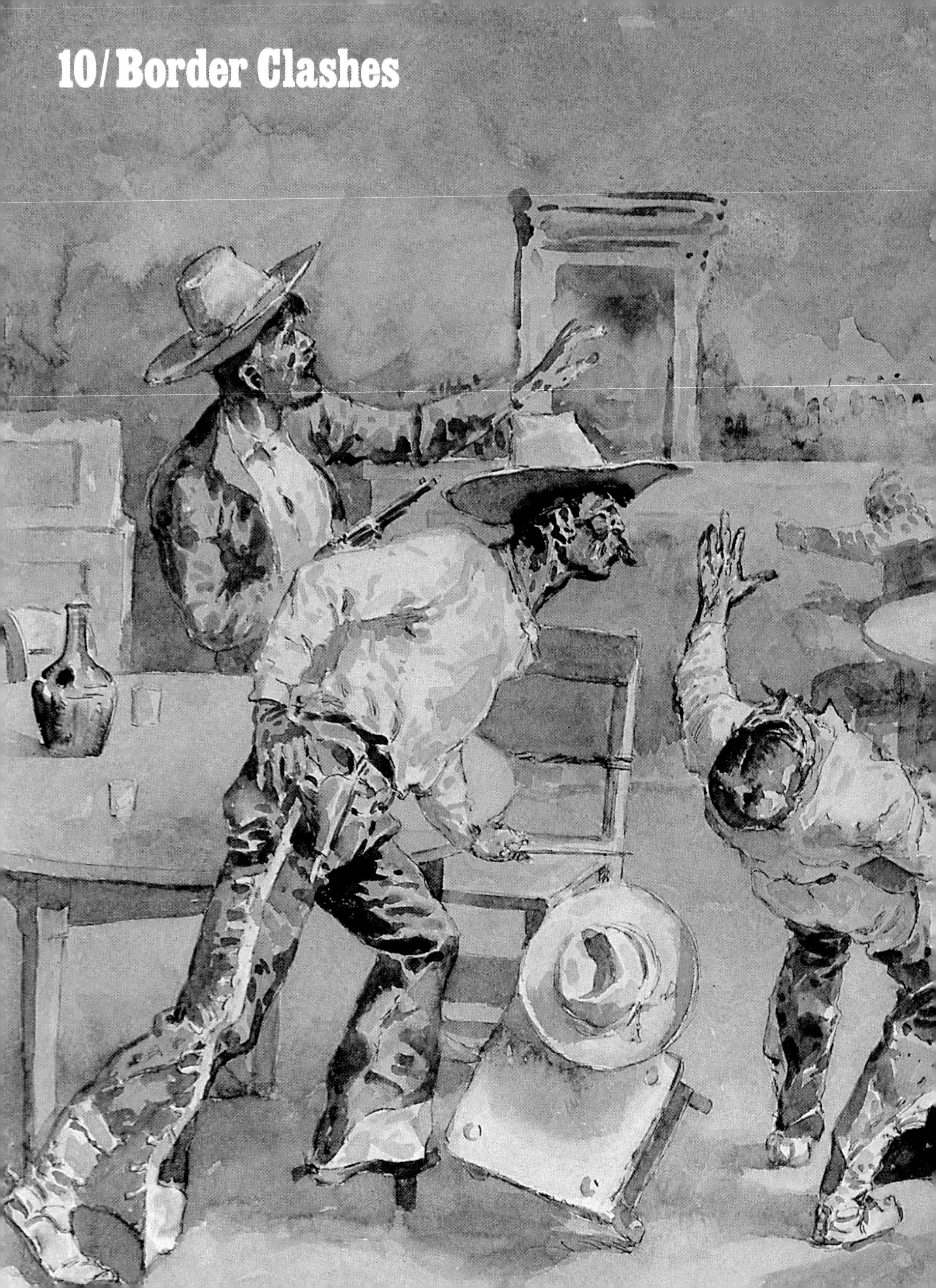

Hostile encounters between disparate ethnic groups and nationalities gave rise to episodes of violent banditry from the time of the war with Mexico until the second decade of the twentieth century. In a sense, the Mexican outlaws who raided California's early gold camps and cattle ranches were guerrillas waging border warfare. Many were United States citizens and yet, as pointed out in Chapter 4, they were victimized by discriminatory laws. The men who came to be known collectively as Joaquin Murieta were undesirable aliens in the land of their birth—a land that, in their view, was not American but Mexican, regardless of the coercive 1848 Treaty of Guadalupe-Hidalgo and 1853 Gadsden Treaty. The Murieta bandits were too far north of the newly established border to make brief raids into the hated American communities and then escape into Mexico. Others, however, were able to use precisely that tactic.

It may be recalled that Tombstone's Old Man Clanton, whose sons were attacked by the Earp gang at the O.K. Corral, was killed in Guadalupe Canyon by Mexicans engaged in rustling American cattle and running organized smuggling caravans between Sonora and Arizona. It may also be recalled that some of the Indian brigands in the Nations considered themselves beleaguered guerrillas, attacking invaders of their sovereign territory or making raids across the border into enemy country. Renegades like Cherokee Bill and Henry Starr, who spoke with loathing of "the white man's government," saw Kansas, Missouri, Arkansas, and Texas as conquered lands held by tyrannical foreign aggressors.

But the most natural domain of border clashes involving outlaws was in the territories adjacent to Mexico, a nation that had unwillingly ceded a vast portion of itself to the United States. For many decades Mexican authorities saw no reason to parry bandit thrusts into the domineering northern giant whose Manifest Destiny they still feared. Brigands were permitted to camp unmolested in the hills of Sonora, Chihuahua, and Coahuila, crossing the border at will as long as they refrained from terrorizing Mexicans.

Almost forgotten now by all but a few studious *chicanos*, Juan Cortinas was the first socially motivated border bandit. He was the son of a prosperous Texas family uprooted from its land by the "Anglos" after Texas was annexed. While wanton killers like William Clarke Quantrill, Bloody Bill Anderson, the Jameses, and the Youngers inflicted their own kind of border warfare on Kansas and Missouri, Juan Cortinas was rallying a small army of Mexican and Mexican-American followers in Texas. He combined the motives and tactics of racial rebellion and nationalist guerrilla insurgency with what some historians have called "social banditry"—meaning that he was one of the very few outlaws who actually upheld the Robin Hood ethic. Like Bill Doolin in the Indian Territory, but on a grander scale, Cortinas dispensed largesse to hungry farmers. He robbed from the Anglos and gave to the Mexicans. If many of his Anglo victims were far from rich, most of the Mexican recipients were poor, indeed. His bitterness toward Americans inspired a rhetoric that convinced his partisans and justified his actions to himself: "To me," he wrote, "is entrusted the breaking of the chains of your slavery."

In 1859, the year when a self-appointed breaker of chains named John Brown led an assault on Harpers Ferry, Cortinas led one hundred men against the little Texas town of Brownsville on the Rio Grande, the only strong American settlement below Corpus Christi. Cortinas and his raiders shot down three American residents, broke open the jail and released the prisoners, pillaged the town, then rode to a camp that was supposed to be secret but was well-enough known to Mexican-Americans to

Preceding pages: Gunman's expression seems self-righteous as well as self-satisfied in Frederic Remington's wash drawing entitled, "Them Three Mexicans is Eliminated." Though he may have satirized Southwestern attitudes, Remington himself felt contempt for Mexicans and Indians. Border atmosphere of hatred made international banditry inevitable. Romanticized ethnic rivalry was still evident in 20th-century picture cards (left) packed with Hassan cork-tipped cigarettes. Cowboy is ambiguously captioned "A parting shot," but Mexican is saying, "Hands up!"

attract flocks of new volunteers. A U.S. Army expedition defeated the *bandidos* in a pitched battle, killing sixty, but the leader and a large number of his men escaped. Thereafter they camped in Mexico and made forays across the Rio Grande. To his countrymen he was a political and military leader, not a bandit, and at one time he served as governor of Tamaulipas.

Then and later, such police and paramilitary groups as the Texas Rangers frequently violated international agreements by crossing into Mexico in search of rustlers, gunfighters, smugglers, and bandits. In 1860 a Texas Ranger force overtook the Cortinas desperadoes on Mexican soil and again defeated them, this time killing thirty. Once more the leader and many men escaped to continue their plunder of American border towns and ranches. The United States then sent troops under Colonel Robert E. Lee into Texas with orders to disregard the boundary, to invest the Mexican desert and badlands if necessary, but to kill or capture Cortinas at all costs. Threatened with a second American invasion, Mexico at last ended its unofficial protection of Cortinas. Captured by the Mexican army, he was imprisoned by the nation of his allegiance, and his career of border banditry was ended. Two hundred and forty-five men had died in gunfights between his Mexican raiders and Americans. But Cortinas was a villain only to white Texans and the United States Government. He was a hero to his own people, a rebel who defied oppression. He was a precursor not only of Pancho Villa, but of today's militant *chicano* radicals throughout the American Southwest.

The next celebrity of border violence was the Apache Kid, an Indian outlaw and therefore anathema to authority on both sides of the international boundary. His real name may have been Has-kay-bay-nay-ntayl, and he was born between 1867 and 1870. He could not have been

more than twenty years old when he became a sergeant of Apache Scouts, working out of the San Carlos Agency under Al Sieber, the celebrated Indian fighter of Arizona and New Mexico. In the mid-1880's, Sieber and his men were scouting for Generals George Crook and Nelson A. Miles against Geronimo's Chiricahuas. Among the white scouts riding with Sieber was Tom Horn, who had not yet abandoned soldiering and detective work for the more lucrative trade of the hired assassin. Most of the trailing and fighting took place in Arizona, but sometimes the scouts followed hostile Apaches into the Mexican mountains. The Apache Kid quickly earned the respect of his white colleagues for his resourcefulness and courage, not only in the campaign against his hostile tribesmen but against smugglers and bootleggers. Gunrunners were hawking their wares to Indians and bandits on both sides of the border. Stolen cattle were also being smuggled in both directions, as were silver and gold, liquor, and assorted merchandise subject to import tariffs.

He might well have become a famous lawman, had he understood the subtleties of white law. While he was working for Sieber, an Indian murdered his father. Sieber tried to persuade him of the need for arrest, indictment, and trial. To the Apache Kid the only need was to obey the mandates of filial custom and tribal law. With a small band of relatives and friends, he tracked down and executed the killer. The avengers then surrendered to Sieber. But during a parley with the military authorities an Apache took fright and started shooting. According to some accounts, the Apache Kid wounded Sieber in the ensuing melee, and it was for this reason that Tom Horn, rather than Al Sieber, was sent to open peace talks with Geronimo.

The Kid and some of his followers fled. Two years later, in 1889, he was so weary of incessant running that he brought his men in to face a court-martial. Convicted of

Top: May, 1870, illustration from American Agriculturist *shows innocent branding operations by Mexicans, but Anglos who came upon such scenes at Rio Grande suspected traditional border rustling. Bottom: Mexican soldiers are depicted fighting off stagecoach robbers in mid-1860's, but Mexican government for years furnished unofficial asylum to bandits who kept raiding activities north of international boundary.*

murder, the young renegade was pardoned by President Grover Cleveland. It was a pose of governmental beneficence combined with a tacit admission that justice to the Indians was not always served by strict enforcement of the conqueror's rule. But in a region terrified of Geronimo the civil authorities felt differently. They immediately indicted the Apache Kid and his closest followers for the killing of a whiskey peddler—another tribal execution—on the San Carlos Reservation before they had surrendered. The Kid and eight comrades, all former Government scouts, were sentenced to seven years at the territorial prison in Yuma. Though evidently bewildered and enraged, they showed little emotion beyond what journalists sometimes characterized as "the Indian's sullen demeanor."

In November, Sheriff Glen Reynolds, Deputy Bill Holmes, and a wagoner named Eugene Middleton left Globe, Arizona, with the prisoners, intending to deliver them to Yuma. Two days later Middleton, barely able to stand, managed to get back to Globe. With a bullet in his neck, he had been left for dead in the Pinal Mountains, where the bodies of Reynolds and Holmes still sprawled. The renegades had broken loose and shot them.

"From that day on," wrote historian James D. Horan, "Arizona witnessed the worst one-man reign of terror, rape, and robbery it had ever known." The Kid was never a political leader or soldier, like Geronimo, fighting for his people. He was simply an outlaw, a bitter man unbalanced by the impact of an alien civilization, seeking vengeance and living on plunder. But while campaigning against Geronimo he had learned from that fine tactician how to hide a trail. His original comrades were soon caught. The Kid himself was too crafty to be trapped or overtaken. He slipped across the border repeatedly, hiding in Mexico's Sierra Madre between forays, sometimes acting alone,

sometimes recruiting raiders. He took an Apache wife, and it was said that she participated in some of the assaults on prospectors and settlers. But the Kid was also accused every time a white man or woman was robbed and murdered by a lone rider. The territorial legislature offered a $5,000 reward for him, dead or alive, and he became the most wanted outlaw on the border. No one knew the

Drawing shows "Texan" Rangers when they abandoned pursuit of Indians and rebellious Mexican guerrillas like Juan Cortinas to fight for Confederacy in Civil War. Inset is photograph of Cortinas in official uniform as governor of Tamaulipas. White Texans and U.S. Army regarded him as most dangerous bandit leader, but to Mexicans and early chicanos he was courageous revolutionary hero.

number of his victims, but everyone believed there must have been scores.

Then, in 1894, the terror inexplicably ceased. A prospector named Edward A. Clark, who had once commanded a detachment of Indian scouts, was camped one night north of Tucson when two Apaches—a man and a woman—tried to steal his horse. He killed the woman and

wounded the man. There was a blood trail, but it petered out and the thief was never found. Clark was sure that it was the Apache Kid, that he had at least one bullet in his back and could not survive, that he must have found some lonely spot in the desert where he could await death. All of which may have been true. Certainly the prospector wanted to believe it, for the Apache Kid had murdered one of Clark's partners several years before. But many settlers believed that Clark had shot some other Indian, or that the Kid had survived the wound and retreated permanently into Mexico where, according to persistent border legend, he raised a family and lived to see a substantial part of the twentieth century.

The last and most famous of the border bandits was Doroteo Arango, known to the world as Pancho Villa. He is now honored as a Mexican patriot, but even his staunchest admirers concede that he was also the chief bandit of Chihuahua.

He was born several hundred miles south of the Rio Grande, in a ranching settlement named for that river. The date was probably October 4, 1877. He was the son of poverty-stricken *peons,* of mixed Indian and Spanish ancestry. The Arangos were, in effect, serfs of a wealthy rancher, Don Arturo Lopez Negrete. Before the boy was in his teens, he was earning a few pesos as a *charro,* or ranch hand, but he and his two sisters led an existence of semislavery. He was flogged twice for running away and was briefly imprisoned after a third attempt. Upon his release, he later claimed, he learned that Arturo Negrete's son Leonardo had raped one of his sisters. Arango killed the rapist and fled to the hills. Along the way he encountered one of the feared *rurales,* mounted state policemen, who helped to subjugate the peasantry for the landowners and the dictatorial government of President Porfirio Diaz. He killed the policeman and took his clothes and rifle.

Knowing that apprehension would mean death, he joined a locally famous bandit troop led by Ignacio Parra. During the 1890's Arango's shrewdness, ruthlessness, and almost foolhardy courage made him Parra's favorite lieutenant. In about 1895 the gang held up a heavily guarded Mexican stagecoach bearing a mine payroll. Parra was mortally wounded and Arango took his place as chieftain, operating in the state of Durango, below Chihuahua, and occasionally venturing northward. Diaz repeatedly ordered the *rurales* and the government military police known as *federales* to rid the country of bandits. Arango was now so well known that he could not use his real name when staying for long in any settlement, and he took the alias Francisco Villa. Soon he was given the less formal name of Pancho by his henchmen. He must have been pleased, for he spoke of a family legend about an ancestor named Pancho Villa who had been a successful bandit.

The Villistas, as he and his horsemen came to be known, fared well rustling cattle and robbing silver trains

Injured man is Al Sieber, Arizona pioneer, chief of scouts in campaign against Geronimo, and later Federal deputy marshal. Most of Indians at right had probably scouted for him, but they became renegades after an illegal tribal execution and eventually earned title of The Apache Kid's Red Devils. Apache Kid himself, standing second from right, was Arizona's most wanted outlaw.

coming from the mines. Occasionally they crossed the Rio Grande and sold stolen herds to Texas and Arizona ranchers. In addition, Villa probably did some rustling north of the Rio Grande, but, contrary to border legend, he sacked no American communities until the United States aligned itself against his insurgent faction during the Mexican revolution.

By the turn of the century he was being called "the Puma" and the "Jaguar of the North," a tribute to his cunning in outwitting *federales* in the mountains of Chihuahua. Generous to those who rode with him, he gathered hundreds of followers. Don Luis Terrazas, the richest and probably most hated landowner in Chihuahua, raised a private army to assist the Federal forces, but the Villistas eluded pursuit or beat their enemies in battle. Then, in 1905, when prolonged drought increased the usual famine in Chihuahua, the Villistas began to distribute cattle, grain, and provisions to the *peons* who hid them, spied for them, and misdirected pursuers. Towns celebrated the arrival of the bandit chieftain with fiestas

and shouts of "Viva Villa!" Unwittingly, he was foresaking brigandage for social revolution.

In 1910 civil disturbances escalated into rebellion. Porfirio Diaz, "strong man of Mexico," had held office ever since a coup d'état in 1876. He had kept a promise to reduce banditry and increase the prosperity of the middle and upper classes. But he had exercised tyrannical power for more than thirty years, too, selling huge tracts of land to the wealthy, endorsing a virtually feudal agricultural system, refusing to educate the peasants, keeping the poor in a state of near-starvation and enslavement. In Chihuahua, where Terrazas acquired seventy million acres, almost half of the land belonged to fewer than 3,000 families, and there were 10 million landless, impoverished agricultural workers. When Diaz invited heavy investment by foreigners, especially Americans, and one American lady purchased more than a million acres of Tehuantepec, the traditional hatred of *gringos* was inflamed. Landless Mexicans were convinced that the Americans were conniving with their oppressors and

would eventually annex Mexico.

Diaz, fearing revolt, had broken a promise to permit the election of a successor, and an idealistic but ineffectual statesman named Francisco Madero called for a national insurrection to begin in November. Though poor at organizing his forces, he might have established a new government if the country had not splintered during the previous years of horror into warring factions led by almost anyone who could command a few guns and horsemen. For a while, Madero's cause was championed by Pancho Villa and a revolutionary named Pasqual Orozco, who joined forces to defeat state troops in Chihuahua. Their success kindled other uprisings, and Madero briefly held the presidency. Orozco, dissatisfied with his award of 50,000 pesos and a generalship, then formed a new group of insurgents called the Red Flaggers. Beaten by General Victoriano Huerta, he lost all power.

As for Villa, he was a bewildered, impulsive, unschooled Indian who genuinely looked forward to immediate Utopia for his countrymen. He was disillusioned by the slowness of reform, not fully satisfied with his own gift from the government of a meat market and bullring in Chihuahua, and incorrigibly attracted to money and horses. In 1912, after quarreling with Huerta over which of them was entitled to a stolen horse, he was sentenced to be shot. The sentence was commuted and Villa subsequently escaped from a jail in Mexico City. With a single companion he reached El Paso, Texas. There, awaiting developments, he established contact with another revolutionary, Emiliano Zapata, an idealistic Indian from lower Mexico, who permitted women to serve as officers in his small army and whose scorched-earth campaign against landowners and their overseers had caused him to be called the Attila of the South.

In 1913, Villa left Texas for Mexico with just eight men. By sheer reckless courage he took villages and then towns, gathering an army as he went. Soon he was the undisputed rebel leader of Chihuahua. With Zapata as an ally he held significantly large portions of Mexico, while Governor Venustiano Carranza of Coahuila controlled comparably large portions. Carranza, feeling powerful enough to reject any binding alliance, considered Villa still a bandit and not to be trusted.

But for a while it was Huerta who seized power in the capital. He had Madero assassinated, together with Vice President Pino Suarez. Shocked by the murder, Woodrow Wilson refused to recognize the new regime. American policy makers were also worried about the possible seizure of foreign holdings in Mexico and the possible alignment of Mexico with enemy nations in the event of a European war. In April, after a minor incident involving the arrest of some U.S. Marines in Tampico, the American fleet converged in the Gulf of Mexico. American forces temporarily seized Veracruz to prevent a German ship from delivering machine guns and ammunition to unfriendly revo-

Preceding pages: Remington painting dramatizes capture of "Chaparral Bandits" by Texas Ranger in 1870's, before Pancho Villa started selling rustled Mexican cattle in U.S.
Left: Villa at time of Mexican Revolution, when he had turned from banditry to partisan warfare. Right: Wearing braided military uniform in group photo, he poses with Emiliano Zapata (holding large sombrero), who was ruthless revolutionary but never joined Villa in banditry.

lutionary factions. Sixteen Americans and nearly two hundred Mexicans were killed. The United States soon heightened tensions by supplying arms to Carranza.

Factional alliances shifted, regimes rose and fell almost overnight, and chaos continued until Carranza's forces, under General Alvaro Obregon, consolidated their control. In 1915 the United States recognized the Carranza government. But Villa battled the new regime. Secretly the Americans permitted Mexican troop movements north of the border, with the result that Villa was soundly defeated in Sonora by unexpected reinforce-

ments aiding another Carranza general, Plutarco Elias Calles. In December, Villa was forced to disperse his army into small, scattered units. To weaken the insurgent's position with the people, Carranza began to institute long-promised land reforms that worried foreign investors. Ironically, Wall Street speculators and wealthy American businessmen with interests in Mexico, who had feared confiscation of their holdings by reformist revolutionaries, began to encourage the revolutionary Pancho Villa, in a few cases actually sending money and arms. But the United States Government was solidly behind

Carranza, and the Villistas therefore remained solidly against the *gringos*.

In 1916, Villa and four hundred mounted troops crossed the Rio Grande to attack a detachment of the 13th U.S. Cavalry, stationed at Columbus, New Mexico. The soldiers suffered a few casualties, but turned back the attack on their camp, whereupon the Villistas sacked and burned the town itself, killing sixteen citizens.

The United States immediately requested Mexico's permission to send troops across the border in pursuit of the raiders. (Elements of the 13th Cavalry had already crossed over but did not remain.) Carranza replied that the troops would be welcome if future raids occurred and on condition that Mexican forces could, in turn, penetrate the United States in search of border brigands. Washington agreed to the reciprocal condition but did not wait for any future raids before sending General John J. Pershing into Mexico with two columns of cavalry. Most of the soldiers were from Negro units that had patrolled the Southwest since the days of Indian fighting. Among the white officers was one who would serve under Pershing again in Europe when the First World War erupted and

Big sombreros, crossed bandoliers, military rifles, and any pistols they could obtain were standard equipment for Villista bandits turned revolutionaries. Villa stands in front row, third from right, among his "generals." Their bristling weaponry prepared them for ambush and also had psychological effect, signaling "no quarter." Dead man is rebel hanged by federales near Torreon in 1912.

would become one of the Second World War's most controversial generals. He was a young second lieutenant, George S. Patton. During the course of the famous Punitive Expedition, Patton led a cavalry patrol (in very modern style, using three Dodge automobiles instead of horses) that killed one of Villa's aides, Colonel Julio Cardenas, and two lesser Villistas.

There were few such successes. Near a Mormon settlement called Colonia Dublan, the Americans captured a few Villistas and they routed a large group at Guerrero, another at Agua Caliente, but Villa himself and most of his men escaped them. The bandit revolutionaries were now operating as scattered bands. Their countrymen, fiercely resentful of the American troops, served as spies, gave the foreigners false intelligence reports, and kept the bandits informed of their whereabouts. Carranza, annoyed at what he regarded as American arrogance and sensing that he was losing favor with his people, restricted Pershing's movements, ending any hope of overtaking Villa.

At Parral supposedly friendly Mexican troops fired on an American detachment. U.S. Secretary of War Newton D. Baker ordered the governors of the Southwestern states to call out their militia, and America's border towns became armed camps. Pancho Villa, former cattle-rustling *peon*, was now an international celebrity, a potential cause of war, and a hero of socialist insurgents.

Pershing sent two cavalry companies into an area forbidden to them by the Mexican government, evidently to provoke Carranza into some action that would excuse further intervention or else bluff him into cooperating in Villa's capture. At Carrizal a large Mexican force attacked when Pershing's men insisted on advancing. Nine Americans were killed and nineteen captured, after which Carranza ordered the foreign troops out of his country. The

In one of his most famous photographs, Villa rides with partisan column that was no longer a bandit gang but disciplined light cavalry. It was force like this that he led into Columbus, New Mexico, in 1916, when 16 Americans were killed.

United States, more concerned than ever about the war in Europe, unwilling to commit overt aggression, embarrassed by Pershing's unauthorized and overbearing action, and still hoping to achieve friendship with its southern neighbor, complied with the eviction notice.

Villa remained on his own side of the Rio Grande, but he was not pacified. In 1919 he kidnapped an American named F. A. Knotts but released him when a ransom was paid. His people now addressed him as General and his acts of violence, kidnapping included, were becoming acts of partisan terrorism rather than simple banditry. Like Juan Cortinas, he had transformed himself from a rebellious brigand into a forerunner of modern political guerrillas and terrorists.

While fending off the Americans, Villa had also been hounded by one of Carranza's generals, Alvaro Obregon. In 1920 Obregon arranged a coup in which Carranza was assassinated, and after some shuffling of positions Obregon became president. To insure peace he granted amnesty to Villa and bought him a large estate. Then he surprised observers by initiating more reforms than Carranza had felt obliged to offer, and by establishing a relatively stable government.

In 1923, while Villa and three bodyguards were passing through the town of Parral in an automobile, they were abruptly confronted by eight men carrying repeating rifles. Before Villa and his companions could draw their guns they were riddled. Evidently the man in charge of the assassination was a politician named Jesus Salas Barrazas. He stepped from a nearby building and put four shots into the dead bandit's head. Investigators counted forty-seven wounds in the corpse. Later Barrazas claimed that the government owed him fifty thousand pesos for his service. He was neither paid nor punished.

There has been speculation that the assassination was ordered by Obregon, who was himself assassinated the following year, or perhaps it was ordered by Obregon's successor, General Calles, who had beaten the Villistas in Sonora in 1915. Calles, though he was an ardent bolshevik, was relatively friendly to the United States and he detested Villa. Like Carranza, he suspected that Villa the revolutionary remained Villa the bandit.

The troubles with Mexico, reinforced by the troubles with the Eighteenth Amendment to the Constitution—Prohibition—had much to do with the establishment of a new police agency, the U.S. Border Patrol, in 1924. During the Patrol's early years a great deal of attention had to be devoted to tracking rustlers and intercepting rumrunners and smugglers. And even in those supposedly innocent years there was traffic in marijuana and the harder addictive drugs. Occasionally, too, border patrolmen had to watch for escaped convicts or other fugitives trying to cross in either direction. The patrolmen sometimes faced dangerous criminals, but the days of border clashes with old-fashioned badmen were dwindling. Mexico and the United States, despite recurrent strains in relations, were trying hard to cooperate in guarding their borderlands. A modern technology of surveillance and swift apprehension was developed while strong, high fences uncoiled for mile upon mile above the Rio Grande.

Today's typical border clash amounts to no more than the interception of an illegal immigrant, desperate to feed his family by laboring in California's lettuce fields or Idaho's potato fields. He is no defiant Cortinas or Villa, but a tragic embodiment of hunger, a gaunt, exhausted man who knows he will probably be caught again and sent back as he has been once or twice already, who knows that neither outlawry nor revolution changed his father's lot and that he must therefore try again and be caught again and try again.

History has elevated Mexican outlaws from status of common murderers and bandits to that of patriots. Panel of mural painted in 1936 by Diego Rivera—a case in point—is entitled, "The Bandit Hero."

11/A Rogues' Gallery

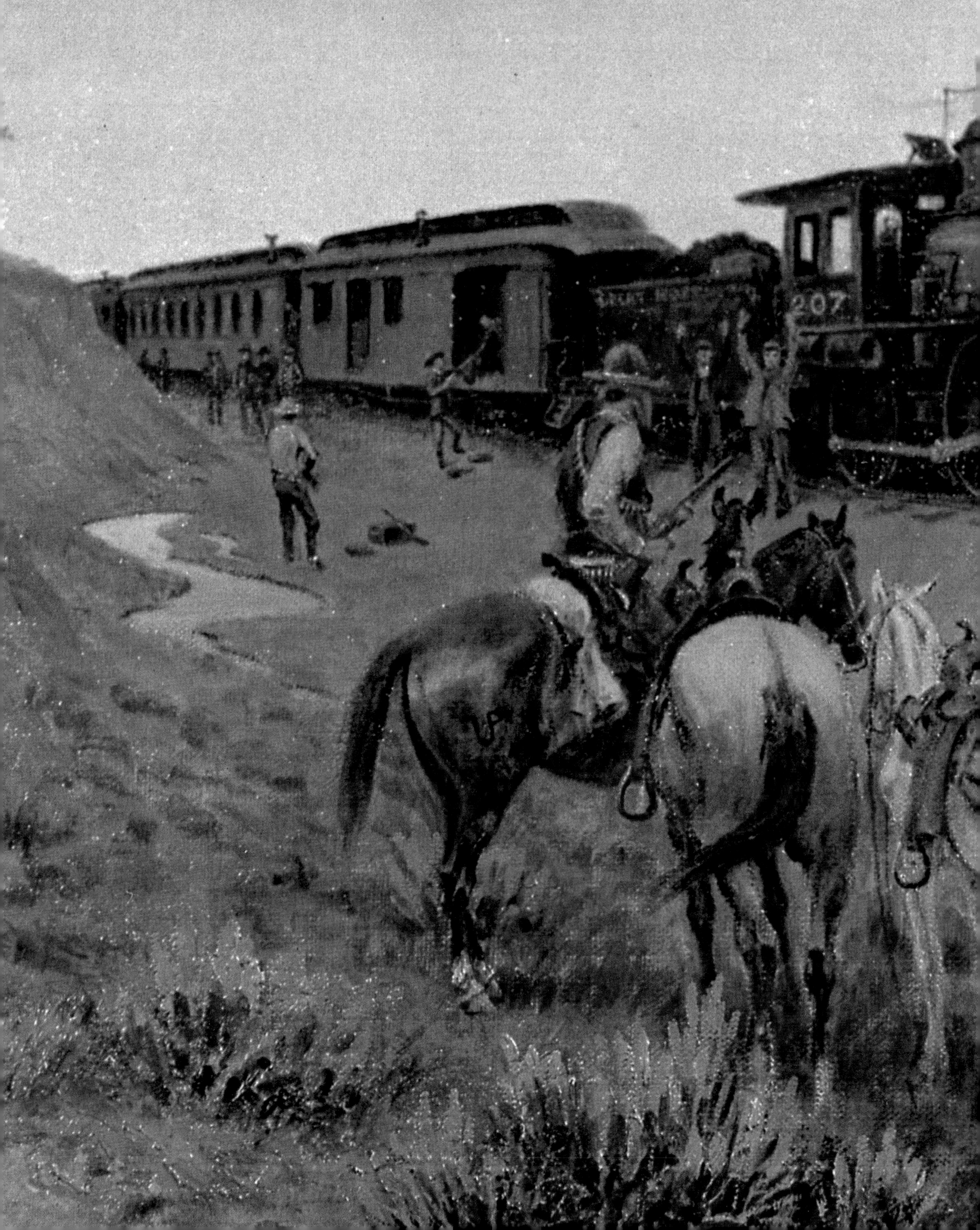

O.C. SELTZER.

There was no way for a rustler to transport herds of stolen cattle or horses inconspicuously, and sometimes buyers were scarce and prices low. Whiskey running and the robbery of individuals usually brought small returns for great risks. Bank robbery brought large, instantaneous profits, but banks were situated in towns where lawmen were headquartered, where posses could form quickly, where the armed citizenry might turn a raid into a debacle, as happened in Northfield and Coffeyville.

Stagecoaches and railroad trains looked so much easier, so much more vulnerable as they rumbled through uninhabited country, slowing to a crawl on grades and hairpin turns, halting to make repairs or clear obstructions. At remote way stations the coaches stopped for water, rest, food, fresh horses; the trains stopped for water and occasionally fuel. Stage lines and railroads carried silver and gold shipments, payrolls, bank deposits, and moneyed passengers. Inevitably, many outlaws were tempted by the moving targets. A few bandits found enormous sums in the strongboxes and express cars, but more often they were disappointed. Some of the most carefully planned holdups ended in ludicrous failure and each new attempt increased the danger of death or capture. Yet in the battle for plunder there were always outlaws eager to replace the casualties, convinced that they could succeed where others failed.

Ever since the opening decades of the nineteenth century, when Captain Lightfoot robbed the Boston stage and Joseph T. Hare waylaid coaches on the Natchez Trace and in Maryland, highwaymen had been following the stage lines westward. As railroads impinged on the horse-drawn trade, outlaws turned their attention to the trains. Some of these desperadoes have been mentioned. Additional names merit inclusion here, in a rogues' gallery of freebooting specialists.

America's first train robbery took place in 1866, near Seymour, Indiana. It was not committed by the James Brothers, as is sometimes said, but by a gang whose leaders were the Reno brothers—John, Frank, Simeon, William, and Clinton. During the Civil War several of the Renos had prospered modestly as "bounty jumpers," collecting a cash bounty for enlisting in the Union Army, then deserting and enlisting elsewhere. At the war's end, when they returned home to southern Indiana, they found small coveys of thieves operating brazenly around Seymour and nearby towns. They consolidated several such groups into a large band. Some of their early profits came from spurious bills printed by a counterfeiter named Peter McCartney, but murder and plunder were more characteristic. By autumn of 1866 the Reno gang controlled and terrorized the lower portion of the state.

It was then that they invented train robbery. Probably inspired by wartime cavalry raids, they flagged down an Ohio & Mississippi Railroad train as it slowed for a curve a few miles from Seymour. The wood-burning locomotive pulled an Adams Express car that carried $10,000 in cash and gold, plus a stout safe containing additional valuables. For almost an hour William Reno and several helpers labored unsuccessfully to break open the safe. Finally they rode away with the $10,000.

The Pinkerton Detective Agency was under contract to protect the Adams Express Company. The agency's founder, Allan Pinkerton himself, came to Indiana to track down the gang. But the Renos were still at large the following spring, and they rode into Missouri and robbed the Daviess County Treasury of $22,065. Evidently thinking themselves invincible, they began using the Seymour railroad depot as a meeting place. Now Pinkerton knew where to find them, but the gang had grown so large that the arrival of a posse would bring on a pitched

Preceding pages: "Kid Curry Holdup," by O. C. Seltzer, commemorates last great train robbery by members of Butch Cassidy's Wild Bunch; it occurred in 1901 near Malta, Montana. Escaping with $40,000, gang avoided mistakes of predecessors like George Parrott, Sam Bass, and Black Jack Ketchum. Left: Shotgun messenger dominates dramatic Remington impression of lonely stage road where robbers such as Black Bart Bolton might lurk. Vulnerability rendered trains and stages prime targets for western rogues.

battle. He therefore planned a ruse to capture John Reno, who was considered the ringleader.

With six muscular volunteers recruited in Cincinnati, Pinkerton arrived at the depot platform and somehow persuaded John Reno to step aboard a car for a private conversation. The instant the outlaw was inside, the train pulled out. Upon realizing what had happened, Frank Reno and a group of henchmen commandeered another train. However, they failed to overtake Pinkerton, and John Reno was sentenced to forty years at hard labor.

Undeterred, his brother Frank led the gang in new forays. In 1868 they robbed the Harrison County Bank in Magnolia, Iowa, escaping with $14,000. Pinkerton again took up the pursuit. With a large posse, he captured the Renos and their most trusted lieutenants at Council Bluffs. The robbers were packed into the local jail. On April 1, 1868, they broke through the jail wall. Over the large escape hole one of them chalked the words "April Fool." In May they stopped a Jefferson, Missouri & Indianapolis Railroad train near Marshfield, south of Seymour. They shot down a guard, forced open the express car, and departed with $96,000 in gold, cash, and Government bonds. The loot was far greater than any the James-Younger gang ever took.

Pinkerton decided to lure the outlaws into a trap. He allowed word to leak that $100,000 was to be shipped through Seymour. The Renos expected a heavy guard but they failed to realize that the express car would contain, instead of gold, a platoon of lawmen. When the bandits threw open the doors they were hit by a barrage. Several were wounded before they fled into a swamp. Two were captured, then three more. The possemen lost all five prisoners to a lynch mob. Not long afterward, Pinkerton detectives captured William and Simeon Reno and deposited them in the prison at New Albany, Indiana. Then Allan Pinkerton traced the others to Windsor, Ontario, a short ferry ride from Detroit, but at that time a wildly lawless town. Aided by local officers, he arrested them.

After weeks of extradition negotiations, Pinkerton and several operatives returned with their prisoners —Frank Reno, Michael Rogers, Miles Ogle, Albert Perkins, and Charles Spencer. The manacled prisoners nearly drowned in the Detroit River when a tugboat collided with their ferry, but they were finally locked up in the two-story New Albany jail. By then the settlers of southern Indiana were forming a vigilance committee, sworn to end outlaw terrorism. In December a railroad engineer died of gunshot wounds inflicted by the Renos during a holdup the summer before. The vigilantes, newly incensed, agreed on December 11 as a "night of blood," when retribution would be exacted.

They gathered at midnight in Seymour, all wearing long red masks. The backs of the leaders were marked with large chalked numbers. They were as well organized and disciplined as a militia company. After cutting the telegraph lines they commandeered the night train to New Albany, cut the lines there, too, left protesting residents under guard in the railway coaches, and rushed the jail. The sheriff was wounded when he resisted. Two county commissioners were relieved of their cell keys. The vigilantes had condemned Frank, William, and Simeon Reno and one cohort named Charlie Anderson. The other prisoners were not molested. The doomed outlaws fought, begged, and wept as they were dragged up the prison stairs to a catwalk rimming the second-floor cell block. Nooses were tightened and the four were thrown over the railing to dangle before the eyes of the other prisoners.

The Southern Indiana Vigilance Committee quietly departed and ten days later published a proclamation and warning, declaring that "it became necessary for this or-

Lynching scene recreates one of several such incidents when captured members of Reno gang were seized from lawmen by infuriated Indiana citizens. After they committeed America's first train robbery in 1866, Renos became powerful enough to terrorize state. Inset is contemporary sketch of ringleader Frank Reno.

ganization to mete out summary punishment to the leaders of the thieves, robbers, murderers and desperadoes. . . . Having lopped off the branches, and finally uprooted the tree of evil which was in our midst, in defiance of us and our laws, we beg to be allowed to rest here, and be not forced again to take the law into our own hands. . . ."

Armed robbery in Indiana subsided for some time afterward.

But another outlaw from the same state, an illiterate orphan named Sam Bass, was soon to make his presence felt farther west. His mother and father had died by the time he was thirteen years old, and Sam had sought shelter, together with several of his nine brothers and sisters, in the home of an uncle named Dave Sheeks. Sheeks worked the children mercilessly. After five years Sam left the Indiana farm. He labored in a Mississippi sawmill for a while and in 1874 accompanied a wagon train to Denton, Texas. After herding cattle briefly, he handled cargo for Sheriff William F. "Dad" Egan, who owned a freighting business. Bass was dismissed when he and a friend named Henry Underwood, having acquired a fast mare, began to devote all their time to the local races. In 1875 Bass and Underwood wandered down into Mexico and up into the Indian Territory, pitting their horse against all challengers. While passing through San Antonio Bass met Joel Collins, a former bartender who convinced him that trail driving and cardplaying would be more profitable than fleecing cash-poor Indians out of paltry racing bets.

They took a herd up to Kansas, collected thousands of dollars for the owners of the cattle, and then went into the Black Hills. At first they probably intended to return the money after using it to win some for themselves in the Deadwood gambling rooms. Instead, they lost it all. They tried freighting and failed at that, too. Then a suggestion came from Jack Davis, a gambler who had been in prison

Above: Newspaper rendition of bank robbery in Missouri shows merciless carnage perpetrated by gangs like Renos and Jameses. Top right: Another Missouri scene shows how railroad passengers were victimized; as a rule, ladies were not immune to bandits' greed, in spite of romantic myths. Bottom right: In dramatization from Illustrated Police News, *masked California road agents go so far as to pluck earrings from terror-stricken women.*

for robbing a Nevada train. He suggested holding up the Cheyenne-Deadwood stage.

Bass, Collins, and three friends (one of whom was probably Davis) tried to block the coach as it came through Whitewood Canyon, outside Deadwood. Bass and Collins had agreed there would be no killing, but when they ordered the driver to stop he whipped the horses to greater speed and an unidentified bandit shot the guard, John Slaughter. Still the coach did not stop. Neither did the next one they attempted to waylay. They hid near Deadwood and kept trying. The next one brought them about $30, and the fourth yielded $3 and a gold watch and chain. Again they tried, and made $6. Eluding capture seemed to pose no problem, but eating did. They decided that train robbery must surely be more profitable.

Bass, Collins, and Davis recruited three Nebraska outlaws—Jim Berry, Tom Nixon, and Bill Heffridge. In 1877, when a Union Pacific train stopped to take on water at Big Springs, Nebraska, they forced their way into the Wells Fargo Express car. The messenger, Charley Miller, told them the safe had a tamper-proof time lock. Failing to break it apart, they almost left empty-handed. Out of curiosity, they smashed open three small boxes and found $60,000 in $20 gold pieces consigned to the National Bank of Commerce in New York. While Collins and Bass loaded the unexpected fortune on the horses, their confederates went through the coaches and relieved passengers of an additional thousand dollars or so.

Collins, the gang's real leader, rode into Kansas with Heffridge, but news of the holdup preceded them. Near Fort Hays they were stopped by a sheriff and a cavalry patrol. They drew their pistols and were killed in the ensuing gunfight. Lawmen were watching for Jim Berry. He had bought six red bandannas from an Ogallala storekeeper who knew him, and a torn remnant of one was found at the Big Springs watering station. When he and Nixon rode into the town of Mexico, Missouri, Sheriff Walter Glasscock was waiting. Nixon got away and was never heard of again. Berry was killed. Davis rode to Texas with Bass and then disappeared as Nixon had.

Near Denton, Bass set up camp with Henry Underwood and another less than famous outlaw named Frank Jackson in Cove Hollow, a ravine pocked with caves and shielded by thick brush. Dad Egan and other local peace officers knew where they were, but the place was almost impregnable. Furthermore, no one in Denton was enthusiastic about killing or capturing Bass; he was a good-natured young ruffian who had never done any harm in that neighborhood. Occasionally he and a few friends ventured out to get supply money, but they fared almost as poorly as they had in Deadwood. During the Christmas season of 1877 they gleaned $11 from the Fort Worth stage. They scored a bit better in a second attempt two months later: the passengers gave up a pair of watches and $70. Another train robbery seemed almost mandatory.

In February, 1878, Bass, Jackson, Seaborn Barnes,

Above: Sam Bass at 16 years of age, before he left Indiana farm to become western badman, and in his 20's when honest employment in Texas began to pall. Left: Wells Fargo Express wagon, heavily guarded and loaded with gold from Great Homestake Mine near Deadwood, where stagecoaches and miners' wagons motivated Bass and three young friends to make Black Hills famous for bungled ambushes.

Tom Spotswood, and possibly Henry Underwood waited at the Allen station for the Houston & Texas Central Express. This time they got $1,280. Only at Big Springs had Sam Bass ever been more successful, and he never was so lucky again. Three more train robberies in the next two months brought the gang a total of $600.

If Denton residents found Sam Bass amusing despite the mounting rewards offered by railroads, authorities elsewhere were less forgiving. He was being trailed by detectives, Texas Rangers, and assorted other lawmen. The Rangers arrested Jim Murphy, an old friend of Bass, for having harbored the outlaws. An offer was made to dismiss the charge if he would help trap the gang. Murphy eagerly agreed. He rode to Cove Hollow and offered his services as a robber. Bass was planning to hold up the bank at Round Rock, and since only Barnes and Jackson were then camping with him at the Hollow he welcomed the extra man. En route, while the outlaws refreshed themselves and watered their horses in a small town, Murphy slipped away and sent a wire to the Rangers: "We are on our way to Round Rock to rob the bank. For God's sake get here."

Major John B. Jones dispatched Captain Lee Hall and four other Rangers. He also sent Travis Deputy Sheriff Morris Moore and Williamson Deputy Sheriff A. W. Grimes, but without telling them why.

As Bass and his men rode into Round Rock, they decided to spend the afternoon idling and reconnoitering, and rob the bank the next day. Murphy again managed to separate himself from the others. Bass, Jackson, and Barnes strolled into a general store to buy tobacco. Each wore a belt holster, with the butt and hammer of a six-gun in plain view, ready for fast drawing. Deputies Moore and Grimes followed the three strangers into the store to remind them about the almost universal law against wearing

sidearms while in a town. Confronted by a pair of badges and assuming they had been recognized, the outlaws drew and started shooting. Grimes fell, with six bullets in his body. Moore, standing behind him, managed to fire five shots before he, too, fell. As the Rangers came running, Barnes tried to mount his horse but pitched to the ground, dead. Jackson got away.

Bass, though Grimes had hit him in the stomach and right hand, managed to ride off. After dark a farmer came into town from Bushy Creek and reported that Sam Bass was lying outside his cabin. The lawmen brought a doctor, but there was nothing to be done beyond waiting for the end. When Major Jones questioned Bass about gang members still at large he replied that "if a man knows anything, he ought to die with it in him." He did so three days later, on July 22, 1878.

In the previous year, when Wells Fargo had compiled lists of stagecoach robbers, Sam Bass had been but one name among more than two hundred. No one can estimate how many highwaymen attacked the stage lines. Surely the most flamboyant and perhaps the most pathetic was Charles E. Bolton—California's legendary Black Bart. He was a tired, embittered old man when he turned to crime for a livelihood, but he was also gentle and chivalrous, a wit, a prankster, and the poet laureate of western badmen. Little is known of his background. He once told Pinkerton operatives that he came from Jefferson County, New York, and that his family had brought him west in about 1830, when he was ten years old. He is believed to have been a farmer for some years and then a drummer, peddling patent medicines. Still later he prospected in the California gold fields, apparently with little success. In the mid-1870's he could no longer abide the scratching at an unyielding frontier for a bare subsistence. He began to take rooms at good hotels, sometimes in San Francisco, sometimes in Los Angeles. He carried a walking stick and bought a diamond stickpin. He wore a bowler, stylish suits, a velvet-lapeled, satin-faced Chesterfield. No one knows how he initially financed his new mode of living. Perhaps his first ventures into larceny were lucrative and undetected.

His first authenticated robbery occurred in 1877, when he stopped the Wells Fargo stage outside Fort Ross, near the Russian River. The strongbox yielded $300 in cash and a check for $305.52. Though the booty was not particularly great, newspapers made him a celebrity, for he was a most unusual highwayman. He always appeared suddenly and alone where a coach had to slow down or stop. He always carried a rifle, which he pointed at the driver or the shotgun messenger but was never known to fire. In a voice described as "deep and hollow," he always issued one command: "Throw down the box." He always wore a long white linen duster that covered him from shoulders to ankles, and over his face a flour sack with eyeholes cut in it.

Several days after the Fort Ross holdup, investigators found the emptied Wells Fargo box in the brush. On a waybill left in the box, the robber had scrawled:

> I've labored long and hard for bread
> for honor and for riches
> But on my *corns too* long yo've tred
> *You fine haired sons of Bitches*
> BLACK BART, the Poet

After that, Bolton left scraps of verse at the scene of each holdup, signing them "Black Bart the Po8." Even the Wells Fargo detectives who tried for years to learn his true identity found it hard not to smile at his doggerel:

> here I lay me down to Sleep
> to wait the coming Morrow
> perhaps Success perhaps defeat

Charles E. Bolton—California's famous Black Bart— in finery evidently purchased with proceeds of stagecoach robberies. For years he left scraps of light verse at scenes of holdups before Wells Fargo detective Jim Hume discovered his identity through laundry mark on handkerchief dropped when he waylaid Sonora stage.

And everlasting Sorrow . . .
let come what will, I'll try it on
My condition can't be worse
and if theres money in that Box
Tis munny in my purse

In charge of the long investigation was James B. Hume, a pioneer criminologist and probably the most successful of Wells Fargo detectives. Black Bart stopped the stage from Quincy to Oroville in July, 1878, and this time he took from the box $379 in coin, a diamond ring, and a silver watch. (Hume reported that the jewelry was removed from the strongbox, not from passengers as related in some accounts. When Bolton was finally apprehended he insisted on adding an interesting disclaimer to his confession: "I never robbed a passenger, or ill-treated a human being.") Only five days after robbing the Quincy-Oroville stage, he struck the coach coming down from La Porte to Oroville, taking $50 in gold specie and another silver watch. Jim Hume distributed a circular detailing the robberies, quoting the verses left behind, and reproducing a facsimile of the bandit's penmanship. Bolton had disguised part of the writing, as if each line were penned by a different hand, but Hume hoped that some characteristics of the robber's script might be recognized. Modern and thorough, he noted in the circular that a "wag" of this sort "would be likely to leave specimens of his handwriting on hotel registers and other public places."

But the search was unproductive until 1883, when by luck Hume obtained a decisive clue. As a stage approached Copperopolis, on the run from Sonora to Milton, Black Bart stepped from behind a rock, pointed his rifle, and issued his customary order. The driver threw down the box, which was heavy enough so that Bolton decided to pry it open on the spot. In doing so he cut his right hand,

and bandaged the cut with his handkerchief before scooping up $4,800. Distracted by the plunder or his injury, he failed to notice a rider approach. The rider handed his gun to the stage driver, who fired at Bolton, inexplicably missing. The bandit leaped for his horse and fled, dropping the handkerchief.

On the square of linen was an inked laundry mark, "F.O.X. 7." Hume and his investigators checked the records of some ninety laundries. Eventually they traced the laundry mark to an elderly, distinguished gentleman named Bolton, who carried a gold-knobbed cane and was registered at a San Francisco hotel. Bolton was sent to San Quentin. After four years he was released, partly because of his age and partly on the basis of exceptionally good behavior in prison. He vanished and there is no record of

Helena, Montana, photographer E. D. Keller made studio portrait of famous manhunter John X. Biedler, probably at time when "X" and Lem Wilson arranged capture of Big Nose George Parrott at Miles City. Far right: In 1879, New York Illustrated Times *captioned this picture, "Four road-agents overpower and plunder two officers and seven soldiers near Bismarck, D.T." Time, place, and type of crime all point to George Parrott's outlaw band.*

his death. Reports reached California that he ended his days in Nevada, once again farming.

For a brief, inglorious period, Big Nose George Parrott displayed more ruthlessness if less elan than Black Bart. Parrott's gang robbed stages and freight wagons in Wyoming, Montana, and Dakota, and sometimes lounged in Miles City between expeditions. Whenever lawmen became obdurate in their peacekeeping duties, he retreated into the Dakota Badlands, the prairies of Montana, or Wyoming's Big Horn Mountains. In January, 1879, a Fort Keogh merchant named Morris Cahn left for the East with $14,000 to buy a large stock of goods for his store. He traveled in a military wagon with an Army paymaster, followed by an escort several hundred yards to the rear. Just beyond the crossing of the Powder River, where the trail dipped into a coulee, the Parrott outlaws stopped the wagon, took the $14,000, and were gone before the escort came within shooting distance. Parrott crossed the Yellowstone and was back in Miles City two nights later, spending large amounts of cash in celebration. After gathering sufficient evidence, Miles City Marshal Hank Wormwood arrested Parrott and some cohorts. They were released on perjured testimony from friends that they had been in Canada at the time of the robbery.

The following year, U.S. Marshal John X. Biedler arrived in Miles City. "X" was a well-known manhunter who had received word from Wyoming authorities that they would pay $1,000 for Parrott. In 1878 unidentified robbers had tried unsuccessfully to derail a Union Pacific

train in order to get into the pay car; two lawmen who trailed the bandits were murdered, and officials in Wyoming subsequently learned from an informer that Big Nose George had led the desperadoes.

X found Parrott and another badman standing in front of John Chinnick's saloon, a shack frequented by the lawless. In front of the shack was an open space of more than a hundred yards. It was doubtful that a man could cross that space if the outlaws disliked his appearance. John X. Biedler limped noticeably and was known by sight throughout Montana. He therefore enlisted the aid of a shrewd and courageous settler, Lem Wilson, who was wearing ragged bib overalls and could hardly be taken for anything but a harmless farmer. Wilson tucked a pair of pistols behind the overall bib and walked straight up to Chinnick's shack.

One of the outlaws demanded, "What do *you* want?"

"I'm going to see Chinnick," Wilson replied and walked past. Miles City's pioneer photographer, L. A. Huffman, succinctly described how Wilson concluded the exploit: "Being at their backs, he gave a command and their hands shot into the air fast."

Parrott was tried in Rawlins, Wyoming, and sentenced to hang. After the jailer's wife thwarted an escape, the citizenry dragged him out and hanged him from a telegraph pole.

A few accounts have mentioned Ben Wheeler as a suspected road agent of the same type and period. Wheeler was nothing more than a spectacularly unsuccessful bank robber. In the early 1880's he served as Assistant City Marshal under George Hendry Brown in Caldwell, Kansas. Brown kept the peace so efficiently that appreciative townsmen presented him with an engraved Winchester rifle. They were almost equally fond of his assistant. Then, in the spring of 1884, the president and the cashier of the bank at Medicine Lodge were killed during a holdup. Citizens, quickly capturing the gang in a canyon, were astonished to discover that the bandit leaders were Brown and Wheeler. The prisoners were jailed but that night a mob came to lynch them. The sheriff resisted. In the confusion the bandits ran. Brown was killed by several rifle bullets and a charge of buckshot. Wheeler was wounded and recaptured. With two other accomplices he was hanged from an elm tree.

Speculations regarding additional crimes by Wheeler seem inconsequential by comparison with the accusations against more notorious outlaws. Newspapers had charged the Jameses and the Youngers with crimes perpetrated simultaneously in locales separated by hundreds of miles. In 1891, California grand juries returned true bills against the Daltons for two train holdups they could not have committed—holdups that might well have been the work of the Sontag brothers.

George and John Sontag owned a quartz mine near Visalia, California, but they wandered far afield to find more profitable employment. In 1892, after an investigation of train robberies near Kosota, Minnesota, and Racine, Wisconsin, Pinkerton detectives identified the Sontags as the bandits. Pinkerton notified American Express, Wells Fargo, and Southern Express that the robbers had been traced to Visalia. Though express messengers were alerted, the pair stopped a train passing through Fresno County. They blew open the express car with dynamite and took $5,000 from a Wells Fargo safe. They escaped a posse, wounding two lawmen in the process, and were joined by a man named Chris Evans, a farmer of evidently savage temperament. Trapped in a barn a few days later, Evans and John Sontag shot their way out,

In small photograph, Ben Wheeler wears his badge as Assistant City Marshal of Caldwell, Kansas. Manacled captives in large picture are (from left) John Wesley, City Marshal Hendry Brown, Billie Smith, and Wheeler, caught after robbery of Medicine Lodge Bank. Gun is Wheeler's .44 single-action, which may have killed bank president and cashier.

leaving behind the corpse of a deputy sheriff, but George Sontag was captured and sent to Folsom Prison.

Peace officers, Wells Fargo operatives, and Indian scouts tracked the badmen through the San Joaquin Valley for nine months. There were several battles, and seven more lawmen were wounded. Evans and Sontag stopped several stages, not alone to rob them but to ask, according to contemporary reports, "if there are any detectives aboard we can kill." In June, 1893, a posse surrounded their latest hideout. Two deputies were killed. Reinforcements arrived and the shooting continued for eight hours while the desperadoes took cover behind trees in a running fight that became known as The Battle of Sampson's Flats. Finally both of them were badly wounded and captured. John Sontag died of his injuries

that night. When George Sontag received the news at Folsom he went berserk. He was shot to death as he scaled a prison wall. Evans was sent to Folsom for life. He escaped in 1893, but was recaptured and returned to prison.

Thomas "Black Jack" Ketchum was more methodical than the Sontags but he may have been equally deranged. He was born in about 1866 in New Mexico, where he remained for most of his life. Although he wore a carefully barbered handlebar moustache and sometimes affected attire that gave him the look of a rising banker, he was an uneducated cowboy who drank heavily, had trouble keeping a job, and easily drifted into robbery. In the Pinkerton archives is a notation describing him as "one of the leaders of the Hole in the Wall Gang"—Butch Cassidy's Wild Bunch. This was not quite true. In the late 1890's, after his

sweetheart married another cowboy, Ketchum left Clayton, New Mexico, rode up into Wyoming, and spent some time in the vicinity of Cassidy's Hole in the Wall lair. He may have ridden with the Wild Bunch once or twice, but he had no part in the leadership. It seems likely that Cassidy would hesitate to trust him in any dangerous enterprise, for Tom Ketchum sometimes exhibited disturbing eccentricities, particularly when he had been drinking. His reaction to being jilted was to beat himself with a rope and club himself with the butt of his single-action. A number of Clayton cow hands witnessed the strange tantrum.

Elza Lay, alias Bill McGinnis, was one lesser light of the Wild Bunch willing to ride back to New Mexico with Ketchum. The two were joined by Black Jack's brother

Sam and another mediocre bandit named G. W. Franks. It is possible that additional riders from the Wild Bunch joined them on one or two raids.

A letter written in 1899 by W. R. Reno, a special agent of the Colorado & Southern Railroad, described the oddly unimaginative forays of the Ketchum gang. Late the year before, the outlaws held up Train No. 1 at Twin Mountains near Folsom, New Mexico. The loot amounted to no more than a few hundred dollars, yet Black Jack and his accomplices held up the same train at the same place three more times. He raided elsewhere, but not often. It almost seemed as if he had an unconscious desire to be captured or a yearning to be immersed in violent battle. The only other logical explanation was that he was satisfied with small successes and too stupid to realize he was courting disaster or to make new plans.

Certainly he took no pains to avoid bloodshed. Reno's letter said that Ketchum had "committed a number of murders" and that Captain John Boyd of Jerome, Arizona, had identified him as the murderer of two men in July, 1899. It was nine days later that the Ketchum gang held up the train at Twin Mountains for the last time, and only two more days before a posse trapped the outlaws in Turkey Canyon, near Cimarron. A wild gun battle erupted and two sheriffs, Edward Farr of Huerfano County and W. H. Love of Cimarron, were killed. Elza Lay was captured. Sam Ketchum and G. W. Franks escaped. Black Jack Ketchum got away, too, but he was shot through the right shoulder and unable to travel fast; he was captured a few days later. Franks dropped from sight. In August, when Sam Ketchum tried to hold up the train at Twin Mountains a fifth time, conductor Frank Harrington shattered his arm with a shotgun blast. He was captured at a nearby ranch. A doctor amputated his arm but blood poisoning had set in. Unaware that he was dying, he

Left: Train robber George Sontag, photographed in Folsom Prison. Far left: Body of his brother, John Sontag, propped up in front of possemen who killed him in gun battle after long pursuit through San Joaquin Valley.

boasted of his brother's banditry. Several outlaws were called Black Jack. Sam Ketchum told a reporter, "I'm the brother of Tom Ketchum, the original Black Jack."

The original Black Jack was being held in jail at Santa Fe. William J. Mills, Chief Justice for the Territory of New Mexico, directed U.S. Marshal C. M. Foraker to produce Ketchum for trial at Clayton, but there were rumors that outlaws would try to rescue their colleague. Justice Mills wrote to Foraker ordering a secret change of plans. The outlaw was to arrive at Clayton on a Tuesday, rather than on Monday as previously scheduled. "Do not inform anyone . . . but leave Santa Fe quietly . . . and take the first train east. There will be a special to take you and the prisoner to Clayton from Trinidad."

Deputy Marshal Frank W. Hall, serving under Foraker, took charge of the prisoner and brought him safely in. Territorial Tax Collector A. L. Morrison, in a letter written to Hall several weeks before, had declared,

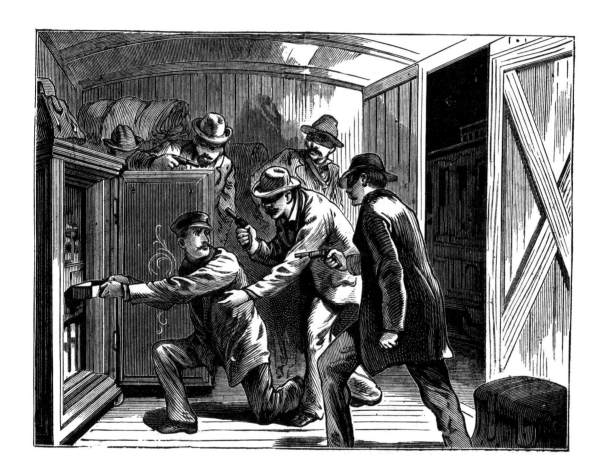

Even in late 19th century, Old World memories influenced America's concept and style of outlawry. 1878 newspaper sketch of bandits in railroad express car was captioned "Prairie Pirates," and 1892 portrayal of gang confronting train's engineer and fireman (in manner of Black Jack Ketchum's band) was titled "The Modern Dick Turpin."

"I hope you will hang the rascally 'Black Jack,' and thus give wide notice to all ruffians to give New Mexico a wide berth." Lawmen throughout the Southwest agreed. There is no certainty as to whether a rescue was really planned; if so, the bandits were outwitted. Hall earned commendations from his superiors and was one of those who received an invitation to the hanging.

In September, 1900, Ketchum was tried for the murder of Farr and was convicted. While awaiting his sentence, he wrote to the editors of the Santa Fe *New Mexican*. He said, in part: "I have never in no wise denied my guilt of the attempt[ed] train robbery on Colo & So [Colorado & Southern Railroad] at Folson neither have I denied participating in the Steins pass train robbery on Sopac [Southern Pacific]. It is the latter which three men named Leonard Alberson Bill Watterman & Walter Hoffman are now serving time for none being guilty. . . . The parties in the Stein pass hold up were myself and the following. David Adkins Ed Cullen-Will Carver-Bronco Bill and my brother S. W. Ketchum. Ed Queen was killed during the attempt. . . . We were also the ones who robbed the Steins pass post office getting but little more than Eleven dollars. . . . I dislike to see innocent men suffer for a crime committee by others. . . ."

A reporter for the *New York Times* wrote that Ketchum watched from his cell window as the scaffold was being erected, that his behavior was nonchalant, that on April 25, 1901, he "leaped" up the gallows steps and helped the hangman adjust the noose. As the black hood was placed over his head, he is supposed to have said, "I'll be in hell before you start breakfast, boys. Let 'er go!" The nervous and inexperienced executioners had adjusted the gibbet weights improperly. When the trap was sprung, Ketchum fell with a rending jerk, and the rope decapitated him.

Above: Two U.S. Deputy Marshals, identified as Steve Birchfield (left) and Pink Peters or Baylor Shannon, with saddles and guns captured from Ketchum gang in New Mexico in 1896. Top right: Black Jack Ketchum's holstered revolver, grouped with his photograph, handcuffs, key to his cell, deputy marshal's commission of Frank Hall (who brought Ketchum to court), and Hall's ticket of admission to Ketchum's hanging. Bottom right: Hangman lowers noose as Ketchum stoically awaits execution.

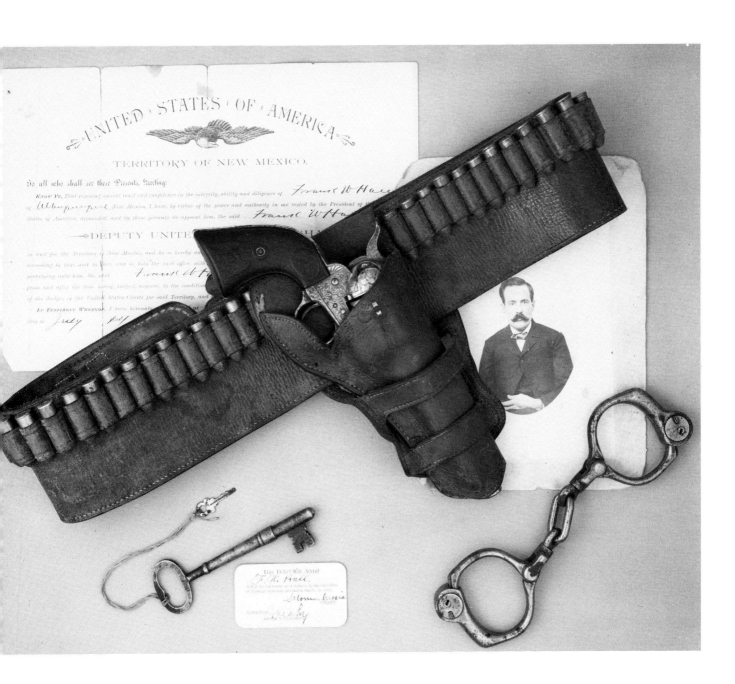

Preceding pages: Hotel on outskirts of Dawson, Yukon
Territory, at turn of century. Klondike gold rush was already
subsiding, but wild frontier conditions prevailed
here and across international boundary in Skagway, Alaska.
Above: Famous picture of Wild Bunch leaders,
taken at Fort Worth studio of John Swartz. Elegantly attired
and gazing into camera with nearly sober expressions,
they are, from left: Harry Longbaugh (the Sundance Kid), Bill
Carver, Ben Kilpatrick (the Tall Texan), Harvey Logan
(alias Kid Curry), and Butch Cassidy. Right: Laura Bullion,
who began as camp follower and became Kilpatrick's
faithful paramour. She sometimes guarded relays of escape
horses and, on last train holdup, handled rifle.

The Wild Bunch was the biggest, the most colorful, and the last of the long-lived western outlaw gangs. After its disintegration there were desperadoes who bludgeoned the outposts of expanding American settlement, but their assaults were brief—the last flashes of frontier anarchy, like brush fires flickering and dying in a gale. Perhaps most infamous among these remnants of outlawry were Soapy Smith in the Klondike and Harry Tracy, an alumnus of the Wild Bunch, in Oregon and Washington. Most of the others were quickly forgotten. The taming of the Wild Bunch coincided with the taming of the last wild towns, the last wild frontiers. The end of widespread marauding was inevitable, as was its beginning.

A series of devastating calamities encouraged the rise of the West's largest outlaw confederation. A terrible drought struck Wyoming and neighboring regions in 1883; beef prices dropped sharply in 1884 and the market crashed in '85; the winter of 1886-1887 was so severe that entire herds perished on the open range. The larger cattle companies dismissed great numbers of cowboys, and some of the unemployed turned naturally to rustling since beef

husbandry was the only trade they knew. Then, as conditions improved slightly, absentee ranchers sought new hands who would work for low pay. A few of them hired drifters and railroad laborers, including fugitives or former convicts who were easily recruited into the rustling gangs. While beef barons counted their losses and the region suffered through lingering depression, there were pockets of contrasting prosperity where small ranchers (both honest stockmen and rustlers) could keep expenses low enough to sell their beef cheaply and make a profit. Settlements like Buffalo, Wyoming, though never conspicuously rich in the manner of the silver and gold centers, were boom towns by comparison with other communities in the cattle country. And they came to be called "rustlers' boom towns."

It was near Buffalo, at the KC Ranch on the Powder River, that Frank Canton's posse fired the first shots of the Johnson County Range War and killed Nate Champion, a leader of the independent ranchers who were struggling against the powerful Stockgrowers Association. Whether or not Champion himself was a rustler chieftain, as alleged, there is no doubt that some of his riders and associates were outlaws. They were the ones (rather than the Canton faction, as sometimes reported) who became locally known as the Red Sash Gang. A cowhand wearing a sash above his gunbelt was flaunting a badge of warning. Few homesteaders, fence riders, or deputies would interfere with his actions.

Some of Champion's colleagues were to help form the Wild Bunch, at first known as the Hole-in-the-Wall Gang. They included Flat Nose George Curry and his rustling partners: Harvey Logan—more widely known as Kid Curry after he adopted his mentor's name—Logan's brothers John and Lonny, Tom "Peep" O'Day, and Walter Punteney, who came to be called Wat the Watcher because he served so often as lookout when the gang abandoned rustling for bank robbery. Harry Longbaugh, a reckless young cowboy who had spent some time in jail at Sundance, Wyoming, may have been a late recruit or may have joined the group by 1892, when Champion had such tight control over northern Wyoming that the law seemed powerless. Only one conviction was obtained in cases involving a hundred and eighty rustling arrests. Longbaugh was not much interested in rustling, however. In 1892 he and two accomplices held up a train near Malta, Montana (where Kid Curry and several other gang members raided another train on the Great Northern line almost a decade later). The accomplices in the 1892 robbery, Bill Madden and Harry Bass, were captured and imprisoned but Longbaugh escaped. Exceptionally fast and accurate with a gun, he became one of the gang's most famous badmen —the Sundance Kid—though he never appeared to be an important member of the Wild Bunch until shortly before it disintegrated.

The rustlers built cabins and corrals and established a stronghold near a creek bottom in a desolate valley called Hole in the Wall. It was situated between Buffalo and Casper, close to the KC Ranch (which has since grown into the town of Kaycee). The basin was a natural fortress, rimmed by steep, rugged buttes and bluffs, including a thousand-foot red rock wall on the north side. There were caverns for hiding, passages for escape, and a main entry pass through which no intruder could make his way without riding under the guns of outlaw sentinels. The narrow gorge, the hole in the great wall, made the place almost impregnable.

Under the direction of George Curry, the gang was large and thriving long before it joined forces with the famous Butch Cassidy, whose original band was headquartered in Utah. Cassidy's real name was George Leroy Parker. He was born in 1866 and brought up on a ranch at Circle Valley, Utah. His father, Max Parker, allowed the place to be used as a way station by rustlers. One of his cowboys was Mike Cassidy, a prodigious pilferer of other people's horses and cattle. Young George Parker became the rustler's protégé, helping to drive rustled steers to Robber's Roost. This particular Robber's Roost was an arid plateau near Hanksville, in southeastern Utah. It furnished excellent lookout points and its approaches were almost as easily guarded as those of Hole in the Wall. Its use taught George Parker how to select a hidden citadel, and he occasionally returned to it in later years.

He did not take the name Cassidy to hide his identity but as a sign of loyalty and admiration for Mike Cassidy. When the old rustler left for Mexico to avoid arrest, his youthful apprentice, calling himself George Cassidy, rode to the booming mine district of Telluride, Colorado. He drove the mules that carried ore from the diggings until he met the McCarty gang—the brothers Tom, Bill, and George, plus Tom McCarty's brother-in-law, Willard Christiansen, who called himself Matt Warner. The only member of the original group who ever reformed was Warner. After a career of train and bank robbery he served a prison term and then actually became a peace officer. Neither he nor the McCarty brothers belonged to the later coterie of Wild Bunch riders, a gang that also had one member who reformed. He was Elza Lay, a gunman for Cassidy and then for Black Jack Ketchum. Like Warner, Lay served a prison sentence and then stayed out of trouble, ending his days working for an oil company.

With the McCarty gang in November, 1887, Cassidy attempted his first train holdup. It took place on the Denver & Rio Grande tracks, about five miles east of Grand Junction, Colorado. The outlaws piled ties on the tracks, forcing the engineer to stop the train. It was a common maneuver. When the express-car messenger refused to open his safe, the bandits took a vote and decided not to rob the passengers. After removing the pile of ties they waved farewell and rode off. It was typical of Cassidy, a mischievous prankster who could outbluff and probably outshoot his most vicious henchmen but was addicted to jokes and grandiose gestures that sometimes amused or puzzled even the lawmen who pursued him.

Though never positively identified, Cassidy was probably the accomplice who aided Tom McCarty in the robbery of the First National Bank of Denver in March, 1889. McCarty, holding aloft a small bottle of liquid which he said was nitroglycerin, explained to the banker that he was desperate enough to kill himself by blowing up the bank. He demanded and got $21,000. Before fleeing he passed the money to a rider outside the bank, then rested in a nearby hotel where he tossed the bottle of water into a wastebasket.

Following the raid Cassidy and his friends established an outlaw community at Star Valley, on the Wyoming-Idaho line. Matt Warner opened a saloon there and papered the back wall with stolen greenbacks. His enterprise lost money, however, because drinks were free to all friends of Warner or Cassidy. The upkeep of the saloon probably increased the frequency of bandit raids.

In June, 1889, Cassidy rode into Telluride and roomed there for a few days while training his horse to stand motionless as he vaulted into the saddle, then gallop away with tremendous speed. The townspeople smiled at the antics of the fancy-riding young cowhand until Tom McCarty and Matt Warner joined him there to expropriate $10,500 from the San Miguel Valley Bank before performing a final exhibition of saddle-vaulting and galloping. The following year the McCarty brothers drifted out to the lumber camps of Oregon, and Cassidy tried his

hand at more or less honest work (relieved only by a bit of rustling now and then) on several Wyoming ranches. In 1892 he became a butcher at Rock Springs and there acquired the nickname Butch. Soon he was accused of emptying a drunk's pockets; though acquitted he left town in a fury. He considered rustling an honorable occupation for a cowboy, and bank or train robbery apparently furnished its own justification in the form of danger, but the charge of rolling a drunk insulted the cocky young outlaw.

He went back to herding cattle, sometimes legally, and then, with a partner named Al Rainer, bought a small ranch to deal in stolen horses. In 1894, when the new partners brought thirty stolen mounts to Star Valley, Sheriff John Ward of Uintah County trailed them, capturing Rainer first and then Cassidy. It was the only time Cassidy was ever taken into custody. He reached for his gun but was stunned by a bullet that grazed his head. Sentenced to two years in the penitentiary at Laramie, he requested a night's leave from the Lander jail before being transferred. Much is revealed about the force of the young outlaw's personality (and about western attitudes toward wayward cowboys) by the fact that the request was granted. Also revealing is the fact that Cassidy kept his promise to return the next morning to become Convict No. 187. Governor William A. Richards pardoned and released him several months before his sentence was completed. The Governor later recalled that he had failed to extract a promise of complete reform, but Cassidy swore to commit no further robberies in Wyoming. Thereafter he often hid in Wyoming, and he helped his gang plan raids and escapes within the state, but did not himself participate in robberies there. In a manner of speaking, he kept his word again.

Almost immediately he established a new stronghold at Brown's Hole in the Uintah Mountains, where the boundaries of Wyoming, Utah, and Colorado meet. With a friend named Bob Meeks and an adolescent New Mexican rustler named Elza Lay, he built a cabin high on Diamond Mountain at a spot still known as Cassidy Point. Matt Warner was there briefly, but was then jailed with two accomplices at Ogden, Utah, for the murder of two prospectors at Dry Forks. Cassidy persuaded Lay and Meeks to help Warner by providing a retainer for Douglas V. Preston, an able lawyer who defended several Cassidy outlaws before becoming Wyoming's Attorney General. To obtain the lawyer's fee they adopted the straightforward course of riding into Idaho and forcibly withdrawing $7,160 from the bank at Montpelier. Because the bank belonged to the American Bankers Association, a major Pinkerton client, detectives constantly followed Cassidy's trail thereafter. But once again it was Sheriff John Ward who made the first arrest, capturing Meeks at Fort Bridger, Wyoming. Meeks drew Idaho's maximum penalty for armed robbery, thirty-two years in the penitentiary. This time the outlaws could find no way to help a captured friend.

It was during the same period that Cassidy and his growing assemblage at Brown's Hole—now including several men from Hole in the Wall—were christened the Wild Bunch. Their Diamond Mountain lair was situated between Rock Springs, Wyoming, and Vernal, Utah. On Saturday nights they rode into one town or the other, depending on whim, and remained until Monday morning, hurrahing the main streets, carousing in the saloons and the cribs known as "disorderly houses" or "hook shops," leaving bullet holes in the walls but inflicting no bodily injury and spending enough rustling and robbery money to bolster the local economy. For a while Rock Springs and Vernal were bandits' boom towns, just as Buffalo had been a rustlers' boom town. The residents, in a tone that seemed almost affectionate, referred to the visitors as the Wild Bunch. When frontier newspapers printed the name, Cassidy and his cohorts took it up proudly.

In the spring of 1897, Cassidy and Elza Lay robbed the mining camp at Castle Gate, Utah. They stole the payroll, $8,000, but the net profit was somewhat less because Lay, an occasional bungler, dropped a full bag of silver. While Cassidy was merrily vandalizing this region, the rustlers at Hole in the Wall were almost in a state of siege. Several times that year they fought indecisive skirmishes with stockmen and peace officers. They feared an onslaught by vigilantes or the National Guard. In August, George Curry and the Logans led nearly a hundred riders out of Hole in the Wall to enlist under Cassidy, who was becoming the region's most celebrated badman. Along the way the caravan pillaged every sheep camp it encountered.

The new arrivals made Brown's Hole probably the largest outlaw camp in the history of the West. And several of the newcomers had already established reputations as vicious killers. Perhaps the worst were the Logans, part-Cherokee renegades born in Kentucky in the 1870's, raised in Missouri, and adrift through Montana and Wyoming during the peak rustling years. At an 1894 Christmas celebration in Landusky, Montana, Lonny Logan shot and killed Pike Landusky, whose daughter had borne the outlaw an illegitimate child. The three Logan brothers then escaped on a buckboard and drove back to Hole in the Wall. There, under the leadership of Flat Nose George Curry, they reorganized their gang and began holding up banks, trains, stores, post offices, and cattle camps. In 1896 Harvey Logan led his brothers back into Montana for the purpose of killing Jim Winters, a rancher who had given information to peace officers. Along the way they boasted of their intent. Word reached Winters and he was ready for them. When he killed Johnny Logan with a shotgun blast, the others fled. But Harvey Logan, the most ferocious of the brothers, swore revenge and eventually made good the threat.

At about the time Cassidy was robbing the Castle Gate gold camp, Deputy Sheriff William Deane attempted to arrest the two remaining Logans and George Curry. They killed him. A couple of months later they rode into Belle Fourche, South Dakota, to hold up the Butte County Bank. With them were Peep O'Day, Wat the Watch Punteney, and the Sundance Kid. The six outlaws got only $100 in silver and bills, and O'Day was immediately captured during a ludicrous struggle to get mounted. First his horse shied. Then, in desperation, he tried to mount a mule but was overpowered. A posse caught up with the others at a ranch twelve miles away. After much wild gunfire that inflicted no serious injury, the bandits were led off to the Deadwood jail. The Logans and Curry promptly escaped and O'Day was acquitted. The bank officials, enraged and convinced that the permissive jurors

Left: Charles A. Siringo, cowboy detective employed by Pinkerton, who spied on Wild Bunch so effectively that he spoiled Cassidy's plans for a "Train Robbers Syndicate." Above: Sundance Kid and his mistress, Etta Place, photographed in New York before taking ship for Argentina.

235

of Deadwood had no intention of convicting those still in custody, dropped the charges.

Soon afterward most of the desperadoes from Hole in the Wall convened at Brown's Hole. Cassidy was so impressed that he proposed the establishment of a new confederation, which he pretentiously dubbed The Train Robbers Syndicate. He had come to the same conclusion as others who were graduating from town raids and rustling to holding up express cars. The Syndicate had a central clique: Cassidy himself, Flat Nose George Curry, the Logans, the Sundance Kid, Bill Carver, Camilla "Deaf Charley" Hanks, Harry Tracy, a cousin of the Logans named Bob Lee, and Ben Kilpatrick, who liked to be called The Tall Texan and was so described on reward handbills. In a way, Laura Bullion was also included. One of the first of the gum-chewing gangsters' molls, she began as a camp follower, passed from hand to hand as she cheerfully admitted, because "they felt sorry for me." The romantically named Tall Texan, illiterate and a simpleton, had never had a steady consort. He fell in love with her and thereafter they were inseparable.

The Syndicate leaders made elaborate plans, concocted a code, and sent riders out to bribe railway employees and scout for banks and mine shipments. But the great scheme was crippled from the outset by a thin, grizzled, laconic vagrant who rode into the outlaw settlement, introduced himself as Charles L. Carter, and, upon being told who his hosts were, became jovial (though he continued to wear his holster tied down to his thigh with a rawhide thong to facilitate a fast draw). After a while, when he serenely admitted being a fugitive charged with murder, he was accepted by the Syndicate. Charles L. Carter was Pinkerton operative Charles A. Siringo, one of the two or three most famous and successful cowboy detectives. He won the gang's confidence completely, then

vanished from Cassidy Point and supplied enough information to J. P. McParland, Pinkerton's Denver superintendent, to reschedule and reroute money shipments, launch an investigation of suspected bribe-takers, intercept and analyze messages, and make scattered arrests of Cassidy scouts. The gang leaders, realizing they had been hoodwinked, delayed operations. For the next few years Siringo and an almost equally famous cowboy detective, Bill Sayles, traveled thousands of miles to trail various members of the Wild Bunch and keep the gang running, thus drastically reducing opportunities for robberies.

But at first no attempt was made to dislodge the bandit nest at Brown's Hole, and newspapers printed editorials to the effect that lawmen were afraid to go in. During the spring of 1898 the governors of Colorado, Utah, and Wyoming finally reacted by agreeing on a coordinated effort to exterminate the Wild Bunch. Before a campaign could be organized, a drunken outlaw called

Swede Johnson shot and killed a sixteen-year-old boy at a steer-wrestling contest on the ranch of Valentine Hoy, an honest cattleman whose land edged Brown's Hole. Johnson then rode off while the victim, Willie Strang, writhed in the dust. On the trail to Cassidy's stronghold he met Harry Tracy and Dave Lant, and soon the three bandits were joined by a whiskey runner named Jack Bennett. Hoy gave chase with a posse of ranchers. The cattlemen surrounded the outlaws in a gorge, and Hoy was killed in the inevitable battle. The posse caught and hanged Bennett, then sent for reinforcements and followed the other badmen, who had slipped past them and out of the draw.

The weather in the high country turned bitterly cold before the posse overtook the outlaws at Lookout Mountain. There was a gunfight lasting seven hours before Johnson and Lant surrendered. The possemen simply picked up Harry Tracy; he was too exhausted and frostbitten to pull the trigger again as they approached. Colorado tried Lant and Tracy on pending charges, while Johnson was held in Wyoming and convicted of the Strang murder. Lant and Tracy escaped, were recaptured, escaped again. Lant returned to Hole in the Wall before drifting on. Tracy headed into the Northwest, later to terrorize Oregon and Washington. Johnson's murder conviction was reversed, and after serving only two years on a Colorado rustling charge he drifted into obscurity.

In the aftermath of the Strang and Hoy killings, spokesmen for the Union Pacific, Adams Express, and various stockmen's associations demanded that militiamen invade and destroy the outlaw camps at Robber's Roost, Brown's Hole, and Hole in the Wall. But J. S. Hoy, brother of the slain rancher, suggested to the Denver papers that each of the three states involved could accomplish the objective faster and more efficiently by simply offering a $1,000 reward for every Wild Bunch member,

dead or alive. Cassidy and his men were enraged and obviously alarmed. They retaliated by attacking Hoy's cattle camps, killing the horses and steers, burning the cabins. Rewards were offered for known members of the band (though not dead or alive), so Curry, Cassidy, and the others attending their councils of war decided the Bunch should stay away from the usual hideouts and keep on the move, at least for a while.

That spring war was declared on Spain. Cassidy, in an excess of patriotic zeal after reading about the frontier cowboys enlisting in Theodore Roosevelt's Rough Riders, proposed to his friends that they form a regiment to be called the Wild Bunch Riders. When reminded that they would be arrested the moment they appeared at any enlistment center, Cassidy decided they might find equal excitement and greater profit by returning to an earlier plan involving the Union Pacific's Overland Flyer. At 2:30 a.m. on June 2, 1899, near Wilcox, Wyoming, a red lantern flagged the train. Cassidy, honoring his promise to the Wyoming governor, stayed away but George Curry, Harvey Logan, and Elza Lay were there with dynamite. When the messenger refused to open the express-car door, they blew it open and took $60,000 in unsigned Adams Express banknotes to which they could forge signatures.

There has been some confusion about the names the badmen were using at the time of the holdup. Flat Nose George Curry was not Big Nose George Parrott, as he is still occasionally called in histories of American crime; Parrott had been hanged almost two decades before. And Harvey Logan was already beginning to call himself Kid Curry in tribute to the man he most admired. Later, when Flat Nose George Curry was dead, Logan achieved greater infamy as Kid Curry.

A tremendous manhunt was organized at Wilcox. Near Salt Creek the bandits made a brief stand against a

*Dead men, held upright by citizens in this
photograph, have sometimes been erroneously identified
as Daltons. "X" drawn on ground is
between feet of Ben Kilpatrick, killed during attempted
train robbery near San Angelo, Texas, in 1911.
Second corpse, labeled "Ed Welch" in one old caption, appears
to be Kilpatrick's accomplice, Howard Benson.*

Above: Trailing ball and chain from his right foot,
prisoner stands in doorway of first jail in Enid, Oklahoma, in
1903, and two other convicts are manacled together
at left. Such towns mushroomed first when homesteading
lands were opened and then after oil strikes, but they
were soon tamed. Right: Texas Rangers Frank Hamer (in dark
hat) and Duke Hudson at Del Rio, Texas, one of
several border smuggling towns they helped tame. Hamer also
brought law to roaring Texas oil towns such as Mexia.

contingent from Casper, killing a posseman named Tom McDonald. The next day there was another fight, in which Kid Curry mortally wounded Sheriff Joe Hazen of Converse County. But Cassidy, as usual, had provided relays of fresh horses at predetermined spots on the escape route, and the bandits outran hundreds of pursuers. They rode to Hole in the Wall but stayed only long enough to divide the loot. Then they scattered. Elza Lay joined Black Jack Ketchum and hid in New Mexico. After the shooting for which Ketchum was hanged, Lay was captured near Carlsbad and sentenced to life in the penitentiary at Santa Fe. Paroled after about fifteen years, he married and settled at Baggs, Wyoming, where he worked as a ranch hand and then as an oil prospector, using the name William McGuinness. George Curry fled to Mexico with a band of horse thieves. Kid Curry joined Cassidy, who was waiting in New Mexico with the Sundance Kid.

In the summer of 1899, before Lay was captured, he participated with Kid Curry, Deaf Charley Hanks, and Sam Ketchum in an attempted train robbery at Folsom, New Mexico—Black Jack Ketchum's favorite spot for holdups. Hanks held the horses, as he often did. The others boarded the first coach as passengers, then climbed up over the coal tender to level their guns at the engineer

and fireman and force the train to stop. The messenger heard them in time to take the money from the express-car safe and hide it. As had happened before, the outlaws rode away without any loot.

More disasters were to follow. In Dodson, Missouri, Lonny Logan cashed a stolen Adams Express note, and Detective Bill Sayles was sent to investigate. Sayles and four possemen caught him in a snow-blanketed field outside the home of a kinswoman, outlaw Bob Lee's mother. He died in the snow. Then Bob Lee was arrested at the Antlers Gambling House in Cripple Creek, Colorado, and sent to the penitentiary for ten years for his part in a train robbery. And in April, 1900, possemen shot down Flat Nose George Curry, who had returned from Mexico only to be cornered at Thompson Springs, Utah. After that, Harvey Logan never used any name but Kid Curry.

The Pinkerton agents, bank and railroad detectives decided that further bloodshed and financial losses might be averted by offering amnesty and money to a chieftain among all these robbers. They offered to hire Butch Cassidy as a guard for the Union Pacific, and negotiations were under way when Cassidy, the Sundance Kid, Deaf Charley Hanks, and Kid Curry decided they might achieve the dream of many outlaws: a strike that would earn them passage to South America. Shortly after Union Pacific Train No. 3 passed the Tipton, Wyoming, station on an August evening in 1900, Cassidy and Kid Curry dropped from the tender to the engineer's cab and brought the train to a stop on a long uphill grade. The express car was supposed to be carrying $100,000 consigned to the Bank of the Philippines, but somehow the railroad detectives had become suspicious and rerouted the money. The bandits blew open the safe, inadvertently using too large a blast, demolishing part of the express car and destroying currency that would have been part of the loot. They collected just $50.40. While Hanks held the horses and Cassidy worked at the safe, the Sundance Kid and Kid Curry relieved coach passengers of several hundred dollars, twenty pocket watches, eighteen lapel watches, and seven gold hatpins and hairpins.

Since the funds garnered at Tipton were hardly sufficient to finance retirement to South America, Cassidy made another "raise," as holdups were called, less than a month later. With Kid Curry, the Sundance Kid, and Bill Carver he robbed the First National Bank of Winnemucca, Nevada, taking $32,640. The popular literature invariably depicts Cassidy as the undisputed leader of the Wild Bunch and the Sundance Kid as his closest friend and most valued henchman. Actually, the Kid participated in only a few of the robberies before the gang began to disintegrate, and the leader was sometimes Cassidy, sometimes—as at Winnemucca—Kid Curry. Among the many reward notices distributed in an effort to apprehend the Wild Bunch leaders was a 1902 Pinkerton handbill offering $4,000 in connection with the Winnemucca robbery. It listed "George Parker, alias 'Butch' Cassidy, alias George Cassidy, alias Ingerfield," and "Harry Longbaugh, alias 'Kid' Longbaugh, alias Harry Alonzo, alias 'The Sundance Kid,'" describing both as "members of the Harvey Logan alias 'Kid' Curry band."

Another myth is that the outlaws clowningly heralded the twentieth century by using bicycles instead of horses to make a fast escape after one of their robberies. What really happened was that Cassidy, inebriated, rode a bicycle up and down the streets of Fort Worth's red-light district to the cheers of girls leaning from the windows of the crib houses. After Winnemucca, the gang leaders assembled in Fort Worth to hide, celebrate, rest, and debate whether to leave the country or try for still another big raise. During an extended binge, five of them—Cassidy,

Longbaugh, Kid Curry, Bill Carver, and Ben Kilpatrick —bought the finest available city clothes and posed for a group portrait at the Main Street photographic studio of John Swartz. Later the Pinkerton office obtained a print of the photograph. The outlaws spent much of their time at the sporting house of Fannie Porter, a brothel-keeper who augmented her considerable profits by harboring fugitives. On a drunken whim Bill Carver married one of Fannie's girls, Lillie Davis. He and Kid Curry then took Lillie and another of the girls, Maud Walker, on a "honeymoon" tour but abandoned them in Denver. Subsequently, Lillie Davis eagerly identified the men in the Swartz photograph for William Pinkerton.

Kilpatrick, having no desire for Madam Porter's protégées or anyone but his mistress, took Laura Bullion to stay with his kin at a ranch near Sonora, Texas. She was using the name Della Rose and was sometimes called The Rose of the Wild Bunch, but she no longer dallied with any of them except Kilpatrick. Carver came to visit the now-monogamous couple, and one day rode into town with Kilpatrick's young brother George. Sheriff E. S. Briant, seeing them emerge from a general store, recognized Carver. When the sheriff and a deputy tried to arrest him, Carver and George Kilpatrick dropped their bundles and reached for their guns. The lawmen killed them both.

In Fort Worth, meanwhile, Fannie Porter lost two of her newest and handsomest girls to the Bunch when Kid Curry took Annie Rogers as his mistress and Harry Longbaugh went away with Etta Place, an adventuress with the appearance of a delicate cameo. Longbaugh and his lovely consort departed for New York City, traveling as Mr. and Mrs. Harry Place and accompanied by a man who introduced himself as James Lowe—Butch Cassidy's new alias.

Soon Mrs. Place's bosom was adorned with an expensive gold lapel watch bought for her, according to tradi-

Top: Dawson City at height of Klondike gold rush, when throngs of prospectors filled streets and saloons, furnishing easy prey for gamblers, footpads, and saloon keepers who dispensed knockout drops and occasionally bullets. Bottom: Saloon in Pecos, Texas, in 1880's, when outlaws still sought refuge in southwestern towns. Seated at faro table in white hat is Jim Miller, one of several badmen who were lynched at Ada, Oklahoma, in 1909.

tion, by Mr. Place at Tiffany's (though it might just as well have been filched from a railroad passenger somewhere in the West). After having photographs made at a fashionable salon, the couple boarded the *S. S. Soldier Prince*, bound for Buenos Aires. Cassidy was to have embarked with them, but a letter from Kid Curry persuaded him to rejoin the Bunch for a last train robbery. On July 3, 1901, as the Great Northern Express No. 3 pulled away from the little station at Malta, Montana, Kid Curry jumped aboard the baggage car. Climbing over the coal tender, he leveled a gun at the engineer and fireman and ordered a stop at a bridge near the town of Wagner. Deaf Charley Hanks was holding the horses there. With him were Cas-

sidy, Kilpatrick, and Laura Bullion. On more than one previous occasion Laura had probably waited with a relay of fresh horses. This time she was at the scene of the holdup, dressed like a cowboy and holding a rifle. She and Kilpatrick guarded the trainmen and passengers while Cassidy and Curry blew the safe open. They rode away with $40,000, mostly in unsigned bank notes and blank money orders. The notes were negotiable as soon as the spurious signature of a bank president and cashier could be affixed—a simple matter of forgery. The money orders could be filled out and cashed with equal ease. While William Pinkerton launched an investigation from Denver, the Great Northern Express Company publicized a

$6,500 reward, and $5,000 more was added by the Union Pacific and the Adams Express Company.

All the robbers but one headed straight back to Fort Worth. Kid Curry made a two-hundred-mile detour to seek revenge, shooting and killing Jim Winters, the rancher who had slain brother Johnny Logan. Soon after that the gang scattered for the last time.

Cassidy boarded a train for New York and from there took a steamer to Buenos Aires to join the Sundance Kid and Etta, who were making discreet inquiries about the availability of Argentine land for homesteading.

Ben Kilpatrick and Laura Bullion were found in St. Louis after passing forged banknotes. Laura went to prison for five years and lived with relatives while faithfully awaiting Kilpatrick's release. He was paroled in 1911, then tried and acquitted of an old charge of murder stemming from a Texas gun duel. Again he was released. A few months later he and a former cellmate, Howard Benson, boarded the Southern Pacific Sunset Flyer No. 5 at San Angelo, Texas. As the train neared Sanderson, they broke into the express car. Benson went forward into a mail car to pilfer it while Kilpatrick ordered the messenger, David A. Trousdale, to open the express safe, which held $50,000 in cash and jewels. Trousdale surreptitiously reached for a large ice mallet leaning against the safe, and with one blow killed Ben Kilpatrick. Then, with

Left: Tent camp set up at Skagway, Alaska, in 1897 by prospectors waiting for good weather that would permit them to pack over Chilkoot Pass into Klondike. At this time Soapy Smith ruled Skagway with his band of cutthroats, relieving men like these of their savings or gold dust. Above: Monte Carlo, miners' favorite gambling house at Nome, Alaska, when new gold strike drew them from Dawson and Skagway to last boom town on arctic coast.

243

PACKERS ASCENDING SUMMIT OF CHILKOOT PASS
COPYRIGHT 1898

the outlaw's gun, he killed Benson as well.

Kid Curry was already dead. Captured in 1901 after shooting two patrolmen in Knoxville, Tennessee, he had escaped and appeared two years later at Parachute, Colorado, using the name Tap Duncan and working as a cowboy. In 1903, after an attempted train robbery near Parachute, he was killed in a night-long gun battle with possemen. Deaf Charley Hanks was dead, too. Hiding in Nashville during the fall of 1901, he had run out of money and tried to cash a forged bond. He was dressed so raggedly that a suspicious bank guard sent for the police and then tried to question him. Dashing outside, Hanks escaped on a passing ice wagon as bullets whistled past. Lawmen, communicating by wire and telephone, spread a dragnet and he was finally shot down.

But Cassidy and the Sundance Kid were thriving in a distant country. James Lowe and Mr. and Mrs. Harry Place had filed for and received an Argentinian homesteading grant—four leagues of land in Chubut Province. By the spring of 1903 they had purchased herds of sheep, cattle, and horses. Perhaps they might have continued to live as peaceful ranchers if a Pinkerton operative named Frank Dimaio had not arrived in Buenos Aires, consulted the local authorities, and distributed stacks of reward circulars. There is also a possibility, however, that honest ranching was only a temporary expedient and a cover while Cassidy and Longbaugh reconnoitered banks, mines, company stores, and the Argentine railroads. In any event, so many would-be reward collectors were hunting for them by 1906 that their ranch was no longer safe. That spring they robbed a bank at Villa Mercedes, San Luis. Etta Place, wearing a stylish English riding habit, held the horses. Some of the $20,000 loot was used to send her to New York for medical treatment; she had fallen ill, and the tentative diagnosis was appendicitis. The Sun-

dance Kid accompanied her part of the way but stopped in Denver. There he got roaring drunk and shot up a saloon, after which he fled back to Argentina. Etta Place disappeared forever after reaching New York.

A few months after their first Argentine robbery, Cassidy and Longbaugh held up another bank at Bahia Blanca, then made their way into Bolivia, where mining companies were hiring drifters as well as native laborers. It was a time of heavy North American and European investment in mining operations, transportation companies, and other newly expanded enterprises in underdeveloped Latin countries. Among the managers, technicians, and employees with special skills there seemed to be at least as many Anglo-Saxon as Spanish names. Even among laborers without special skills there were plenty of aliens, some of them wanted for crimes committed in the States. If they wished to work few questions were asked. For a while Cassidy and Longbaugh slept in the barracks of the Concordia Tin Mines at La Paz, where they worked as wranglers and mule drivers. Cassidy called himself Santiago Maxwell and Longbaugh was Enrique Brown.

They disappeared from the mines long enough to establish a brigands' camp in the rain forest and to rob a mine train at Eucalyptus. They returned, then vanished again, this time to roam through adjacent portions of Bolivia, Peru, Argentina, and Chile, robbing banks, stores, trains. In North America they had already been immortalized by an early movie entitled *The Wild Bunch*. Like another early film called *The Great Train Robbery*, it inspired at least a few naïve young thrill-seekers to attempt imitation. The emulators were no more successful with trains and banks than Pearl Hart had been with stagecoaches. While police in the States were being harrassed by amateur bandits, two ruthless professionals were introducing the methods of the genuine Wild Bunch

Two views of Chilkoot Pass in 1898. At top,
prospectors too impatient to await spring thaw have formed
awesome cavalcade up steep, hard-packed trail.
At bottom, large encampment has been established during bad
weather or difficulties over customs inspection by
Northwest Mounted Police. Some prospectors returned to
Skagway—temporarily, they thought—only to be
tossed dead into alleys or off wharves by Soapy Smith's men.

to the pampas. In autumn, 1907, while seizing several thousand dollars from the Compania Mercantile at Rio Gallegos, Argentina, they killed the company manager and wounded his assistant. In several countries, military patrols began searching for the *Yanqui* desperadoes.

The last holdup occurred early in 1909, when Cassidy and Longbaugh learned of a mule train that would be carrying a payroll to the Aploca Mine in Bolivia. There was a suitcase full of money strapped to one of the saddle mules. They stopped the drivers and took the mule bearing the money—a big, silver-gray animal, easily recognized. They fled into the mountains, to the village of San Vicente, fifteen miles from the holdup scene. There an innkeeper recognized the stolen mule and sent for a detachment of Bolivian cavalry stationed nearby.

When the soldiers arrived, the outlaws were resting in a patio containing a hut and enclosed by an adobe wall. An officer shouted to them to surrender. Accounts differ as to whether Cassidy or Longbaugh fired the first shot. As a soldier fell dying, some of his companions surrounded the wall while others began firing through the gate. The outlaws, well supplied with ammunition, continued to return the fire until late in the evening. Then there was silence. The soldiers waited for the light of morning and then went in. Butch Cassidy and the Sundance Kid were dead. Some witnesses reported that both had been shot by the soldiers, others that one or both, realizing the impossibility of escape, had committed suicide.

By the turn of the century the dangers of outlawry in the United States were beginning to outweigh the temptations. Regions where money could be found were becoming thickly populated and protected by police. Harry Tracy, after escaping from the jail at Aspen, Colorado, had decided against returning to the Wild Bunch. Instead he made his way to Seattle and then Portland, where he was unknown and where no plague of holdups had concentrated the forces of the law. For a while he worked on a railroad. In a saloon one day in 1898 he met a gambler and petty thief named Dave Merrill. Before long he had married Merrill's sister Rose and settled in a cottage on the Willamette River at Portland. He and Merrill then initiated a wave of armed robberies. Wearing false-face masks of the sort made for children's parties, they held up saloons, stores, and logging offices.

Because Merrill could not resist boasting, a police informer soon learned the identities of the "false-face bandits." Detective Dan Weiner arrested Merrill, who forthwith agreed to lure Tracy into a trap. Tracy fired at the arresting policemen, then leaped aboard a Southern Pacific locomotive, forced the engineer off, and would have raced the train away if a conductor had not pulled the emergency brake cord. He went to prison still unaware that his brother-in-law had betrayed him. In the penitentiary Tracy bribed a guard and arranged for a recently freed convict to smuggle rifles and a rope ladder to him. In 1902 he and Merrill broke out. Tracy killed six guards and Merrill shot down a prisoner who tried to interfere.

The escape brought on the greatest manhunt in western history. Volunteers were deputized to assist peace officers and the two hundred and fifty men of National Guard Company F. Literally thousands of searchers combed northern Oregon and the lower half of Washington.

At a farm where Tracy held a family hostage while resting and eating, he saw a newspaper article about Merrill's role in his arrest. He killed his partner before going on. He forced the owner of a fishing boat at Olympia to take him up to Seattle, and after robbing a saloon continued northward. At Bothell he shot down three possemen, then doubled back and killed several more near

Top: Troupe of actresses—who may well have doubled in brass beds as employees of Soapy Smith—at cloud-dappled Happy Camp, en route to Klondike. Bottom: Miners with pack train in Dyea Canyon, bound for same destination.

Seattle. Before he was finally cornered he had killed ten pursuers, while receiving only a single wound in all the gun battles.

Early in August, 1902, a posse found him at the Eddy Ranch, near Creston, Washington. When they closed in, he was helping his captive hosts to build a barn. A bullet hit Tracy's leg, ending any hope of escape. As he lay in a wheat field, watching armed men picketing the hedgerows around him, he put the muzzle of his rifle against his head and pulled the trigger for the last time.

There were still a few wild towns in the States, a few pockets of outlawry, but after the turn of the century such places were tamed fast. Troublesome Texas border towns like El Paso and Del Rio were ideal ports of entry and exit for rumrunners, thieves, fugitives, narcotics smugglers, and purveyors of stolen goods. But at the end of the First World War, even before the Border Patrol was established, the Texas Ranger force was substantially increased and other law-enforcement agencies were similarly strengthened. As the border difficulties subsided, an oil boom gathered force in Texas and Oklahoma. Oilmen's camps grew into tent and shanty towns and sometimes more permanent settlements. The populations of some communities grew by many thousands in a few weeks, without benefit of organized government or law enforcement. Yet the opportunities for brigands were not what they had been in earlier wild places.

An exemplary case was that of Mexia, an oil-boom town southeast of Dallas, but until 1921 a quiet country settlement of about twenty-five hundred inhabitants. That fall a driller struck oil and some thirty thousand newcomers choked the streets. Those looking for work in the oil fields were outnumbered by gamblers, speculators, swindlers, bootleggers, robbers, pimps, prostitutes. Stills peppered the woods outside town, bars opened to dispense bootleg liquor, and the hotel was turned into a gambling house—the first of eighteen, some of them mere tents erected in the business district. Suddenly the town was lawless and the older citizens were afraid. They appealed to Governor Pat Neff, who called in several undercover agents and then sent for Ranger Captain Frank Hamer, a lawman soon to become famous for tracking down Clyde Barrow and Bonnie Parker as motorized, macadamized crime replaced old-fashioned outlawry.

The undercover agents reported that Mexia's crime was concentrated in two bootlegging and gambling establishments called the Winter Garden and the Chicken Farm, where guards searched the customers and patrolled the premises with shotguns, pistols, rifles, and submachine guns. The agents also reported that peace officers from Limestone and Freestone counties were dealing openly with the criminals. Hamer arrived in Mexia with twenty-two men, including a pair of Federal agents. They shot their way into the two establishments, captured the owners and many henchmen, and confiscated gambling equipment, more than six hundred quarts of whiskey, a large cache of narcotics, and an arsenal of weapons. Within three days after the Rangers rode into town, hundreds of arrests had been made. However, local graft-takers, fancying themselves latter-day Roy Beans, began to warn suspects whenever a search warrant was issued. The Governor declared martial law and sent in the National Guard. Faced with such a show of power, the corrupt local officials ended their cooperation with the remaining rumrunners and vice peddlers. In less than two months one of the wildest of the new boom towns had been domesticated. Law and order came equally fast and forcefully to other such communities.

The last of America's truly wild frontiers opened in Alaska with the discovery of gold in the Yukon's Klondike

Region in 1897 and another lode at Nome, Alaska, the following year. The Yukon was Canadian territory but was choked with Americans, and the gateway to the Klondike was Skagway, Alaska. There were two ways to reach the Klondike diggings. One was to steam from Seattle up to Norton Sound, below Nome on the western arctic coast, and then east all the way across the Alaska Territory on the Yukon River. A much shorter, though more dangerous and rigorous way, was to steam from Seattle to Skagway, then pack over the Chilkoot Pass to Lake Bennett, the Yukon headwaters, and build boats to go downriver to Dawson. That was the favored route.

As word of new gold discoveries spread, men by the thousands arrived. Among them, inevitably, were unscrupulous adventurers, fugitives, outlaws who came not to mine for gold but to prey on the miners. There was an old song that had been popular during all the gold rushes since the Forty-Niners had pushed to California, and had probably been sung as far away as the Argentine. Once again in Alaska men gathered in saloons and sang a raucous chorus: "Oh, what was your name in the States?/Was it Thompson or Johnson or Bates?/Did you murder your wife and fly for your life?/Say, what was your name in the States?"

Dawson was a raw Yukon outpost where quarrels were settled in the saloons or in the snow and mud with guns, knives, clubs, and boot heels, but Skagway was worse, especially after the arrival of Soapy Smith.

Jefferson Randolph Smith of Georgia was tall, handsomely bearded, soft-spoken, well-dressed, and merciless. He was born in 1860. In San Antonio at the end of the Reconstruction Period he mastered several shell games and the art of never losing at three-card monte. During the early 1880's he toured the gold camps from Denver to Leadville, fleecing the miners. He became a small power in Denver politics, though he was charged with four murders. Released three times for lack of evidence, he was tried and acquitted in the fourth case.

One of his favorite quick-money schemes was to set up a peddling stand in a small town or gold camp, load it with bars of soap, and shout to a gathering crowd that several of the bars were prizes—packed with a twenty-dollar bill inside the wrapper. He was selling chances, not soap. He was, after all, not a peddler but a gambler. The skeptics watched as a stranger bought a bar, unwrapped it, and whooped with joy upon uncovering a twenty-dollar bill. No one else found a prize but a lot of soap was purchased at high prices before Smith and the stranger moved on.

In 1892 Soapy Smith opened a saloon and gambling hall called the Orleans Club in Creede, Colorado. Neither the drinks nor the games were honest, but at first there were few complaints because the owner quickly took control of the town. He organized fellow swindlers and thieves into a Gamblers' Trust, installed himself as president, and gave orders to all local officeholders. He survived several gunfights and many threats before the citizenry was seized with the fervor of reform. But when newly elected, honest officials ordered him to move on, he showed little resistance. The local silver lode was dwindling.

He returned to Denver but found himself so unwelcome that a long visit might have proved foolhardy. Next he appeared in Butte, Montana, where he probably was caught cheating at cards in the Clipper Shades Saloon. In any event there was an altercation that ended in his shooting down saloonkeeper Jack Jolly. He left hastily to seek opportunities in the lower Northwest. The police of Portland and Seattle were giving him cause to consider another precipitate move when the great Klondike gold strikes occurred.

At Skagway he found conditions ideal. Canada's Northwest Mounted Police visited Dawson, but Skagway was on the American side of the boundary. Deputy Marshal Frank Canton, brought from Wyoming to Alaska at the request of trading-post owners who foresaw a wave of lawlessness, was iced-in hundreds of miles away on Big Minook Creek, and in the spring he planned to push on to Dawson, too far away to be a threat. When Smith disembarked at Skagway there were only two lawmen to patrol Alaska's entire Yukon River District.

A candle could be sold for a dollar, a cord of firewood for twenty-five. Prostitutes, gamblers, and footpads were arriving daily from the States. When the onset of winter froze the Yukon River and kept prospectors in town, thousands of men had little to occupy them but drinking, gambling, and womanizing. Smith assembled a gang of armed cutthroats and became ruler of Skagway. He opened two drinking, gaming, and whoring emporiums, The Mining Exchange and Jeff's Place. His crooked gamblers took large sums of money from the customers, as did the bartenders who sold his whiskey at inflated prices. A man who lost no money at the tables or the bars was in danger of being knocked senseless, robbed, and tossed into an alley.

Smith's employees began plundering the warehouses on the harbor wharves and holding up men in the streets. A minister was robbed of funds he was raising for a reform movement. A woman was robbed and murdered in her own room. In 1898, a few days after Smith, astride a white horse, led the town's Fourth of July parade, a henchman named Ed Fay killed a new deputy marshal. Some of the townspeople could bear no more. They organized a vigilante committee to hang the murderer. Smith notified them that if they attempted a lynching his men would enforce law and order. The committee was sufficiently intimidated to cancel the hanging, but the community's leaders then joined the vigilantes and the movement gained momentum. One of the organizers was Frank Reid, a civil engineer who had laid out the town of Skagway and was ready to fight, even to risk his life, to make it decent.

Smith could not believe that the vigilantes, now calling themselves the Committee of 101, would risk armed conflict with his men. While the meetings were in session he lured a miner into one of his saloons and robbed him of $2,700 in gold dust. A committee spokesman gave Smith until four that afternoon to return the money. When Smith replied that he had more armed men than the vigilantes could muster, another committee meeting was held in a warehouse. Reid and three companions stood guard outside to prevent any of Smith's men from entering. Smith himself appeared, carrying a rifle. When Reid told him he could not pass, Smith fired. Reid fell, then raised his revolver and put a bullet through Soapy Smith's heart. Reid clung to life for twelve days, and died knowing that all of Smith's gang had been shipped at gunpoint to Sitka and Seattle. Every one of them was sent to prison.

At precisely the same time, rich gold deposits were discovered at Nome, and in a single month two thousand men left the Dawson-Skagway area for the new strike. Eighteen thousand were panning Nome's beaches when the rush peaked in 1900. A coastal Eskimo village had become the last wild boom town of the North. In a book called *A Dog Puncher in the Yukon*, Arthur Treadwell Walden described his adventures during five years on that frontier, and he described Nome as he found it in 1900:

> Robbery of every description was in full swing. . . . The men down here seemed to be more quarrelsome than they were in Dawson. . . . At one time it was proved here that all three sheriffs and deputy sheriffs had done time in the peniten-

tiary. One of them made his living by robbing the drunks he arrested.

One day two men and I were given a dose of knock-out drops. . . . As we had had a drink in three different saloons, it was impossible to tell which one had done the trick. Two of us were already busted and lost nothing, but the other man was robbed of six hundred dollars.

That was also the year when Judge Arthur H. Noyes was appointed to Nome's judicial district and arrived with his silent partner, Alexander McKenzie. Noyes neglected to try the five accused murderers who were being held for his arrival, but he was most energetic about drawing up and signing fraudulent papers taking into receivership five of the richest claims on Anvil Creek. McKenzie then set out with a group of armed hirelings and evicted the rightful owners.

It was a performance in the old style, worthy of Sheriff Henry Plummer's gang or Wyatt Earp or Soapy Smith. But Plummer had been lynched a generation earlier, and Smith's recent revival of piracy had been stopped by a vigilante's bullet. Earp was right there in Nome at the turn of the century, running the Dexter Saloon and casting about for the kind of triumphs that seemed to come so easily to shrewder men like Noyes and McKenzie. However, Earp had already suffered a face-slapping by Marshal Albert Lowe and conditions in Nome were so disappointing that he would soon return to the States. Noyes and McKenzie, too, were mistaken in their appraisal of time and place. The age of brute force was drawing to a close. Overt piracy was already such an anachronism that the robbed Nome miners felt no need for a vigilance committee or the hired guns that once guarded against claim jumpers and fought range wars. They simply sent delegates to San Francisco to seek legal redress.

McKenzie served a short prison term as a result, and Noyes was removed from the bench and fined a thousand dollars. The miners retrieved their property. Already a detachment of Army troops had been dispatched to Nome to maintain order. By 1905 a telegraph station was operating from nearby Port Safety, and Nome's residents could communicate speedily with the authorities in Canada and the States.

The gold veins were declining. The fishing industry and lumber would soon be of more interest than prospecting. The universal human need for stability had proved as strong as the imperative of Manifest Destiny, spreading west and north to the farthest sea. Constables patrolled the streets of towns in the Far North as they did in New England. The badmen were gone, the frontiers civilized.

Jefferson Randolph Smith, southern gambling man who became scourge of Skagway on far northwestern frontier. One of America's last old-fashioned badmen, he was killed by one of America's last vigilantes. In death he looked childishly innocent, as if he had merely done what was expected.

Picture Credits

Cover: Glenn Shirley Western Collection

THE PAINTED WEST
9: Paine Art Center & Arboretum, Oshkosh, WI. 10-11: TG. 12-13, 14-15: Amon Carter Museum of Western Art, Fort Worth, TX. 16: TG.

CHAPTER 1   LEGEND AND REALITY
18-19: NYPL. 20: CP. 22, 23: GS. 25: Shelburne Museum, Shelburne, VT. 26, 27: CP.

CHAPTER 2   AMERICA'S FIRST BADMEN
28-29: Aberdeen Art Gallery and Museum, Scotland. 30, 30-31, 32, 33: Bucks County Historical Society, Doylestown, PA. 34: CP. 36: NYPL. 37: CP. 38, 39: NYPL. 40: CP. 41: NYPL.

CHAPTER 3   WESTERN EXPANSION
42-43: TG. 44: Division of Commerce and Industrial Development, Jefferson City, MO. 46-47: NYPL. 47 (inset): EPC. 48: LC. 49, 50: State Historical Society of Missouri, Columbia. 51: LC. 52 (left): State Historical Society of Missouri, (right) GS. 53, 54 (top): State Historical Society of Missouri. 54 (bottom): LC. 55 (top): BB, (bottom) EPC. 57: GS. 60: CP. 61 (top): Wells Fargo Bank History Room, San Francisco, CA, (bottom) NYPL.

CHAPTER 4   WILD TOWNS AND VIGILANTES
62-63: Courtesy of the E.B. Crocker Art Gallery, Sacramento, CA. 64: TG. 65: EPC. 66-67: BB. 67 (bottom): Wells Fargo Bank History Room. 68, 69: LC. 70: Wells Fargo Bank History Room. 70-71: Courtesy of New York Historical Society, NY. 73: EPC. 74: California Historical Society, San Francisco. 75: GS. 76: California Historical Society. 77 (top): Courtesy of the Oakland Museum, CA, (bottom) Montana Historical Society, Helena. 78: LC. 79: Montana Historical Society. 81: TG.

CHAPTER 5   LAWLESS LAWMEN
82-83: TG. 84: LC. 86-87, 87 (bottom): CP. 86 (bottom): UOL. 89, 92: CP. 93: BB. 94 (top): Bianchi Leather Products, (bottom) BB. 96-97: EPC. 101: Wadsworth Atheneum, Hartford, CT. Ella Gallup Sumner and Mary Catlin Sumner Collection.

CHAPTER 6   GUNFIGHTS AND FEUDS
102-103: TG. 104: Whitney Gallery of Western Art, Cody, WY. 105: UOL. 106-107: R. W. Norton Art Gallery, Shreveport, LA. 110-111: CP. 112-113: Denver Public Library, Western Collection. Photo by Poley. 113 (top): NYPL. 114: TG. 115 (top): UOL, (bottom) Carl

Breihan. 118 (top & bottom left): GS. 118 (bottom right): UOL.

CHAPTER 7   THE RANGE WARS
120-121: CP. 123 (top): UOL, (bottom) Bettmann Archive. 124: EPC. 125: GS. 126: Bettmann Archive. 127: GS. 129 (top): New Mexico Department of Development, Santa Fe, (bottom left & right) GS. 132: UOL. 133, 134: Wyoming State Archives and Historical Department, Cheyenne. 136-137: CP. 139: Wyoming State Archives and Historical Department.

CHAPTER 8   THE FORT SMITH GALLOWS
140-141: Oklahoma Historical Society, Oklahoma City. 142, 144, 145, 146, 148, 149: GS. 152: UOL. 153, 154: GS. 156: Oklahoma Historical Society. 158: GS. 159: Kansas State Historical Society, Topeka. 160: Oklahoma Historical Society. 161 (top): Cunningham Collection, (bottom) GS. 162: NYPL. 163 (top): Bettmann Archive, (bottom) Kansas State Historical Society. 165: UOL.

CHAPTER 9   SOME BADWOMEN
166-167: UOL. 168: CP. 169: Montana Historical Society. 170-171: BB. 171 (top): CP. 172: GS. 172-173: Oklahoma Historical Society. 174 (left): UOL, (right) NYPL. 175 (left): LC, (right) EPC. 177, 178: NYPL. 179: Bancroft Library, University of California, Berkeley. 183 (top): NYPL, (bottom) UOL. 184: Arizona Historical Society Library, Tucson. 185: Amon Carter Museum.

CHAPTER 10   BORDER CLASHES
186-187: Amon Carter Museum. 188: CP. 191 (top): CP, (bottom) NYPL. 192-193: CP. 193 (inset): 194, 195: UOL. 196-197: GS. 198: BB. 199: CP. 200-201: BB. 201: LC. 202-203: BB. 205: NYPL.

CHAPTER 11   A ROGUES' GALLERY
206-207: Carl C. Seltzer. 208: Amon Carter Museum. 211: NYPL. 212: CP. 213 (top): State Historical Society of Missouri, (bottom) CP. 214-215: LC. 215 (left): UOL, (right) CP. 217: Wells Fargo Bank History Room. 218: Montana Historical Society. 219: CP. 221 (top): UOL, (bottom left & right) Carl Breihan. 222: BB. 223: UOL. 224: CP. 225: NYPL. 226: UOL. 227 (top): Bruce R. Douglas, (bottom) EPC.

CHAPTER 12   THE LAST WILD FRONTIERS
228-229: CP. 230, 231, 234: UOL. 235: BB. 236: CP. 238: UOL. 239: GS. 241 (top): BB, (bottom) UOL. 242-243: LC. 243, 244: BB. 247: LC. 251: Denver Public Library, Western Collection.

Index
Italic numbers refer to caption locations

King, James, 76
King, Luther, 98
Kloehr, John, 156
Klondike, *230*, *240*, *246*, 248-249, 251

L

Lake, Frank, 158
Lake, Stuart N., 100
Lane, Senator James, 46, 49
Langtry, Lily, 88, *97*
Lay, Elza, 223, 232, 234, 237, 239
Lee, Bob, 236, 239
Lee brothers, 151
Lee, Robert E., 190
Lefors, Joe, 138
Leonard, Bill, 98
Liddil, Dick, 56
Lincoln County War, 126-130
Lindsay, T. S., 161
Little Big Horn, 85
Little Britches, *see* Stevens, Jennie
Logan, Harry, *230*, 231-245
Logan, Lonny, 235, 236, 239
Longbaugh, Harry, *230*, 232, 235, *235*, 236-246
Longley, William Preston (Wild Bill), 93, *104*, 105, *106*, 109-116, *115*, 122
Loomis family, 40
Love, Harry, 70, 71, 72-74
Lowe, Albert, 100

M

Macnab, Frank, 128
Madame Moustache, 179
Madden, Bill, 232
Madero, Francisco, 198
Madsen, Chris, 157, 158, 161
Maledon, George, 143
Marcus, Josephine, 100
Martin, Michael, 37-40, *38*
Mason, Joe, 94
Mason, Sam, 32-35
Mast, Milton, 115, *115*
Masterson, Bat, 85, 87, 91, *92*, 94, 95
Masterson, Jim, 94, 157
Maverick Bill (1884), 133
McCall, Jack, 60
McCanles, David, 59
McCarty gang, 232, 233
McCarty, Henry, *see* Billy the Kid

McCloskey, Bill, 128
McCorkle, John, 49
McDougal, (Cattle) Annie, 181, *182*
McElhanie, Bill, 152, 153
McKenzie, Alexander, 251
McKenzie, Robert, 75
McKowen, Johnson, 110
McLaury, Frank, 98, 99
McLaury, Tom, 98, 99
McLean, Frank, *92*
McMahon, Frank, 119
McMasters, Sherman, 99, 100
McParland, J. P., 137
McSween, Alexander, 123, 126, 128
Meeks, Bob, 234
Merrill, Dave, 246
Middleton, John, 176
Miller, Clell, 56
Milton, Jeff, 119
Moderators, 26
Moore, Eugenia, *see* Quick, Florence
Morco, Happy Jack, 90, 91
Morgan, Pat, 117
Morose, Martin, 119
Morton, Buck, 128
Murieta, Joaquin, 21, 70, 72-74, *72*, 189
Murphy, Jim, 216
Murphy, L. G., 123
Murrell, John, *36*, 37
Muskogee, 92

N

Newcomb, George (Bitter Creek), 152, 153, 155, 157, 158
Nickell, Willie, 138
Nix, E. D., 157
Nixon, Tom, 214, 215
Norton, John (Brocky Jack), 90
Noyes, Arthur, 251

O

Obregon, Alvaro, 204
O'Day, Tom, 231, 235
O. K. Corral, gunfight at, 98-99
O'Keefe, Tom, 123
Orozco, Pasqual, 198
Overland Company, 79
Owen, J. G., 92

P

Parker, Bonnie, 248

Parker, George Leroy, *see* Cassidy, Butch
Parker (Judge) Isaac C., 24, 143-147, *145*, *147*, *149*, 164, 165, 176
Parker, Judy, 152
Parra, Ignacio, 194
Parrott, (Big Nose) George, 218, 219-220
Parsons, E. B., 85
Patton, George C., 203
Paul, Bob, 98-100
Payne, Ransom, 161
Pershing, John J., 201, 203
Philpot, Bud, 98
Pierce, Charlie, 155, 157, 158
Pinkerton Detective Agency, 209, 210
Piratical and Tragical Almanac, The, *32*
Pitts, Charlie, 56
Place, Etta, 182, 235, 240, 243, 245
Plummer, Henry, 58, *60*, 69, 79
Pony Express, 136
Pool, Dave, 49
Porter, Fannie, 182
Powers, Bill, 155, 156
Prostitution, in frontier West, 169-170, *176*, *178*
Punteney, Walter, 231-232, 235

Q

Quantrill, William Clarke, 31, *46*, 49, *49*, 52
Quick, Florence, *162*, 181

R

Raidler, Little Bill, 157, 158
Rainer, Al, 233
Rangers, 24
Range wars, 138
Red Legs, 46
Red Sash Gang, 231
Reed, Jim, 172, 174
Regulators, 24-26
Reid, Frank, 250
Remington, Frederic, 89, *106*, *118*, *158*, *189*, *198*, *209*
Reno brothers, 31, 209, 210
Rice, Sally, 35
Ridge, John Rollin, 74
Ringgold, John, 95
Ringo, Johnny, *see* Ringgold, John
River piracy, 32-33

Road agent, 21, *41*
Roberts, Betsy, 35
Roberts, Susan, 35
Roerig, Peter, 98
Rogers, Annie, 182
Rogers, Isaac, 162
Roosevelt, Theodore, 80
Rose of the Cimarron, *see* Dunn, Rose
Runnels, Randy, 65
Rush, Dave, *142*
Russell, Charles M., *115*
Ruxton, George Frederick, 24

S

Sampson, Sam, *154*
Sampson's Flats, battle of, 222
Samuel, Dr. Reuben, 50, 52, 53
San Francisco, 70, 74-79
Sawyer, Lew, 114
Sayles, Bill, 236, 239
Scarborough, George, 119
Schieffelin, Ed, 95
Selman, the Constables, 119
Seltzer, O. C., 80, 104, *209*
Setter, Bill, 35
Shadley, Lafe, 157
Sharkey, Tom, 100
Shelby County War, 24
Sherman, William, 79
Short, Ed, 155
Short, Luke, *92*, 95
Shown, John, 92
Sieber, Al, 190, *194*
Simmons, Dell, 157
Sims, W. H., 91
Sippy, Ben, 96
Siringo, Charles, *235*, 236
"Skinners," 31, *41*
Slade, Joseph A., 80
Slaughter, John, 95-96
Slayback, Alonzo, 65
Smith, Bill, *142*
Smith, Jefferson Randolph (Soapy),
    180, 231, 249-251, *251*
Snively, William Daniel, 35
Sohn, Alf, 157
Sontag brothers, 220-222, *223*
Spear, John, 109
Speed, Dick, 157
Spence, Pete, 99
Spicer, Wells, 99

Standish, Miles, 21
Stanley, Henry Morton, 60
Starr, Belle, 70, 151, 152, 156,
    170, *172*, *174*, 176
Starr, Henry, *156*, *158*, 164-165
Starr, Pearl, 172, 173, 175, 176, 179
Starr, Sam, 151, 176
Starr, Tom, 174
Sterling, John, 90
Stevens, Jennie (Little Britches),
    181, 182
Stewart, Henri, 143
Stewart, Virgil, 37
Stilwell, Frank, 99
Story, William, 92, 145
Stuart, Charles, 114
Stuart, Granville, 80, 133
Stuart, James, 75
Stuart's Stranglers, 80, *80*
Sufrin, Mark, 105
Sundance Kid, *see* Longbaugh, Harry
Sutton-Taylor Feud, 110-111, 117
Sweetwater (Texas), 91
Sydney Ducks, the, 74

T

Taylor, Jim, 117
Tensleep Murders, 139
Terrill, Edward, 50
Texas Rangers, 109, *192*, *198*, 216, *238*
Thomas, George, 114
Thomas, Heck, *149*, 151, 157, 158, 161,
    161, 176
Thompson, Ben, 90, 91, 95, *95*, 117
Three-Fingered Jack, 21
Tilghman, Bill, 155, 157, 158, 161, 181
Timberlake, James R., 56
Tolbert, John, *142*, 149
Tolbert, Paden, *142*
Tolby, F. J., 108
Tombstone (Arizona), 70, 87, 91, 95
Tonto Basin War, 138
Tracy, Harry, 231, 236, 237, 246-248
Train robbery, begun by Renos, 209
Tunstall, John H., 123, *125*, 126, 127
Turpin, Dick, 41
Tutt, Dave, 59

U

Underwood, Henry, 212, 215, 216
Upson, Ash, 122

V

Vasquez, Tiburcio, 21, 76, 80
Vega, 108
Vermillion, Texas Jack, 100
Vigilantes, 24, 75, *78*, 79, 80, 210, 250
Vigilantes of New Granada, 65
Villa Pancho, 194-205, *198*, *203*
Virginia City (Montana), 69
Virginia City (Nevada), 85, 113

W

Walden, Arthur Treadwell, 250
Wallace, Jim, 161
Wallace, Lew, 130
Ward, John, 234
Warner, Matt, 232, 233, 234
Watson, E. A., 176
Watson, Ella (Cattle Kate), 135,
    182, *182*, 183
Watson, Peg Leg, 137
Webb, Charles, 105, 117
Weightman, Red Buck, 157, 158
West, Little Dick, 157
Wheeler, Ben, 220, *220*
White, Fred, 96
White, G. S., *142*, 151
Whitney, Chauncey B., 90, 91
Whittaker, Sam 75
Wichita (Kansas), 87, 92, 132
Wild Bunch, *230*, 231, 234
Williams, Marshall, 98
Wilson, Floyd, 164
Wilson, John (Kid), 164, 165
Wilson, Lem, *218*, 220
Wolcott, Frank, 135, *135*
Wormwood, Hank, 219
Wyeth, N. C., *44*

Y

Yellow Bird, *see* Ridge, John Rollin
Yoes, Marshal, 152
Younger, Bob, 56, 69
Younger, Cole, *46*, 49, 50, *50*, 52, 53,
    53, 56, 69, 152, 153, 172
Younger, Jim, 49, 50, *50*, 52, 53, 56
Younger, John, 50, *50*
Yountis, Ole, 157, 158

Z

Zapata, Emiliano, 198, *198*